ROBERT A. M. STERN

BUILDINGS AND PROJECTS
2004–2009

ROBERT A. M. STERN

BUILDINGS AND PROJECTS
2004–2009

Edited by Peter Morris Dixon

With a conversation between Paul Goldberger
and Robert A. M. Stern

THE MONACELLI PRESS

Library of Congress
Cataloging-in-Publication Data

Stern, Robert A. M.
Robert A.M. Stern : buildings and projects,
2004–2009 / edited by Peter Morris Dixon ;
with a conversation between
Paul Goldberger and Robert A.M. Stern.
p. cm.
Includes bibliographical references.
ISBN 978-1-58093-234-9
1. Stern, Robert A. M. 2. Robert A.M. Stern
Architects. 3. Architecture—United States—
History—21st century. I. Dixon, Peter Morris.
II. Goldberger, Paul. III. Title.
NA737.S64A4 2009
720.92'2—dc22
2009027487

Printed in Italy

10 9 8 7 6 5 4 3 2 1
First edition

Designed by Pentagram Design

www.monacellipress.com

Acknowledgments

Partners

1969–
Robert A.M. Stern

1969–1977
John S. Hagmann

1988–
Robert S. Buford

1989–
Roger H. Seifter
Paul L. Whalen
Graham S. Wyatt

1999–
Alexander P. Lamis

2000–
Randy M. Correll
Grant F. Marani

2008–
Augusta Barone
Gary L. Brewer
Melissa DelVecchio
Sargent C. Gardiner
Preston J. Gumberich
Michael Jones
Daniel Lobitz
Meghan L. McDermott
Kevin M. Smith

This is the sixth volume in the series documenting buildings and projects. It is particularly meaningful to me because it marks forty years of practice, a good many years during which my passion for the art of architecture has never flagged. When I embarked on the independent practice of architecture, mine was but one of a few voices in a small revolution questioning the prevailing dogma by calling for an architecture that takes its place in history, rather than against it. The voices of forty years ago were in time heard and grew in number, and as a result, it has been a great pleasure to see the conception of contemporary architecture broaden to allow for many points of view.

The work documented in this book has been accomplished collaboratively, in a partnership beautifully managed by Robert S. Buford, where I am joined by fifteen collaborating design partners as well as associates and very many others whose names are listed in the project credits at the back of the book. I thank each of them, and all those who have worked with us, for their creative input and professionalism. An architect is only as good as his clients, and over the years those who have entrusted us with the realization of their goals and aspirations have been wonderfully supportive.

Like the work it documents, this monograph is itself a team effort. In our office Peter Morris Dixon, Jonathan Grzywacz, and Harjit Jaiswal worked with me to gather the material and keep it focused. My partner Augusta Barone, along with Gaylin Bowie and Megan Glaves, oversaw the production of drawings for publication; Dana Esposito compiled the credits. Michael Bierut, one of the most gifted graphic designers of our time, with whom I've had the good fortune to work since he arrived in New York from his native Ohio twenty-nine years ago, has, working with his colleague Yve Ludwig, designed a book that unifies and clarifies the full range of our work.

The contributions of wonderful photographers, in particular Peter Aaron of the Esto group, who has documented our work since the start, are essential. I have enjoyed and benefited from a long and productive association with Gianfranco Monacelli, who has published my work from the first, and his managing editor Elizabeth White, whose steady manner and keen appreciation of architecture has kept this book on track. Lastly I thank Paul Goldberger for pushing me, in the conversation that follows, to say something intelligent about my life in architecture.

Contents

Robert A. M. Stern
and Paul Goldberger
A conversation

PAUL GOLDBERGER: Bob, forty years of practice is an extraordinary thing, all the more because you continue at such a rapid pace. I remember the office over the storefront on West Seventy-second Street, which was probably smaller than your reception area is right now. Let me first ask you if there's anything you miss from those early days when it was a kind of office on a shoestring.

ROBERT A. M. STERN: "Office on a shoestring" sums it up perfectly. What one does miss, of course, from when one is brand new in practice, is the thrill of the first or the second or the third commission or telephone call as it were. And the very close camaraderie of a few people. But there is no question that a larger office—and I'm not sure how much larger "larger" should really be—provides one with all kinds of other things and a more solid professionalism. You avoid some of the horrible mistakes that many small practices make, both technical errors in execution of the work and mistakes in terms of how to position the firm and how to write a contract and a hundred other things.

I was thinking of that, actually, as I was waiting for your arrival. Of course, it was much nicer in some ways when it was smaller and I knew everybody. And I knew them warts and all, and they knew me warts and all. Now I think they know me warts and all and I'm not sure I know them.

But there are people in our practice today who don't go back to day one but do go back to say, day three. People who have been here thirty years or more and are now partners, and we have a close camaraderie. But of course, many others who came to the practice later have also become partners and associates.

PG: It is remarkable, though, that there are some people who really spent their entire careers here.

RS: I'm always disappointed when people leave. But I recognize that for some people, for many people, it's a good thing to do. Find their own way. Sometimes people don't work better in a different environment than the one they're leaving, but they think it's going to be better, that the grass will be greener. Sometimes, they think they're going to be able to do it on their own, and they suddenly discover that independent practice is not for everyone or not for them. Some chose to return to the nest. But we've spawned a lot of firms.

PG: You know, for a while, it seemed right to compare Robert A. M. Stern Architects to a practice like Delano & Aldrich or John Russell Pope or James Gamble Rogers, great eclectic firms of the 1920s, '30s, and so forth.

But given that they were less concerned about formal innovation than they were about careful, conscientious re-use of historical form and given the sheer volume of work you now have, larger than any of those firms, I think even in their heyday, I wonder to whom would you want to be compared, ideally?

RS: There were no really large firms in the time of the architects you mentioned, to my knowledge. None that was very large. McKim, Mead & White and Daniel Burnham set the model, but it was just the model for big practice, not the reality. It's only since the founding of Skidmore, Owings & Merrill in the late 1930s and after that the large firm taking on many different kinds of work began to emerge.

I like to think that we are able to compete with different firms for different kinds of work, that we can compete with a KPF or a Skidmore for a corporate project and other firms for other kinds of work. Maybe we're sui generis, egomaniac though such a claim might be.

PG: We all know you are sui generis, so the question is therefore, perhaps the firm also is?

RS: We run our practice differently. First of all, we run side by side with certain partners who are doing the kind of work we did twenty, twenty-five years ago, relatively small scale, and other partners who are running large projects. And in between are the institutional projects, which tend to be a bit of one and the other.

But we have people who move around in the practice from one kind of work to the other. And I think people enjoy not doing the same kind of project over and over again year in and year out. People who might not want to be specialists, but would rather be generalists. And that's the way I think we are.

One thing that's different from any other firm you might compare us with: we have always kept ourselves to one office.

The condensed energy of this place—the bumping into each other in the halls and on the stairways and so forth, of the people who are all really involved in the projects—is an essential ingredient in our ability to work together successfully.

PG: So you prefer the challenge of airplane travel to the sacrifices one makes having branch offices.

RS: Yes—especially now that I get my partners to travel.

PG: How do you keep quality up at this volume?

RS: My job in the office—certainly in the last ten years or so—maybe fifteen years—has been to set the agenda for projects and then be the quality control. We'll go this way; we'll go that way. We'll look at this set of alternatives or that. A design direction for a project emerges under my leadership and once that happens, my job is to see to its nurturing and to its survival in the rough-and-tumble of budgets, value engineering, and construction. I constantly meet with the architects working on our projects that are in intensive design development. As they move to the next stages, we meet less frequently as more technical issues come on board, but whenever there's a decision that involves a significant intersection between idea and realization, then these projects are brought back to me. I think I can say that I am ultimately responsible for what we do, good or bad.

PG: You set each project's initial design direction.

RS: Yes. Usually I sit down with a partner and other key people. I've done it collaboratively since the day John Hagmann and I started. The notion that an architect locks himself in his closet, so to speak, and invents a project is, I think, a foolish one and not operative for me. Not operative for most people.

PG: Let's talk about the role of history today: how does one justify doing work that is so reliant on historical precedent in the twenty-first century? Is that different from doing so in the twentieth century? Or if it was justifiable in the twentieth, is there any reason it should be any different in the twenty-first?

RS: I don't see how any art can proceed—I regard architecture as an art—without climbing on the shoulders of what went before it. The modernist argument may have provided a necessary call to do some house-cleaning almost a hundred years ago. But modernism has become a style and an ideology. In fact we now live in a period of revived modernism in which architecture students and young practitioners are doing things that make me smile. I mean, I wouldn't be as blatantly devoted to some of my precedents as they seem to be to Case Study houses in California.

I think that all architecture comes from what went before. And how carefully one hews to precedent or how many liberties one takes, in my view, is part of a larger set of judgments as to what is, or could be called, "appropriate." Appropriate from every point of view, especially from the site, the cultural expectations of a community and of the specific client. It's not a matter of what mood I'm in that morning or which book happened to land on my desk that afternoon.

PG: One of the ways you got into history, I think, was through Robert Venturi's work. And you in fact, played a huge role in bringing him to the world's attention by publishing the excerpt from *Complexity and Contradiction in Architecture* in 1965 before the book itself was published.

And early in your practice, your work seemed to rely very heavily on Venturi's own work, and then it diverged and became more literally historical as he, in fact, became even less reliant on history. Can we talk a little bit about that divergence?

RS: Well, first I would say that my interest in history as a practicing architect was first released, if you will, by Paul Rudolph who always talked about historical precedent. At the Yale School of Architecture, he would say, "You can do it like Mies; you can do it like Wright; like Le Corbusier," as though they were all historical figures even though Mies and Le Corbusier were still very much around. But he respected non-modernist architecture and especially traditional urbanism as well. And he would tell students, "You know, really, you would do better to walk through the Yale residential colleges."

PG: I remember that was quoted at the symposium in conjunction with the rededication of Rudolph Hall.[1]

RS: But because of the way Bob Venturi wrote about his own work and proposed a response to modernism, and especially the argument of Le Corbusier, of course, made it suddenly all very vivid for me that one could indeed engage in an active way in new form-making as well as in the ideas behind that form-making.

Rudolph was nervous about making historically specific buildings, although very recently and as a result of the symposium that we had at Yale[2] I saw a scheme that I'd never seen of Rudolph's, the first scheme for the Jewett Art Museum [at Wellesley College] which was based on the Doge's Palace. I would say not just based on the Doge's Palace, but very close to being the Doge's Palace.

PG: But of course, Rudolph himself was derivative from time to time within the modernist canon. There's no question that the A&A building at Yale could never have had its present form if the Larkin Building had not existed.

RS: All architecture is based on other things. That's what gives the architecture historians something to do every Monday morning, to continue to trace sources. But there grew up a myth in the 1920s and '30s which I don't think should be attributed to Le Corbusier, but much more to the architect-educator Walter Gropius and to the engineer turned historian-polemicist Sigfried Giedion, that architects shouldn't look to the past. The past was dead. And everything was the future. It's important to remember that in Le Corbusier's great polemical book *Vers Une Architecture,* which was mistranslated as *Towards a New Architecture*—

PG: Yes, it's *Towards an Architecture.*

RS: Yes—it's important to remember that Le Corbusier's book is laced with references to the past as a standard to which the new world should aspire to. Venturi, whose *Complexity and Contradiction in Architecture* is as important to the second half of the twentieth century as Le Corbusier's book was to the first, also talked about the past, not just as a standard to be measured against, but as a direct source of design inspiration. I had been a little bit interested and knowledgeable about, for example, Lutyens, but as Venturi talked about him, I began to see a second architecture, a parallel to modernism in the twentieth century, that was modern in spirit but not futurist. I had already been involved in researching the life and work of George Howe. Howe's pre-modernist world was a parallel world.

1. Rededication of Paul Rudolph Hall and dedication of the Jeffery Loria Center for the History of Art, Yale University, November 7–8, 2008.

2. *Reassessing Rudolph: Architecture and Reputation,* Yale School of Architecture, January 23–24, 2009.

And that parallel world has still not been given its just place in the larger tapestry that is nineteenth- and twentieth-century architectural history. And today, who knows where we are?

Politically we're at a very interesting moment as we speak, with a new President and a trashed economy and everybody speculating about what will happen next. But certainly, the kind of irrational exuberance of a great many buildings that we have seen either built or projected in the last few years is not going to be around with us again for a while.

PG: I think we will have fewer buildings of any kind, exuberant or not, for a little while. But let's go back to how we look at history.

RS: Venturi was very, very important. But Venturi changed in his own point of view between *Complexity and Contradiction* and *Learning from Las Vegas.* So that may be where he and I diverge in our approach in architecture. But when you're very young, you have many mentors from the present and from the past. Philip Johnson wanted to be Mies, but was obsessed with Soane and Schinkel, and Paul Rudolph struggled to be Wright, Mies, and Le Corbusier all together, and on and on it goes. I wanted to see what I could do in real terms with what I was observing and learning from Bob Venturi, who helped me learn from Lutyens and McKim, Mead & White and Michelangelo.

PG: Interesting, actually, now that you've made that comparison, because I think the movement in your work somewhat away from Venturi and towards a more literal historicism is roughly the same time into your practice as Philip Johnson's movement away from Mies.

RS: Oh, that is interesting. I would have to do mathematics for that.

PG: I'm doing some mathematics in my head now, and I think at roughly a decade of practice, it was visibly different.

RS: I don't want to dwell on this topic too much, but it's interesting that in the recent literature on Le Corbusier, which finally begins to sort out the man from the myth, the practice from the pretensions, we begin to understand how very many years it took him to figure it out.

To begin with, he worked within the languages of things he saw around him that he admired and he thought he could build upon.

PG: And then there was this retroactive attempt to make it all seem like Athena springing full blown from the head of Zeus.

RS: I will not be subject to such a retroactive analysis; neither Zeus nor Athena am I!

PG: I do think, though, that we are more generous toward history now than a few years ago. I mean, the eclectic architects from McKim, Mead & White on through the architects of the 1920s, '30s, '40s that we've mentioned are certainly not written out of history now. They may not have quite the central role that perhaps they should, but they're not unknown figures.

RS: The profession as a whole does not embrace the possibility of continuing the formal line of thinking that was represented by those eclectic architects. But the public does. The public is quite interested in and willing to accept modernist architecture, but typically assumes that it is the architecture of the corporate world. When we get into the world of institutions, governmental or educational to name but two, and into the world of the private house, things are a bit different. True, there are people who will commission modernist houses or modernist buildings on campuses, but by and large, the public does look askance at the modernist experiment as being associated with regimented corporate life.

We just completed Comcast Center in Philadelphia, which is firmly in the modernist grain. We didn't propose to put ornamental embellishments on it. Yet it is not without historical memory: it's a prismatic obelisk. But does it have historical character? I'd say no. Sir John Soane said that character in architecture came from moldings. What for a glass-wrapped skyscraper? What kind of moldings? Mies used moldings. They were the I-beams on the Seagram Building, which literal modernists decried as decoration. Mies used those I-beams decoratively to give that building character, which is why so many Miesian buildings with tighter budgets disappoint by comparison. At Comcast, we probably don't have as many moldings as Mies would, but we tried to give it a certain character all its own through the shaping of the mass and the use of two different types of glass and the intricate details of the public spaces.

Comcast and Fifteen Central Park West, coming virtually at the same time, represent two seemingly distinct approaches. Fifteen Central Park West gained its character not just from the sculpted handling of the rooftop or the use of stone, which is very important for the luxury it embodies and for how it takes the light, but also, because it allowed us to indulge in a certain level of detailing of moldings that imbues it with a distinct character unto itself, but one not disconnected from what that went before.

PG: I think I'd like to pursue that a little bit more. Soane is an incredibly interesting architect, although I think his remark about moldings has to have been somewhat sarcastic.

RS: No, it wasn't a remark. It was one of his points in his [Royal Academy] lectures on architecture. I had occasion to look it up.

PG: But he was an architect who also did such extraordinary things with space.

RS: The idea of space was never talked about until the late nineteenth century.

PG: I remember Kurt Forster making that point at the writing symposium at Yale about a year and a half ago.[3] I didn't mean that we should push

3. "Writing About Architecture," Yale School of Architecture in conjunction with the Whitney Humanities Center, Yale University, October 8, 2007.

through Soane's writings to find some reference to space because I know we will not find it. But that doesn't mean that Soane didn't conceptualize space all the same.

RS: I used to say to Philip Johnson—we would have these wonderful discussions—I think they were wonderful to him, but they certainly were for me—and I said, "Philip, there's no such thing as architectural space. It's the walls that bound it. You see the walls and how they're configured, and how the light plays against them—that's important. Then you get architectural space. But architectural space in the abstract? It's undefineable. So I'm ambivalent about the term "architectural space." I am that old-fashioned. I think maybe the old guys were right. Don't talk about it. Just make it.

PG: Yes, but I guess what I would say is, you're right that they didn't talk about it, and you're right that architectural space became one of the modernist crutches. Even though Philip didn't list it as one of his crutches, it in fact became an excuse to avoid doing and thinking about and addressing a whole crux of other issues.

RS: I think most modernist space is not even interesting. I would not like to be known as the slice of ice cream between two crackers.

PG: Are you thinking of the Barcelona Pavilion?

RS: You want to get this: I hate—

PG: You hate the Barcelona Pavilion?

RS: I loved it until I visited it. And I've now been there twice. I just feel that you sit down and hang on for your dear life in that so-called room—the space is so movemented, so flowing. But then, to be fair, it wasn't intended as a place to be in but one to move through. However, on the level of the details, the intelligence of the Barcelona Pavilion is fantastic. Nonetheless—ce n'est pas moi.

PG: Maybe the issue is almost semantic. Because obviously, something makes Sir John Soane's breakfast room very different from the room even right next door to it in that very same house.

RS: Well, the arrangement of the walls, the ceiling, the use of reflective surfaces, mirrors and other things, the way the light comes in. It may yield a fantastic spatial effect, but I think the idea of a space-driven architecture is a semantic notion.

PG: I think we're really arguing words, because we both know that you will feel something quite extraordinary, say, if you go into Borromini's St. Ivo.

RS: But here's where I will draw my point a little bit differently about architectural space. Often, in the twentieth century and the early twenty-first century, modernist architectural space has been measured and applauded almost by direct relationship to size. Exalting, intimidating;

for all its pretension that modernism was the architecture of democracy, most of its great rooms—and I prefer the word rooms to spaces—are just intimidating. No detail, no moldings, no character. Just space, that is void. Architecture for me is more than big space, more than awe-inspiring void.

PG: Let's talk about Yale a little bit. You've been remarkably catholic as a dean, I think to the surprise of some and the pleasure of all. You have been very broadminded in making the school the center of a wide range of viewpoints and dialogue.

What do you think your most important influence as an educator has been? Has it been the way you've run the school? Has it been the way you've run the office? Has it been a combination of the two?

RS: In the office I probably do educate people in the sense that as part of the design process I say let's look at this or that building. And sometimes they look at me as though they were deer caught in the headlights, if they don't know what building I'm referring to or why I find the reference interesting, not to say relevant, to the task at hand.

But I don't use my time in the office consciously educating people, although we have an elaborate program of education. I believe that when you leave architecture school, you frequently really begin to need to become independent, to open your eyes to the wider world and to develop your own ideas—and not be led by a teacher.

But really, my teaching—that's what I do at the university, for a long time at Columbia and now at Yale.

At Columbia, I think I had a very strong influence on a lot of people; some of whom came to work for me, like Tom Kligerman or John Ike, who started their own firm, or Gregory Gilmartin who then went on to work for Peter Pennoyer, or Pennoyer himself who also was a student and then worked for me. My impact as a teacher was particularly strong in the late 1970s and '80s when the nature of architectural discourse was wide open to many possibilities. People were looking to the past in their various ways as a means to get beyond the kind of deadening last gasps of the modernist International Style. You know, Peter Eisenman and I have been great friends for forty years, united by an antipathy to the kind of vacuous practice that proliferated in the late 1960s and '70s.

In returning to Yale, I wasn't intent on pushing my own agenda. I enjoyed my time as a student at Yale, which was open to so many crosscurrents, and Rudolph's own personal search for what was right, which was constantly shifting, including the fact that he had Venturi teach there. Only later did Bob become critical of Paul—most unfortunate. One of the accidents of history—they really had much more in common than not.

When I became the dean, it was my idea to build upon Yale's tradition of open discourse. The visiting critic system at Yale is its principal hallmark,

4. *Architecture or Revolution: Charles Moore and Architecture at Yale in the 1960s,* Yale School of Architecture, November 2–3, 2001.

going way back before any other school had visiting critics. I have used the visiting critic system to bring a wide range of architects to New Haven—established leaders and rising talents alike—whose interests range from traditionalism to modernism. Variety of approach is part of the school's DNA, and it's certainly part of mine.

However, beyond opening up to the diversity of isms, I think the important thing about architecture schools is that they be centers of culture—architectural culture. Symposia, publications, discourse—reaching out to the larger community not only of alumni, but to the larger community of practice and scholarship, and to the interested general public.

If you are a true believer in only one point of view, that's okay. But it does tend to pull your antennae in, tends to make you a monoculturist. I am not a monoculturist.

PG: One of the other contributions I think you've made recently is helping people to understand that neither was Paul Rudolph a monoculturist, although history has kind of painted him that way. And getting a much broader, deeper, more nuanced and subtle view of him I think has been nearly as important as the physical restoration of the building.

RS: I think they're both extremely important. And I think what we have been doing at Yale is to look at quite a few architects of the previous generation whose importance as teachers and builders has been overlooked though their legacy is keenly felt by those who were their students. Perhaps we've looked a bit prematurely or slightly the wrong way around at some, like Charles Moore, whom we may have too closely linked to the student unrest of the late 1960s.[4] But I think that our studies on Jim Stirling and Kevin Roche, which are coming forward, lead to an important and productive re-examination of the recent past. And architecture schools—certainly ones like Yale with tremendous resources—I'm talking not only about money, but also faculty resources and libraries and archive resources—are obliged to take this on.

Certainly the few museum architecture departments don't seem to see the need to do this; they apparently prefer to concentrate on current trends.

PG: Let's move back more definitively towards your built work as opposed to the work in teaching. A few minutes ago, you brought up Comcast and Fifteen Central Park West together. It's a fascinating comparison, because as you pointed out, they're both large scale projects, both done at more or less the same time, and I would guess neither could have taken quite its form had it been done by some other hand. In other words, each has something to market as a Stern project, and yet they're very, very different. Can we talk a little bit about all that those projects mean?

RS: We went through many schemes leading to Comcast. The project began in 2000 as a developer-driven speculative tower. And then the disasters of the dot.com collapse, and then 9/11/2001, halted the scheme. It then went forward in fits and starts with different agendas. But when it once got going seriously with the expectation that a very high-tech company, Comcast, would be its principal tenant, it became clear that the building had to embody the culture of modernity, especially that of electronic communication.

How do you do that? Well, make it very modern in materials, and make it as environmentally responsible as possible. The opinions of many to the contrary, I have nothing against glass buildings and have explored their possibilities when appropriate in the past. I did propose, you may recall, in the second *Chicago Tribune* competition (1980) an all glass building but I gave it a classical shape, that of a column in keeping with a narrative that had to do with newspapers. Now, that was done for polemical purposes. But it was not uninfluential, I would argue.

PG: It was around the time of Philip's PPG building,[5] was it not, which was a gothic shape in glass.

RS: I don't know which preceded which. But that's not important, except to say that the material glass is no more or no less a viable material to me than any other. The materiality of a building affects shape, but not always. In Philadelphia, the most significant formal concern was not with material expression but with context. The task was to deal with the skyline that had grown up almost overnight in the late 1980s in the wake of the second Tribune competition with what I would say are some very ambitious buildings, some high-striving skyline buildings, but all rather fat in their cross sections. Buildings that aspired to the slender profile of the Chrysler Building but ended up rather differently. So at the many design meetings I had with our client, I kept arguing for something very, very simple. Paring it back and making it a simple shape like a tapered obelisk, and even resisting the introduction of what many obelisks, I suppose, have, which is a pyramidal top.

Why resist the pyramidal top? In part because it's very difficult technically to ventilate such a top. And for another reason, I just thought cutting the building off, leaving the suggestion of the pyramid off the top might be more interesting.

Then, working with Nancy Rosen, our art consultant on the project and others, we set out to find the right public art for the lobby. Art had to be in the building. And I thought that Jonathan Borofsky's piece, as soon as I saw his proposal for it, was just brilliant. I think it brings people into dialogue with the building in a way that public art should but very seldom does. It's not some abstract piece planted on a plaza, but a witty celebration of the monumentally scaled winter garden.

And then the last thing was someone—it was not my idea, but I embraced it instantly and pushed it along as fast and as forward as I could— someone said, "How about a video wall?" And we had the idea of working

5. Philip Johnson with John Burgee, PPG Corporate Headquarters, Pittsburgh, Pennsylvania, 1979–1984.

with David Niles to make a wall that would just have continuous video, taking advantage of the most advanced technology that one associates with a company like Comcast.

It's amazing: the whole back wall of the lobby—which can be seen all the way from the street across the plaza in daylight, it's that bright. For twelve hours a day, it projects an endless program; there are repetitions, but it is constantly being reprogrammed. And it's not advertising. It is that idea that Venturi has of electronic decoration on the wall of the building. But it is not a substitute for architecture; it is decoration. And it's not commercial. There was much discussion about that, but I argued that the wall not be an extension of the Comcast brand but instead should be just a fantastic thing the Comcast company gives to the world.

Brian Roberts [CEO of Comcast] got into it and went the whole nine yards. The most amazing thing about it: the digital machinery has to rest every so often. And when it rests, it projects an image that matches exactly the wood paneling that clads the rest of the lobby's walls. So you could walk in there and just see paneling—and all of the sudden, it goes away. Electronics and architecture as one.

PG: And so some of it, in effect, is actually a video image of paneling?

RS: Yes. And it runs wall to wall in the lobby from—I've forgotten the height, but it's somewhat above your head to the ceiling. It's amazing.

PG: I would think actually that, in a way, might almost be the most Venturi-esque of all aspects of doing that. Using video imaging to create something that looked somewhat like a wall.

RS: Yes, probably. But more directly it connects back to my experiences on Times Square and Forty-second Street, which are not unimportant. And my experiences with the Walt Disney Company, and how to engage the public. There are wonderful, silly things that happen on this electronic wall. There's a whole Charlie Chaplin sequence. I didn't design any of the sequences. David Niles and his team did. He's quite a brilliant producer and a world-class character. He's down in 26 Broadway. You should talk to him.

PG: The great Carrère and Hastings Building?

RS: Yes. Outside, cool place—but dreary inside. It could be fixed up for about $200 million.

So anyhow, that goes backwards. It's always easier to go backwards, in a way. It goes backwards to Forty-second Street, which also goes backwards to my time with Disney, and my interest in and unabashed and unembarrassed delight in communicating with a larger public.

I'd like to have all my colleagues in the profession hold me in respect, but I would also like that respect to be part of a larger public agenda. Too many artists and architects seem content to make art and architecture just for each other, and not for the larger world. Now there is an elite, and I know about the elite and I'm interested in the elite, and I'm probably part of the elite—the cultural elite, let's say. But I think there is a time and a responsibility for people involved in the visual arts—especially in the art of architecture, which is a social art, the public art of architecture—to connect to the larger issues of the day and to engage people who have no connection to a building that may be designed except that they are stuck on the street where that building is.

PG: They see it every day.

RS: You can build a suburban house on a generous lot any way you like. Put landscape and a wall around it and it's your own castle. But when you build in the public realm, you have to be mindful of the experiences the public will have. And they may be dazzled by certain buildings from time to time, but they may also grow tired of them and discover that on second glance some of those buildings contribute very little to their daily lives in the city.

PG: But it seems to me that one of the fallacies of thinking today is we tend often to believe, or the architectural profession often tends to believe, that public or popular appeal and let's say, serious intellectual content are mutually exclusive, are a zero-sum game. That the more a building has of one, the less it must have of the other. Whereas in fact, throughout history, buildings have both been appealing to a wide range of the public and have revealed themselves on deeper levels to those who come with a more intellectual inclination to them. No?

RS: The great churches—the baroque churches of Rome of the Counter-Reformation were built to get people in and to engage them in the liturgy.

PG: They were pieces of architectural showmanship.

RS: Absolutely. I know there are many, many other periods in the history of architecture when that has been true. It's too bad that when you scan histories of the twentieth century, you see an architecture that is largely private. The so-called icons of twentieth century architecture tend to be houses, whether they are Frank Lloyd Wright's houses, Mies's houses, or whomever.

Now one thing you could say is, "Isn't that great?" It's the architecture of democracy. That every average person or at least middle-class person can perhaps engage in building a house—the Case Study houses, let's say. But all of those are private, and they don't often give out very nice odors, so to speak, to the public realm. When they're isolated like the Farnsworth house or the Glass House, it makes no difference. But when you see the Case Study houses in situ in Los Angeles, with their frequently unfriendly walls and garage doors facing streets, with no suggestion of discourse between the people who live in the house and the people who occupy the street, then I'd say, "Well, are we asking the right questions? Is this the right model for us?" My answer is no.

So I learned that. How did I learn that? By looking at the porches of the nineteenth-century architecture, which Scully introduced to me. These porches were perfect mediators between the public realm of the street and the privacy of the house. And then, one always learns from younger people as well, and certainly Andrés Duany and Lizz Plater-Zyberk—Andrés worked for me for one intense summer—got me focused on another way of looking at the vernacular, and of course, also of looking at the suburb. I was a city boy who held suburbs in contempt. But influenced by Andrés and Lizz, I became very interested in the suburb as an insufficiently understood model of development: I came to revere the garden suburb for its contributions to urbanism as a whole and to see its potential for the redevelopment of cities.

While art museums have been the focus of many architects undertaking public work in my generation, we have devoted a lot of thought to the problems of public libraries. Our Nashville Library, for example, is classical, on axis with the great Strickland Capitol, surrounded by quite a few other classical buildings as well as the usual ragtag of post–World War II downtowns—a struggling downtown, I would think is a better word. Our classical design combined perfectly with the most advanced programming to realize a building that was embraced by every kind of person in Nashville, because classical buildings don't represent factional elitism in our society, as is often argued, but in fact provide a kind of unifying force. Classical architecture is still the great international style. It is the international style of civicism as perhaps the glass box, as we were saying, or modernism, is the international style of corporations.

The great historian Henry-Russell Hitchcock, writing in the 1950s, called the International Style the architecture of bureaucracy. But I think nobody wants to say that very publicly today. Maybe I can stick my neck out. My head is about to fall off it anyhow . . . But I think that characterization holds true.

PG: I think that makes some sense. But that doesn't mean one absolutely must go in the classical direction for an institution and the international style of direction for a corporate building, does it?

RS: Well, I don't know. I never say what one must automatically do or not. I simply think of situations that exist. Take the case of IIT as a campus. I would say many people may admire it for itself, but most people would find it hard to see it as a model for a campus of an academic institution. For a car company, yes, as at the GM Tech Center. But for a place of higher learning, I'm not so sure. Certainly, when the Air Force Academy, which I admire very much on its own terms, was built, it looked totally corporate.

PG: Only the chapel saved it from being completely corporate.

RS: Well, and the costumes—I mean, the uniforms. They used advisors like Cecil B. DeMille and Edith Head who were brought in to orchestrate for the new Air Force, so the cadets looked like they were out of a Hollywood musical. What saves the place is its unbelievable site.

In a university like Yale, we have stylistically new buildings from the 1950s that grow out of the tradition of the International Style, though very interestingly, not one of Yale's significant modernist buildings from the '50s really represents the corporate model of that tradition, though some of the architects responsible for their design were involved in their other work. For example, Gordon Bunshaft's Beinecke Library is not a glass building, and it does not look like a corporate office building in any way, shape, or form. And Saarinen's Morse and Stiles Colleges and Ingalls hockey rink don't resemble his buildings for IBM or General Motors.

PG: All those buildings, I might say, also look much better now than I ever thought they were when I was a student. They've aged well.

RS: They've aged well because by and large, they were well considered in terms of context and symbolic representation. They connect in particular ways to core values of a particular institution. They also look better to you now because times have changed since you were a student, and, dare I say, you like the rest of us know much more about the difficulties of designing buildings and the vicissitudes of taste and so deal less with first-glance impressions. We must never forget that in art or anything else, we go through cycles. As in our views of whether our economy should be regulated or not regulated, so too with our views of what is appropriate in art.

When the Beinecke Library was built, my voice was but one of hundreds of voices saying, "This is the wrong building at the wrong time in the wrong place." Now not only does every parent with a child touring the university want to visit the Beinecke, but virtually every architect who comes to Yale at the invitation of the School of Architecture asks to see it, the hockey rink, and of course the New Haven Coliseum, the last sadly torn down.

So architecture is for the long haul, provided it eludes the wrecker's ball. But I think the point I was making is that in every case, even in the case of the way Kahn handled the glass wall in the Art Gallery extension, it's the way language—classical or modernist—is used, is molded to the demands of physical context and symbolic expression, that is crucial.

The only building at Yale that was a glass box—

PG: —was the computer center.

RS: And it was intended as an expression of computers. So, trite though it was, it was expressive. Buildings need to be expressive. As Rudolph always said, the problem with modern architecture is it runs the gamut of emotions from A to B. I believe he was paraphrasing Dorothy Parker on Katharine Hepburn.

PG: You're absolutely right. Can't beat you on the references, Bob, I must say.

We've let ourselves drift down so many interesting roads that I don't think we've said quite as much as we should about your recent work. And we were starting to compare Comcast with Fifteen Central Park West. But then in fact, we just talked about Comcast. Let's talk about those two again together, and a little bit about Fifteen Central Park West, which is certainly the pre-eminent large-scale residential building that the firm has done in New York.

RS: Well, Fifteen Central Park West belongs to both the history of architecture and the history of real estate. It has garnered a tremendous amount of attention simply because of the tremendous response the building has had in the marketplace.

But I would like to say there were other buildings that came onto the scene at the same time with similar ambitions that didn't do quite that. So I do think architecture was here a perfect handmaid to the client's purpose. And what do we build buildings for, if not to meet the client's purpose?

The Bilbao Guggenheim was built to put Bilbao on the map. Fifteen Central Park West was to show that you could have a fantastic new building that embodied what the marketplace regards as the extraordinary qualities of apartment house living that go with the pre–World War II era in the late 1920s and early '30s, and combine it with accommodations that met the kind of lifestyle—what a dreadful word, but I will use it—the way people live today.

You know, in the case of Comcast and Fifteen, they are parallel because both had excellent developers. At Comcast, we had a principal tenant who ended up occupying almost the entire building and was intent on being part of something very good and special. One of the reasons most of the recent skyscraper office buildings are so bland is there are no great corporate tenants. There's nobody behind them any more intent on immortalizing a corporation or branding the buildings, if you will, seeing them as an expression of their corporate or even personal genius, as in the case of Walter Chrysler and his building in the 1920s.

So, in any case, at Fifteen we have the Zeckendorf brothers, who are heirs to probably the most distinguished name in New York real estate over three generations. And a sense that this was an unforgettable site, a site that had sat there waiting for its moment for a very, very long time, first to be put together, and then to find the right combination of building.

We labored long and hard as to whether the building would be clad in brick or stone. It was a difficult decision to make, involving lots of potential extra expenses. Many, many very fine memorable, prestigious apartment houses in New York, including the Beresford and the San Remo and the Dakota are brick.

But the Zeckendorfs also felt that buildings like 740 Park and others were special, and partially, perhaps, their aura was bound up in the use of stone. It didn't take a lot of persuading for me to say stone would be great; that led to a lot of detailed discussion, because stone cladding represented a significantly greater investment. From a technical point of view, our use of stone is completely twenty-first century, set into precast panels which would have been exactly the way we would have done the brick as well, and hoisted into place. It's not laid up stone by stone. The thickness of the stone, the way you handle certain handset pieces at the bottom of the building, the molding of the shapes which you can do now with the computer; there's nothing about the way Fifteen Central Park West was built that isn't absolutely as state-of-the-art as any other skyscraper in New York.

However, the stone cladding isn't the issue. It's that the limestone performs so beautifully in the New York light. The use of the stone makes the building glow. Its every detail—its moldings, the shadows of ironwork against its surfaces, the way it takes the building's corners and its sculpted skyline profile—these are the ways the stone helps make the composition sing. The decision to clad with stone had many consequences: for example, glass-walled buildings are perceived to afford more "view," to be "glassier," as it were. A glass curtainwall also provides more views to the apartments from the outside looking in; glass-walled buildings seem to be more transparent, as if that were a public benefit. But does the public benefit from endless views of private accommodation? Especially at night? And from the inside, the argument is that occupants will see more through an all-glass facade. But inside, you still have columns in glass buildings, a problem made clear fifty years ago at Mies's 860 Lake Shore Drive; structure definitely frames down the window, whether one set in masonry or a glass curtainwall. And with column-to-column glass you have the problem that most people prefer not to live in a goldfish bowl. They want curtains for sun control, for privacy, and most of all to soften their living environment. They want a bit of cocoon, no matter the view. They want windows that are open to the view at certain times and closed off from it at other times. In a curtainwall building, where do the curtains go when they're open? They cover up some of the glass. If you follow this line of discussion, you realize that if you have large windows set into a wall, you can allow people to be freer in their decoration and personalizing of their space—while still enjoying the view, made more immediate by virtue of being framed.

When Bill Rubin was curator at MoMA he took all the frames off all the pictures. He even took the frame off the picture of Cézanne's painting of himself taking his picture to the framer, which was extremely strange.

This deframing was much discussed and criticized because the frame, at least until abstract expressionism, was part and parcel of the picture: the frame is part of the window. And the window is in the wall. And the wall has depth, and maybe you can't make today's walls as thick as those in the Dakota, but you can make them quite a bit thicker than a tissue of glass, and that thickness, as it were, gives you a chance to hide mechanical equipment, also gives you the chance to shape the embrasure of a window to create the deep space of a view. I'll go with the thick wall and deep window embrasure any time. It brings the view into deep focus.

PG: Yes, it does. It creates a sort of intensity as opposed to letting the view be wallpaper.

RS: I guess the only other person I haven't talked about in my pantheon of modern architectural heros is Louis I. Kahn, who did talk about light. Kahn made me see the magic of light, of light that is treated almost as a solid and is shaped by the embrasured windows through which it enters a building. Light is what makes rooms. I don't ever remember Kahn talking about space. He probably did, but I do remember him talking about light.

PG: I'm not sure. But you go to the Rochester and the Unitarian Church, and suddenly you understand.

RS: I went to Rochester when it was still under construction. Rochester is the grayest place I can think of, except for Buffalo. It was a snowy day. We had to sort of wade our way in, and when we got inside! I knew about those light monitors, but I didn't know that they would have this kind of special glass in them, as I recall now. Not clear glass; I think it's fritted. Anyhow, the light coming in was amazing. Amazing.

I love so much about what architecture can give us. I get so frustrated when I hear architects say it must be one way or another at any given moment. Architecture can be so many different things. But most architects are, like Auntie Mame said, suckers just starving to death.

PG: Life is a banquet. And most poor sons of bitches are starving to death.

RS: Right. Architecture is a banquet and most architects—

PG: —are starving—

RS: —are starving themselves and their clients to death. And you may quote me on that.

PG: All right, will do.

RS: I read the Auntie Mame book and saw the Broadway show, but it's the musical versions I remember most vividly. You know why my architecture might be different from other people's? I've never gotten over my love affair with American musical theater and film.

I remember reading—I guess I must have been at Yale at that time— Rudolph's vivid assessment of the lobby for the United Nations building.

Architectural Forum had asked a number of architects to comment on it in when it opened. Rudolph said the lobby reminded him of a Hollywood musical called *One World* with Rita Hayworth dancing. Such a put-down, but such a knowing and witty remark.

And it just shows you that Rudolph was also very interested in the experience of how you move through space that the movie musical explored in depth; he surely was a guy who went to the movies to look at musicals. I don't go to the movies to—let's put it this way: *Last Year at Marienbad* was not my idea of a garden stroll.

PG: Let's talk a little bit more about your current work before we conclude.

RS: Well, we've talked about Fifteen Central Park West and Comcast. We've also been working on a series of buildings at universities where the academic setting is not the fantastic, established, made-for-Bob-Stern setting like the Harvard Business School, or the Yale campus. Places like the University of Nevada in Las Vegas, where we've just completed a building. This campus is located just off the strip. Our building, Greenspun Hall, is an extremely sustainable building realized in a very demanding climate. It uses the most advanced hardware in the most surprising and, when you think about it, most traditional of ways. For example, we took the photovoltaics and arrayed them as the purlins of a pergola stretched across a courtyard that, as a result, is at once shaded from the sun and therefore pleasant to use most of the year, while harnessing sunlight to power the building. It's an extremely interesting building.

Or at the University of Nebraska, where we were invited to design a quilt museum. To protect the fabric, quilts have to be shown virtually in the dark. So what do you do? Build a big blank box? No. That would be dreary. Our building therefore combines a glass lenticular structure housing public space with a brick box punctuated as appropriate to light staff offices and educational facilities. The glass room welcomes the visitor. In its detailing we strove to represent the woven character of the quilts studied, stored, and displayed. Metal mesh forms scrims to help tamp down the bright sunlight, so that as you come in and move up the stepped ramp that takes you to the galleries, your eye is being adjusted from the bright Nebraska sunshine—winter and summer alike—to the low level of light curators demand to protect the quilts in the galleries. It's quite a nice little building, a landmark at the point of intersection between the university's East Campus and the city of Lincoln.

PG: The other point that probably should be made about all the work, but isn't often enough, is that in fact, for all its reliance on history, almost nothing you've done ever has a precise precedent. That it is, in fact, inventive with the tools of history. Is that not fair to say?

RS: I would say that's true. Sometimes we come closer to precedent and sometimes we're further away. At the Harvard Business School—for the

Spangler Center or for the Bloomberg extension to the Baker Library—
we were working on a campus of historical buildings in the Georgian
style, and in the case of Baker Bloomberg attaching ourselves to one
of them.

So I tried to stick quite close to the language of the place. But in
other buildings, like the Ohrstrom Library at St. Paul's School, the
interpretation of precedent is freer. The character is Gothic, but the
literalness is not there.

PG: That's my point.

RS: Yes, but there is nothing wrong if you set out to make a copy. If you
can make a really good copy, you're a pretty good architect in my opinion.
Most architects can't do it. "Eyes that do not see," Le Corbusier said; they
can't make a good copy.

PG: It's an act of enormous skill and subtlety.

RS: *Gone With the Wind* is not *The Odyssey,* but it's an amazing book; it puts
the reader into an historical period and gets that reader to experience
it in a particular way. It's true to the past and to the present. And we
don't have enough of that history as commentary in our contemporary
architecture. I think that we do ourselves tremendous disservice as
architects. That's because we still have the Fountainhead complex that
we are going to a) invent it, and b) if it isn't built just the way we want,
we're going to blow it up. Grow up architects. Grow up is what I say.

PG: Yes, but on the other hand, it's also true, as you know—let's put it this
way. There's something that differentiates Lutyens from Sir Herbert
Baker. Right?

RS: Well, each of us has a gift. And you can only work with the gift you've
been given and the way you've developed that gift. But I would say of
Lutyens that there are many projects he did that were totally involved
with the specifics of an existing building—he frequently added on to
buildings in a seamless way—and many times he reinvented the past for
something totally new. And as to Baker: he's much greater than many
credit him with being. The early houses in Capetown and the capital at
Pretoria are amazing.

Some think we shouldn't be giving people a blue ribbon for reinvention.
But I'm not so sure. Reinvention can be wonderful. But very few people
can do it well. A sign of a great architect, it seems to me, is the capacity
to reproduce and reinvent. I leave innovation to geniuses. I admire the
ability to just dig in to somebody else's work or building and understand it
and carry it forward. I'm troubled by the notion that every new building
should speak its own language—it can produce a babble. Today we have
urban babble. We have campus babble. How many college campuses
have been completely ruined by self-important babbling? How many in
charge of campus architecture have mindlessly followed the winds

of fashion, departing from the original idea only to end up in an incoherent wilderness?

I love to work in a place that has a defined context that is appreciated. I love to work in a place where the context is clear but not necessarily familiar to me. I like to try new things, to speak architectural languages that are new to me. I like to play against type, because sometimes when you play against type, you do your best work. Because the situation is new, you have to ask questions. You struggle. You have three-in-the-morning sickness feelings in your stomach, and you wake up and you try to think of what to do. That's good.

That's the fun of practice—especially this practice, which has evolved not out of a deliberate strategy, but out of situations, as it were. I didn't have a clear plan forty years ago. If you had asked me in 1969 what I thought Stern and Hagmann would be doing in forty years, I would have had no idea. I certainly could not have predicted what Robert Stern Architects is today. I probably would have thought we would be doing small houses for people in the suburbs or on the beach, which was becoming the playground for beginning architects in the 1960s, and I thought maybe we would work our way up to small libraries and suburban schools. How ironic. Except for one charter school in Bedford-Stuyvesant, I have never designed a grade school. Not that I'm not interested in them. But nobody has ever asked.

PG: We haven't talked at all about your international work. What makes that notable?

RS: Typically, when an architect from a country like the United States is hired, that architect is expected to bring to bear not only the technical expertise that the firm's practice presumably embodies, but also some special insights that can be called American, or British, or Western European, if you lump them together.

On the other hand, to go and build in a new part of the world, new to us, that is, as U.S.-based architects, and simply translate what one has done from one place to another, at first blush seems really wrong. But then there is the second blush. Maybe it's right. Maybe that's how ideas get transferred and then evolve. When I think of my first time in Japan with an architectural commission, I made it my business not only to familiarize myself with traditional Japanese architecture and contemporary work by Japanese architects, but also with buildings by English architects of the late nineteenth and early twentieth century, and of course those by Frank Lloyd Wright. Now the English architects tended to build English stuff. Wright, of course, built his own way, but he had already been so imbued with Japanese culture that in some inexplicable fashion it was American Japanese.

Building in an exotic locale is not a new problem. It goes back to our colonial period. Yet an American Georgian building is identifiably different enough from an English Georgian building, but part of the same language. I think about why this is so all the time.

PG: It does sound as if you've really tried to structure the firm as a serious commercial enterprise that is always connected to architectural ideas and the experience of learning about buildings.

RS: We try to make money. But we are run on ideas and on principles. We love clients because we love designing buildings.

Buildings and Projects
2004–2009

Encinal Bluffs
Family Compound

Sited atop a bluff overlooking a spectacular stretch of Pacific coastline, the elements of a single house are disposed into independent structures organized around garden courts in the manner of a traditional hill town. Limestone rubble walls, exposed rough timber framing, and old terra cotta roof tiles reinforce the hill-town character. In place of a traditional fountain square, the focus is a courtyard with an edgeless pool, framed by a deep loggia at its north end, formal living and dining spaces to one side, and the master bedroom suite and guest accommodations to the other. A network of smaller courtyards and intimate gardens designed in collaboration with Deborah Nevins are interconnected by half-hidden pathways. Broad shaded terraces and outdoor staircases celebrate the steeply sloping site.

Inside, simple, planar plaster walls are offset by intricately framed wood ceilings; steel casement windows and doors, a distinctly Californian reference borrowed from the region's Mediterranean revival of the 1920s and 1930s, complete the vocabulary.

Shellstone pathways meander past a horizon-edge spa to a beach house below.

Below: Beach house.

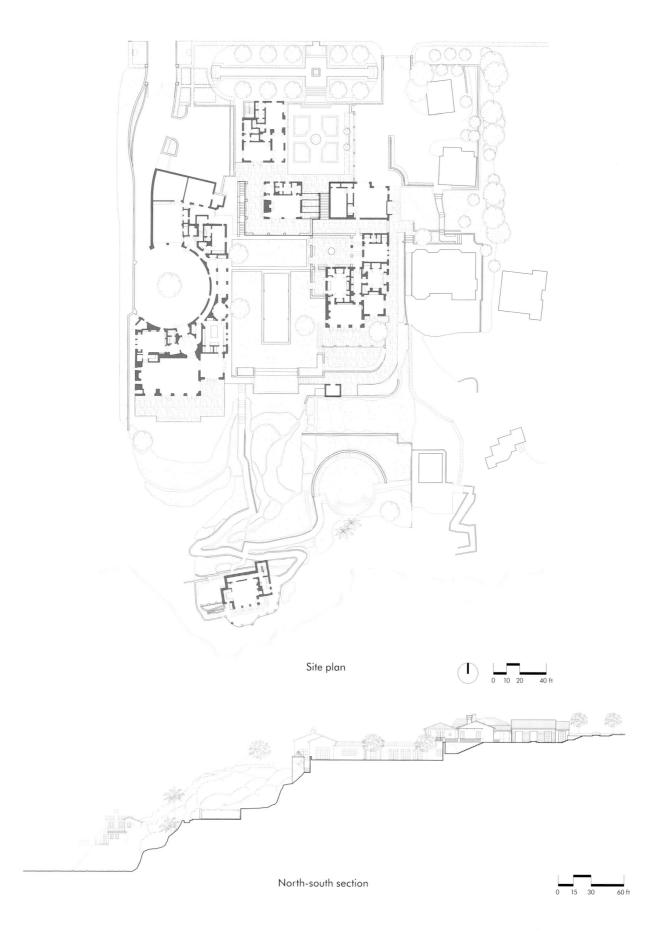

Site plan

0 10 20   40 ft

North-south section

0   15   30   60 ft

Top: Fountain court.

Middle: Lavender
garden.

Bottom: Beach
house from above.

Left: Entry hall.

Right top:
Dining room.

Right bottom:
Living room.

Overleaf: Aerial
view looking north.

Residence on Kiawah Island

Kiawah Island
South Carolina
1995–2003

Among the models for this oceanfront house are the rustic shingled cottages by McKim, Mead & White for the Montauk Association on Long Island. Like them, this house has a relatively simple, rectangular, gabled mass scaled down and softened by secondary gables and dormers, bay windows, and, at the main floor, a broad wrap-around porch.

In accordance with government flood guidelines, the habitable spaces in the house are set a full story above grade. The ensuing battered and shingled foundation walls form a plinth that is appropriate to the Tuscan columns of the main porch. At the entry facade, the brick chimney bisecting the center gable counterpoints the strongly horizontal base.

The principal rooms on two floors are arranged en suite with rhythmically disposed, deeply angled bays opening views to the sea. A hidden stair leads to a home-office aerie on the third floor.

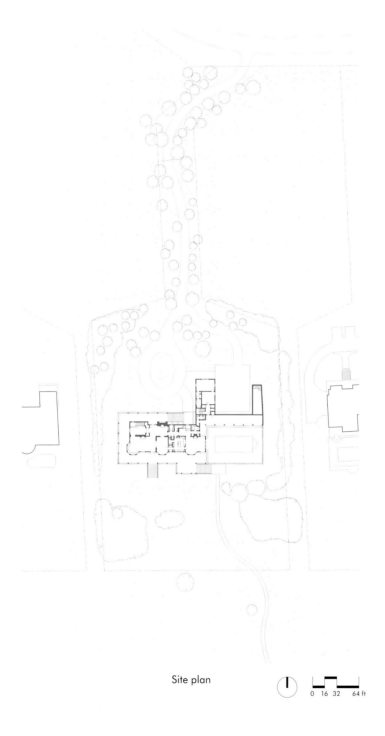

Site plan

0 16 32   64 ft

Left top: Third-floor study.

Left middle: Living room.

Left bottom: South porch.

Right: Porch at third-floor study.

International Storytelling Center

Dedicated to the preservation and promulgation of oral storytelling, the International Storytelling Center is being realized in stages. Located at the edge of the most urban stretch of Main Street in Tennessee's oldest and best-preserved town, where it forms a courtyard with the historic Chester Inn, the new building makes its own distinct statement, announced on the skyline with a fifty-foot tower. In keeping with Jonesborough's small scale, the new building is organized as a series of components that negotiate the difficult slope between Main Street and a new park.

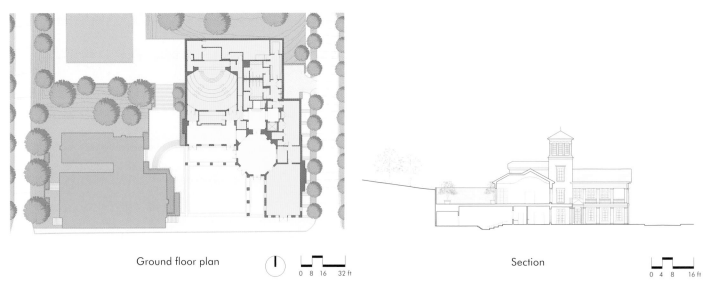

Ground floor plan

0 8 16   32 ft

Section

0 4 8   16 ft

Southwest Quadrangle

Georgetown University
Washington, D.C.
1996–2003

A 780-bed student residential quadrangle, 1,200-seat dining hall, and an underground combined 800-car parking garage and bus maintenance facility represent the first project to be realized as part of our master plan for Georgetown University's 102-acre campus. Together with a new residence for Georgetown's Jesuit Community designed by another architect, the residential quadrangle and O'Donovan Hall surround a half-acre south-facing plaza that opens to views of the Potomac River as it forms a new entrance to the university.

The residences are organized on their upper floors as "neighborhoods" for a maximum of forty-two students. The ground floor, incorporating a mailroom, library, and recreation, meeting, and music-practice rooms as well as five faculty apartments, is penetrated by a vaulted open-air gallery connecting the new quadrangle to playing fields and future buildings to the north. O'Donovan Hall, a freestanding dining facility, incorporates two 580-seat dining halls and a 40-seat private dining room with associated serving kitchens. Reflecting Georgetown's traditional architecture, especially Healy Hall, its signature building, the new buildings are clad in red brick with buff-colored cast stone trim and dark gray slate roofs.

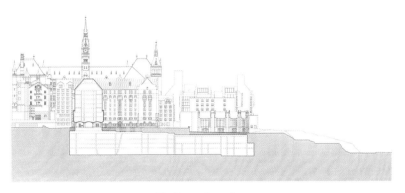

North-south section

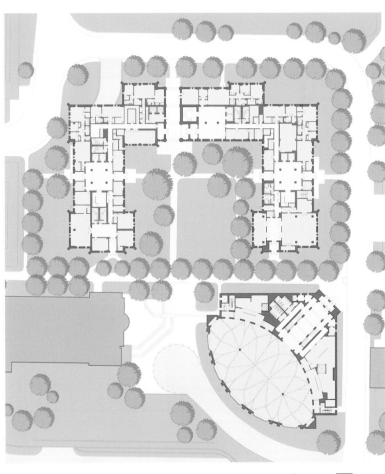

Ground floor plan

0   20   40   80 ft

Left: O'Donovan
Dining Hall from
Library Walk.

Right top: Upper
dining room in
O'Donovan Hall.

Right bottom: Detail
at south facade,
O'Donovan Hall.

Residence in Napa County

On an expansive site with views of the Napa Valley and distant mountains, a series of variously scaled stucco-faced and tile-roofed volumes are arranged linearly along an axis of circulation to form a relaxed grouping that straddles its knoll and defines implied and real courtyards. A garage set apart from the main house by a walled garden and a rubble-stone-faced guest house by the pool nestle into the hillside to open up views from the main house and to minimize the impact of building on the site.

Top: Entry (west)
facade.

Bottom, from left:
View from northeast.
Walled garden.
Dining wing at west
facade.

Left top:
Living room.

Left bottom:
Dining room.

Right bottom:
Dining pergola.

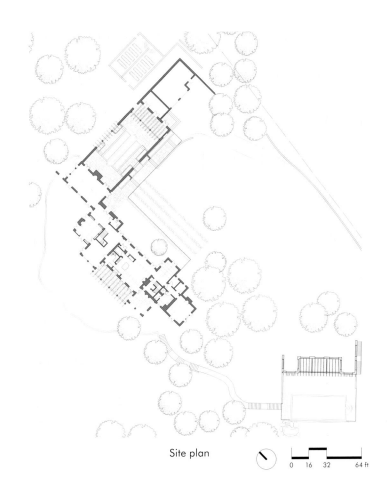

Site plan

0   16   32   64 ft

West elevation

0 10 20   40 ft

Guild Hall

East Hampton
New York
1997–2009

A five-year program of rebuilding an almost eighty-year-old facility (Aymar Embury, 1931) resulted in the reconfiguration of the lobby, galleries, and garden; the creation of a new education center, administrative offices, and a museum shop; and the complete technical upgrading and physical restoration of the beloved John Drew Theater.

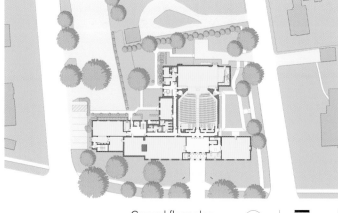

Ground floor plan

0   20   40   80 ft

Left: Entry (north)
facade from Main
Street.

Top: Main Street
facade from
Dunemere Lane.

Middle: Woodhouse
Gallery.

Bottom: Gift shop.

Residence
on Long Island

A long two-story mass with lower service wings connected by curved hyphens forms a square entry court. The plan arranges the principal formal rooms in an enfilade along the south to afford each an unobstructed ocean view, while broad galleries link the informal living and service areas to the east and west.

Crossing the site in a sweeping arc, the main drive passes the pool and tennis complex, treated as a secret garden, rising to the house, which is set as far back as possible on the deep site to dramatize the approach. Deborah Nevins's landscape design of plantings grouped en poché along the edges of the property enhances the somewhat abstract and solitary presence of the house between the broadly expansive lawn and the open sky.

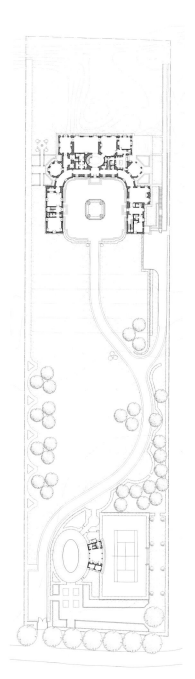

Site plan

0   20   40   80 ft

Left: Entry.

Right top: Stair hall.

Right bottom: Gallery.

Below: West terrace.

Residence
in Palo Alto

Palo Alto, California
1998–2004

Distinguished from its neighbors by its formal street presence, achieved by a symmetrical facade with a pedimented loggia and a broad welcoming terrace flanked by lawn and symmetrically positioned flowering magnolias, this house, true to its Palladian model, Villa Pisani, has a clear bi-axial plan adjusted to modern living in the north wing, conceived as an asymmetrical service addition to an original structure. In contrast to the formality of the street elevation, the garden facade, with its pergolas and balconies, provides a more relaxed backdrop for family life. The L configuration of the house and pool allows the principal interior and exterior spaces to enjoy a southwestern exposure and views toward a spectacular hundred-year-old California live oak that dominates the garden.

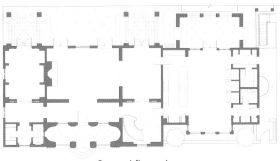

Ground floor plan

Second floor plan

0 4 8   16 ft

Left: Entry portico
looking to living
room.

Top: Garden (south)
facade.

Bottom left:
Gallery looking to
living room.

Bottom right:
Stair hall.

Miami Beach
Library

Reinforcing the characteristic relaxed modernism of Miami Beach, the 45,000-square-foot Florida keystone, terra cotta, and stucco library facing Collins Park is entered under a bold portico carried on an inverted tapering column. Inside, a double-height lobby visually connects the various functional areas to each other. The ground floor contains a 140-seat auditorium, the general library collection, and a café which opens onto a walled garden with a fountain. The second floor includes a large children's library, a young adult section overlooking the lobby, and a reading room for local history and special collections.

Left: Entry.

Right: Lobby.

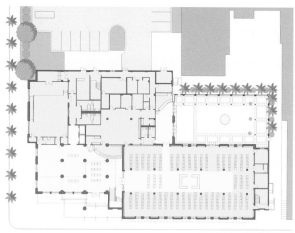

Ground floor plan

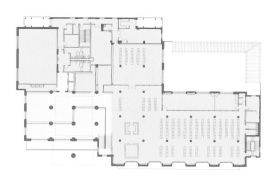

Second floor plan

0 10 20   40 ft

Left: Lobby.

Right top: Children's
reading room.

Right middle: Seating
area in children's
reading room.

Right bottom:
Meeting room.

Peter Jay Sharp Boathouse

Swindler Cove Park
Upper Manhattan
New York, New York
1998–2004

Located on the Harlem River immediately south of Sherman Creek, the Sharp Boathouse reestablishes the historic presence of recreational boating facilities on Manhattan's northern waterfront. The boathouse is a public facility conceived and developed by the New York Restoration Project, a non-profit, privately funded organization working to restore neglected landscapes to active public use. This project is part of the rehabilitation of the blighted shoreline undertaken by New York City and State agencies.

To avoid harming the fragile intertidal environment, the painted board-and-batten wood-framed boathouse has been designed as a floating structure, as were the earlier boathouses located on the site. Access to the facility from the promenade atop the nearby embankment is through a gated entrance and down a series of ramped fixed piers leading to floating docks. The first floor of the boathouse contains storage space and a launching area for sixteen boats; administrative, exercise, and meeting rooms are housed on the second floor, where spectators may view crew practices and races from the vantage of a generously proportioned deck sheltered by an expansive bracketed metal roof. The design of the boathouse was taken forward by our colleague Armand LeGardeur after he left our office.

Left: Deck looking
to boat storage.

Right top: View
from embankment.

Right middle: View
from embankment.

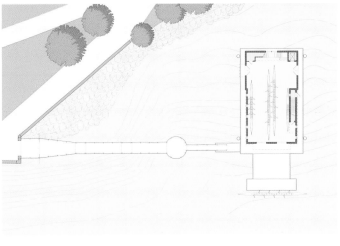

Site plan

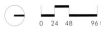

0 24 48   96 ft

Clearwater
Public Library

Clearwater, Florida
2001–2004

Top: Detail at
west facade.

Bottom: View
from southwest.

Taking full advantage of a dramatic site on a bluff overlooking Coachman Park and the intercoastal waterway, the three-story, 90,000-square-foot library is a deliberate attempt to create a locally recognizable landmark that will help catalyze the redevelopment of the city's ailing downtown. The library presents an urbane and dignified face to Osceola Avenue, reserving its more exuberant expression for the park, where large windows are shaded by a broad extension of the undulating roof that forms a superscale porch. Controlled natural daylighting supplements and reduces artificial lighting requirements, and rainwater is captured and re-used for irrigation. Building materials were selected for their appropriateness to local conditions and sustainability, as well as their beauty and utility.

Left: Popular
materials reading
room.

Right: Seating
area in main
reading room.

Right: Café
from above.

East-west section

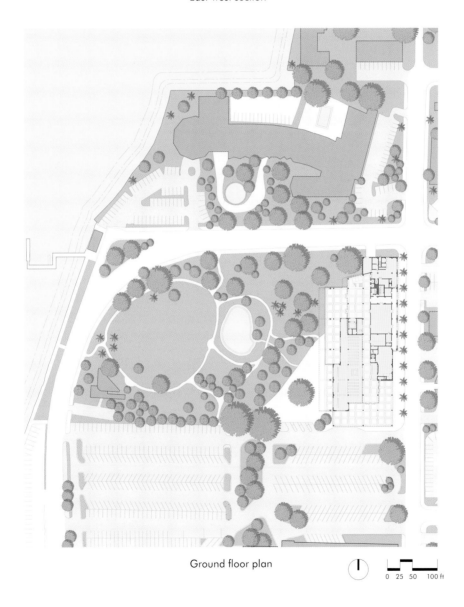

Ground floor plan

0 25 50   100 ft

Perkins Visitor Center

Wave Hill
Riverdale, The Bronx
New York
1998–2004

Top: Gift shop.

Bottom: Side entry.

With splendid views overlooking the Hudson River and New Jersey Palisades, Wave Hill is an internationally respected public garden and cultural institution offering educational programs in the arts and sciences. Our design for the Perkins Visitor Center, incorporating a fire-devastated turn-of-the-century garage, provides a skylighted, timber-trussed gift shop and accessible visitor amenities, workspace for the horticultural staff, and a walled service yard that shields service vehicles and maintenance activities from visitors' view.

Below: Main entry.

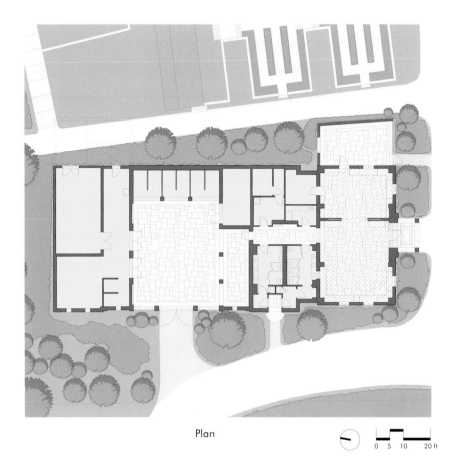

Plan

0 5 10   20 ft

Site plan

0 50 100   200 ft

Informatics and Communications Technology Complex

Indiana University /
Purdue University
Indianapolis, Indiana
1998–2004

Forming the northeast corner of a new academic quadrangle at the gateway to a sprawling post–World War II campus, this 207,000-square-foot building houses a variety of functions relating to information technology, including the global operations center for Internet2 as well as classrooms and offices for the Schools of Music, Library and Information Sciences, and Informatics.

At the intersection of the building's two wings, a top-lit four-story atrium connects the public street with the quadrangle. This arrangement was initially adopted to permit the building to be separated into two construction phases. Funding subsequently was found to realize both wings at once.

Our design combines different textures of locally produced Indiana limestone with large, lightly-tinted windows and silver-gray metal detailing. At the fifth floor a pergola shades a south-facing faculty roof terrace while a curving glass wall at the first and second floors brings natural light to student lounge and study areas adjacent to classrooms.

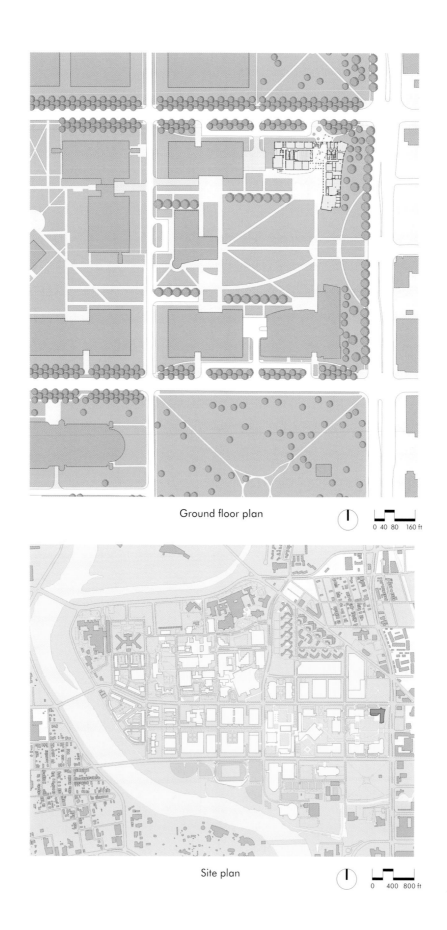

Ground floor plan

0 40 80   160 ft

Site plan

0   400   800 ft

Left: Entry at West
Michigan Street.

Right top: Atrium.

Right bottom:
Lounge.

House in Tidewater Virginia

1999–2005

This shingled house, showcasing the owners' collections of art objects and paintings, occupies a wooded headland site with panoramic views of Hampton Roads and the James River. In order to open views in at least two directions from most rooms, the house is configured as a broadly gabled main mass with an extended service wing that is both lower than and set back from the former. Borrowing from the shipbuilding traditions of the area, the main roofs are gently bowed and hull-shaped. The principal formal rooms are in the larger portion of the house, while the master bedroom suite is in the "tail." A tower that recalls those of traditional shingled architecture in New England, as well as the lighthouses of the Virginia and Carolina coasts, anchors the composition at its southern end.

Site plan

0 15 30   60 ft

Top: View from south.

Bottom left: East
facade from
the James River.

Bottom right: Entry
(north) facade.

Below: Living room.

Sterling Glen of Roslyn Senior Living Residence

Roslyn, New York
1999–2007

Left: Entry (east) facade.

Right: Entry.

Remediating an environmentally compromised site in close proximity to the historic village of Roslyn while providing the community with a new waterfront park, Sterling Glen reestablishes a clear connection between the downtown and the harbor that had been lacking for generations and reinforces the historic character of Roslyn's colonial and colonial revival architecture.

Site plan

0 75 150 300 ft

Below: View from
second-floor porch to
Hempstead Harbor.

Zubiarte Retail and Leisure Complex

Bilbao, Spain
1999–2004

Right: Entry.

A key element in the revitalization of the city's riverfront, Zubiarte (Catalan for "between the two bridges") forms part of Cesar Pelli's master plan for the area of land immediately to the west of Frank Gehry's Guggenheim Museum. Zubiarte plays its part in Pelli's extension of the Ensanche, the nineteenth-century street grid of Bilbao, with the new north-south streets realized as glass-covered pedestrian arcades that break up the big block into four distinct buildings as they lead to the river. Although Zubiarte takes its place within the rectilinear discipline of the Ensanche, it addresses the river with a distinctive sweeping arc of terraces and broad flights of stairs descending to a new waterfront boulevard and promenade. Visitors entering the city across the Puente Deusto, one of the city's principal entry points, are welcomed into the building under a boldly cantilevered glass marquee.

Patterned brick and stone facades both inside and out refer to the predominant building materials and forms of the city while providing a variety of detailing that helps break down the scale of the overall structure.

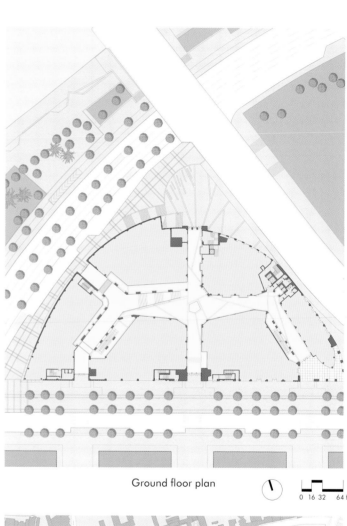

Ground floor plan

0 16 32 64 ft

Site plan

0 150 300 600 ft

Left top: View from Abandoibarra Park.

Left bottom: View looking east along Calle Lehendakari Leizaola.

Right: View looking west past the Guggenheim Museum (Frank Gehry & Associates, 2002).

Residence in California

Perched on a terraced site affording panoramic views of the city 900 feet below, the Pacific Ocean to the west, and the mountains to the east, this white-painted brick house evokes the casual glamour of Hollywood's heyday. House and garden are designed as one, with a carefully orchestrated sequence of spaces leading from the broad central gallery that runs the length of the house parallel to the southerly views, past the living room with its dramatic vista of sloping lawn, to an elliptical garden, and then to a hidden garden and lower terrace, where a pavilion commands a horizon swimming pool hovering over the city below.

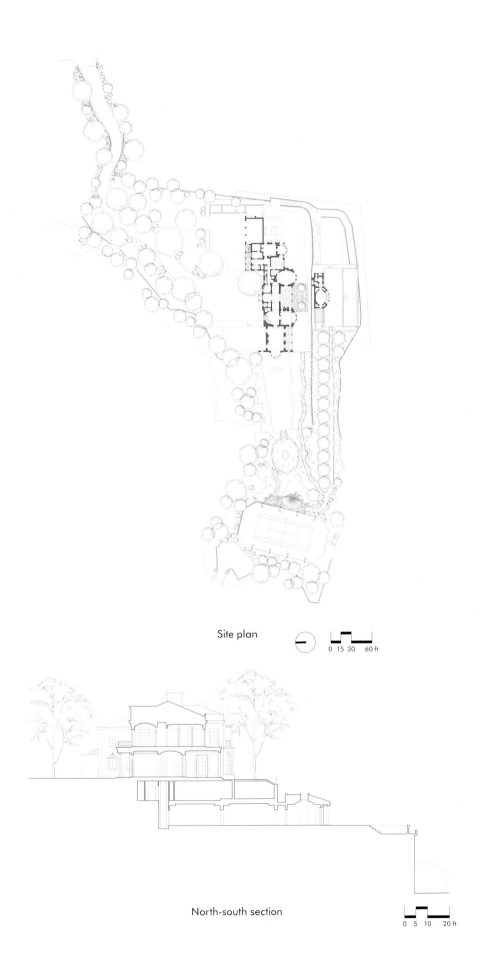

Left top: West facade.

Left bottom: South facade of main house and pool pavilion.

Site plan

0 15 30   60 ft

North-south section

0 5 10   20 ft

Left: Stair hall.

Right top: Living
room.

Right middle: Library.

Right bottom:
Stair hall looking
to gallery.

Residence at West Tisbury

Martha's Vineyard,
Massachusetts
1999–2004

Left top: Entry (south) facade.

Left middle: West terrace.

Left bottom: View from northeast.

Right: North facade at living room.

A compound of houses and outbuildings on a generous site commanding views north across Vineyard Sound has as its principal focus the main residence, designed as an aggregation of various elements grouped around a wind-sheltered south-facing courtyard and overlooking a meadow, orchard, and pond restored after fifty years of neglect.

Below: Entry (south)
facade.

Left top: Guest house.

Left bottom: Guest
cottage.

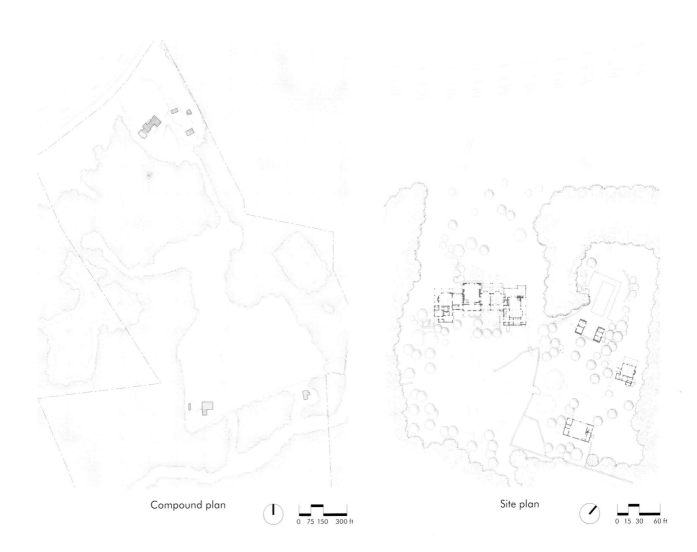

Compound plan   ⊕   0 75 150 300 ft

Site plan   ⊘   0 15 30 60 ft

Below: Squash barn.

Musiskwartier

A 9,600-square-meter mixed-use project, the centerpiece of a strategy to reclaim a formerly industrial part of the city through the creation of a market square surrounded by new buildings incorporating ground-floor retail with residential accommodation above, is carefully woven into and around existing historic buildings, in an idiom that complements but does not mimic them. A glass-covered arcade offers shoppers shelter during the long, rainy Dutch winter, and provides an important connection from the established shopping destination Land van de Markt through to the new market square on the Brouwerstraat.

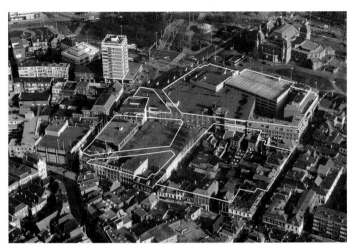

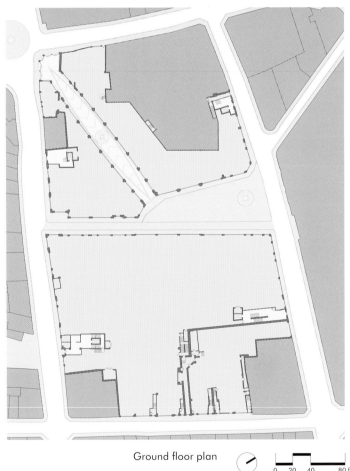

Ground floor plan

0   20   40   80 ft

Below: New plaza.

Top: Residences at rooftop court.

Bottom: Retail passage.

Folly and Pool Cottage in Sonoma

Clients for whom we had designed a house in San Francisco asked us to complement their existing weekend house in the Sonoma Valley with accommodations for entertaining and a pool house that doubles as a guest cottage. Atop a hill at the entry to the property, oriented to spectacular views south to the Sonoma Mountains and east and north over the valley, a reading room, a kitchen wing, and a dining pergola with adjacent barbecue frame an entry lawn. Downslope, a pavilion is situated amid mature Arbutus and tall live oaks, with a south-facing pergola overlooking the pool. The two structures share a common vocabulary inspired by northern California farm vernacular with a nod to the work of Bernard Maybeck and a common palette of cedar board-and-batten siding, corrugated metal roofs, Sonoma stone walls, and bluestone paving. A new main house is under construction on the brow of the next ridge.

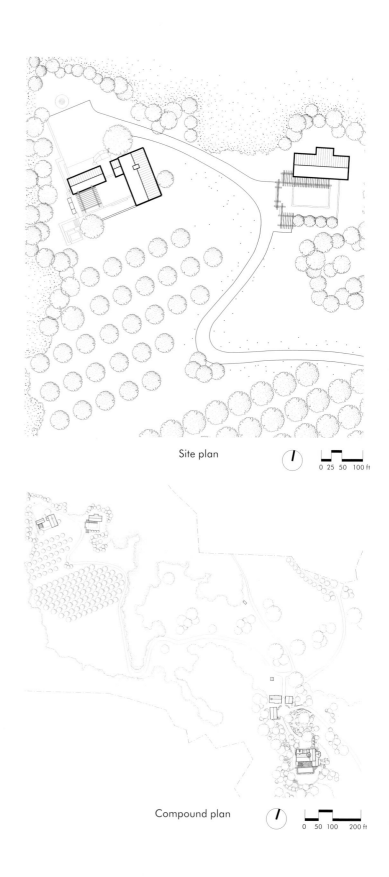

Site plan

0 25 50 100 ft

Compound plan

0 50 100 200 ft

Left: Living room.

Right top: Entry.

Right middle:
Living room looking
to dining terrace.

Right bottom:
Dining terrace.

Below: Pool terrace.

143

Aging and Allied Health Building and Gill Heart Institute

University of Kentucky
Medical Center
Lexington, Kentucky
1998–2002

Housing eleven of the College of Allied Health's previously dispersed departments, the Office of the Medical Center Chancellor, and a 90-bed geriatric inpatient nursing care and teaching facility, the Aging and Allied Health Building is linked to the Gill Heart Institute by a bridge deliberately designed to realize a new southern gateway to the university's Lexington campus. The red brick, Indiana limestone, and matching cast stone vocabulary of the buildings intensifies the watery federal-style character of the historic campus core.

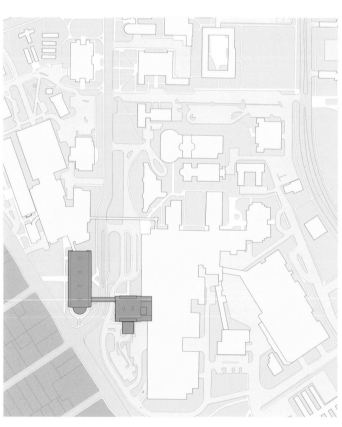

Site plan

0 75 150 300 ft

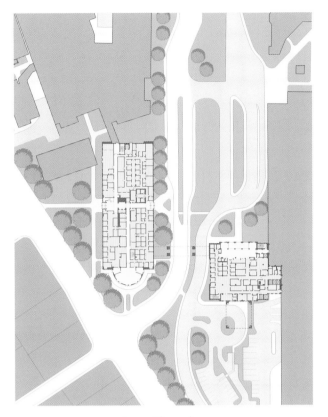

Second floor plan

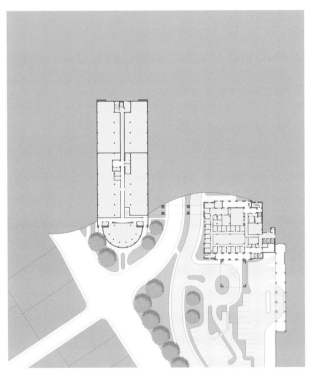

Ground floor plan

0   30 60   120 ft

Residence
in Edgartown

Martha's Vineyard,
Massachusetts
1999–2003

To transform a sprawling, architecturally undistinguished house deemed too new to tear down, an existing one-story entry was replaced with a two-story gambrel-roofed addition that contains a spacious hall, staircase, and library on the first floor and a master suite upstairs. The loftlike living, dining, and kitchen wing of the original house was reworked to provide discrete rooms and a new south-facing dining-room pavilion. Awkwardly placed awning windows were replaced with large, simple double-hung units; detailed trim was introduced throughout. A new pool house and spa building were designed to reflect the cottages found on the picturesque streets of Edgartown.

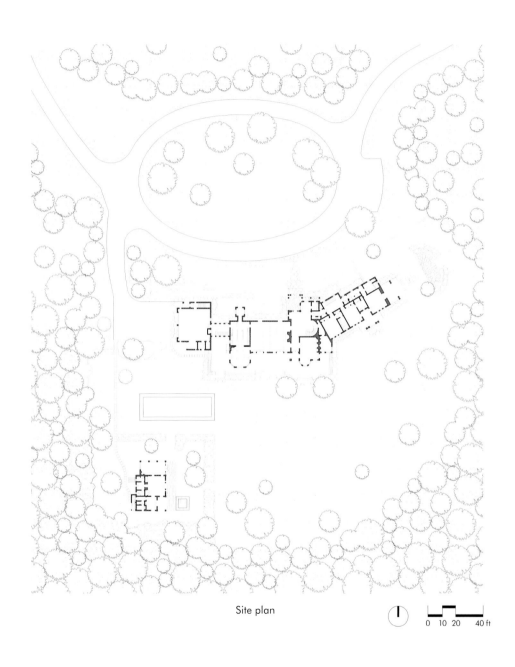

Site plan

0 10 20   40 ft

Residence on
Salt Spring Island

Salt Spring Island,
British Columbia
1999–2005

The southerly tip of a narrow peninsula
provides a secluded spot for the house with
panoramic views of both Ganges and Long
Harbours and the neighboring islands,
animated by the comings and goings of fer-
ries and float planes. A boathouse on Long
Harbour, a teahouse to the west adjacent
to the entrance drive overlooking Ganges
Harbour, and a spa pavilion situated at the
south end of the point join the U-shaped
main house that wraps around an entrance
courtyard sheltered from the strong, often
cold, prevailing southerly winds.

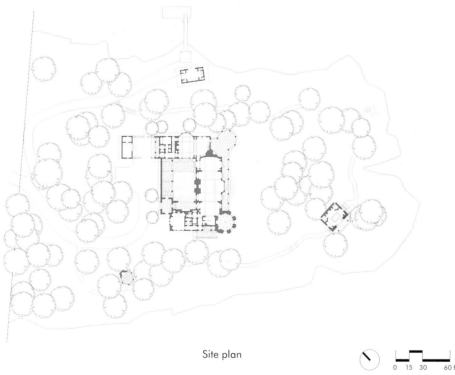

Site plan

0 15 30   60 ft

Left: Library.

Right top: Living hall.

Right bottom: Entry hall.

Talisker Club Park

Park City, Utah
1999–2008

Yielding center stage to the remarkable landscape, the golf clubhouse is treated as a group of pavilions with generous porches and overhanging eaves, stone and wood finishes, and large windows.

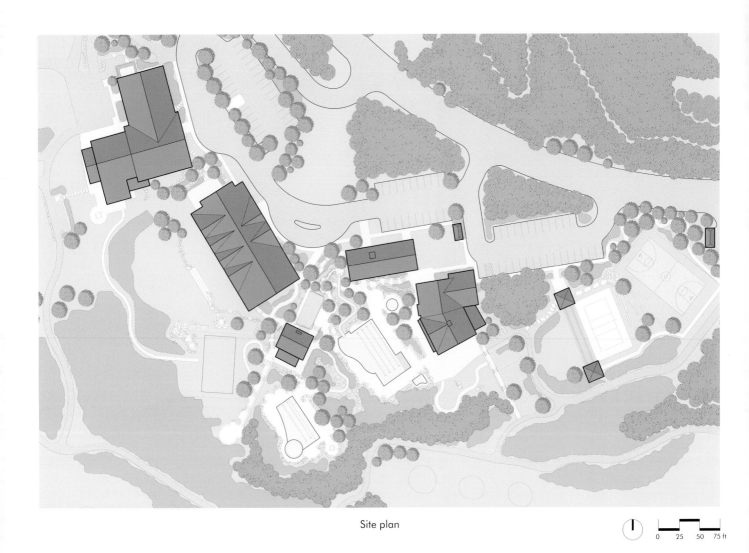

Site plan

0   25   50   75 ft

Top: View looking northwest.

Middle: Member services building.

Bottom: Pool terrace looking to activity center.

Top: Stair to pool terrace.

Bottom: Porch at member services building.

Feil Residence Hall

Brooklyn Law School
Brooklyn, New York
2000–2005

Our firm's second building for the Brooklyn Law School provides apartments catering to the needs of law students, many of whom are returning to school after other careers, and communal amenities on the ground and top floors. Classical detailing recalls our 1994 classroom building addition two blocks away in Brooklyn's Civic Center, but the new building's red brick cladding makes it clearly a part of the increasingly residential neighborhood that the students now call home.

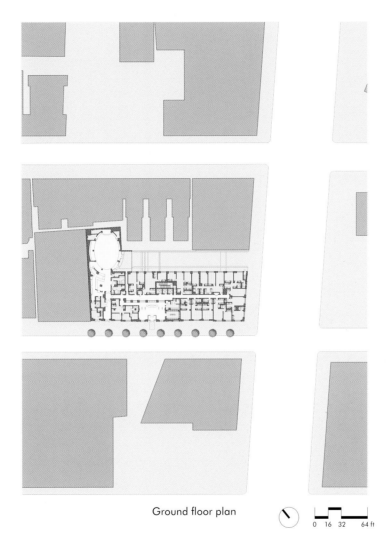

Ground floor plan

0 16 32   64 ft

Below: Entry on
State Street.

Comcast Center

Philadelphia, Pennsylvania
2000–2008

The tallest LEED-CS Gold certified building in the United States, this 58-story, 1.25 million-square-foot faceted obelisk is clad in silvery high-performance glass with ultra-clear, low-iron glass at the corners and crown. A half-acre south-facing public plaza designed in association with the Olin Partnership and a 110-foot-high light-flooded public winter garden create a civic gateway to the building and to the subterranean concourse of Suburban Station, Philadelphia's primary commuter rail station. The winter garden features a double-skin glass curtain wall with sunscreens and louvers that optimize daylight and views while moderating daily and seasonal thermal performance. Radiant heating, thermal extraction, and displacement ventilation combine to provide exceptional energy performance for this civic-scaled space. The winter garden houses *Humanity in Motion,* a commissioned installation by American sculptor Jonathan Borofsky, and in the lobby, *The Comcast Experience* is a high-definition video installation by David Niles.

Below: Skyline view
looking northwest.

Overleaf: Skyline
view looking west.

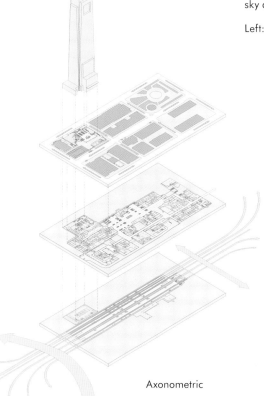

Far left: Plaza and south facade with winter gardens and sky atria.

Left: South facade.

Axonometric

Floor 55

Floor 42

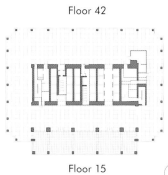

Floor 15

0 16 32   64 ft

Top: Stair from winter
garden to concourse.

Bottom, from left:
Lobby.
Entry at plaza.
Detail at winter garden.

Right: Jonathan
Borofsky's *Humanity
in Motion* in the
winter garden.

Below: Stair from concourse to winter garden, looking to David Niles's video wall *The Comcast Experience*.

Northrup Hall

Trinity University
San Antonio, Texas
2000–2004

Left top: View from
southeast.

Left bottom: Covered
walkway from entry.

Right: Acequia and
covered walkway
at entry.

The Trinity University campus, planned
in 1952 by O'Neil Ford, a noted regional-
ist modernist architect, includes many fine
buildings designed in a distinctive and
consistent palette of brick, metal, and glass.
Our design for Northrup Hall, the new
principal entry to the campus, builds upon
and expands the architectural language of
the earlier buildings, using similar materials but adding energy-responsive elements
such as brises-soleil, covered walkways, and
a drought-resistant landscape. The building
houses student services, development, and
central administration offices.

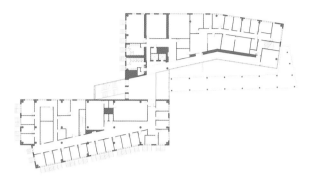

Second floor plan

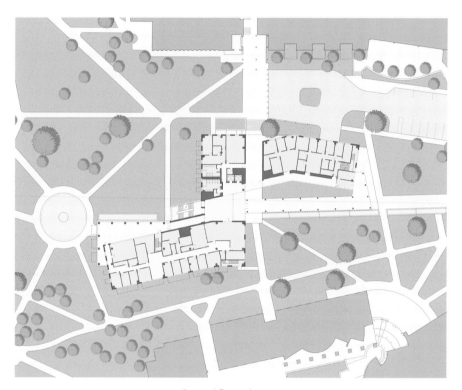

Ground floor plan

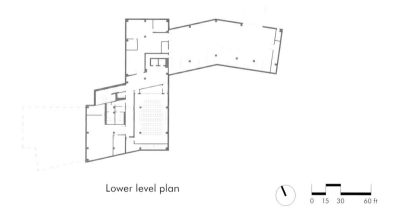

Lower level plan

0 15 30   60 ft

Left: Detail at fourth floor looking to San Antonio skyline.

Right top: Lobby balcony.

Right bottom: Seminar room.

187

Residence in East Hampton

East Hampton, New York
2000–2004

Replacing the owners' long-time former residence with the French country-style residence they had always wanted, this house is entered through a garden courtyard on the north. On the south, facing an expansive garden and lawn, two pavilions frame the principal facade.

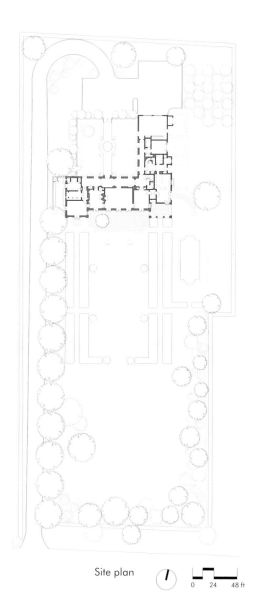

Site plan

0   24   48 ft

Top: South facade.

Middle: Dining room.

Bottom: Loggia
looking to garden.

Left top: South facade
from garden.

Left bottom: South
terrace.

Right: Loggia from
garden.

Tribeca Green

Battery Park City
New York, New York
2000–2005

In keeping with the Battery Park City Authority's mandate for environmentally sustainable design, Tribeca Green, our second apartment building in Battery Park City, is LEED Gold certified. A mechanical penthouse clad in photovoltaic panels and a green roof on the fifteenth floor are among the energy-conserving features.

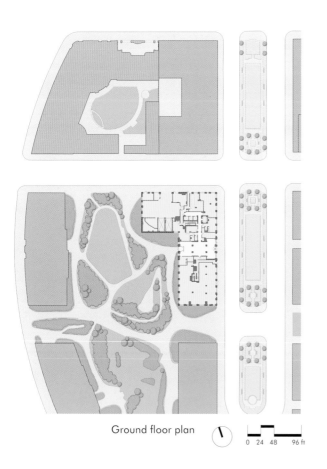

Ground floor plan

0 24 48   96 ft

Left: View from North
End Avenue.

Right top: Entry at
North End Avenue.

Right middle: Lobby.

Right bottom:
Concierge desk.

Dining Hall

The Taft School
Watertown, Connecticut
Project, 2006

To replace an outgrown 1950s facility, this proposal combined a renovation of the 1913 Horace Dutton Taft dining hall and a new 250-seat dining hall, employing traditional Gothic forms and details realized with waterstruck red brick, cast stone, slate roof tiles, stained white oak, and terra cotta floors to seamlessly extend the palette of the school's historic buildings.

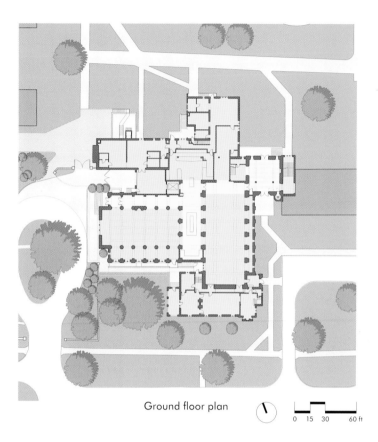

Ground floor plan

0   15   30   60 ft

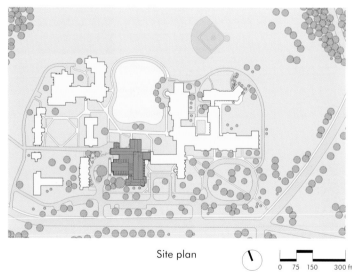

Site plan

0   75   150   300 ft

Top: View from campus entry.

Bottom left: Renovated dining hall.

Bottom right: New dining hall.

Columbus
Public Library

Columbus, Georgia
2001–2005

Respectful of the prevalent red-brick classicism of the region, but in a contemporary way, the three-story library rises to a lantern that has become a municipal beacon. A broad stairway leads directly from the lobby to the rotunda gallery on the second level, off which is the library's gently curved, generously scaled main reading room.

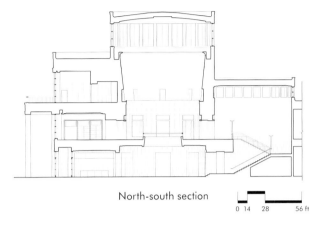

North-south section

0 14 28 56 ft

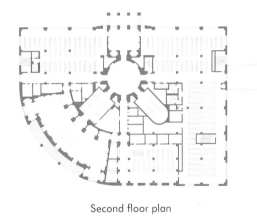

Second floor plan

Ground floor plan

0 20 40 80 ft

Top left: Lobby.

Top right: Main Stair.

Right: Rotunda at second floor.

Middle left: Bradley Memorial reading room.

Middle right: Reading Room.

Bottom left: Children's services desk.

Bottom right: Children's reading room.

Cottage at Michaelangelo Park

San Francisco,
California
2001–2006

Right: Garden
looking to guest
house and studio.

Set in the center of a city block some forty
feet below its south-facing street-level
entrance, this cottage enjoys views of San
Francisco Bay and Coit Tower. A stair
leads down to a studio and guest quarters;
across a garden, a reception hall topped by
an octagonal lantern gives onto a loft-like
living and dining room and, tucked into the
slope below, a media room and master suite.

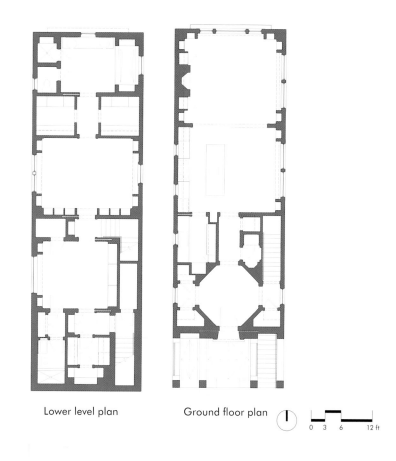

Lower level plan   Ground floor plan

0 3 6   12 ft

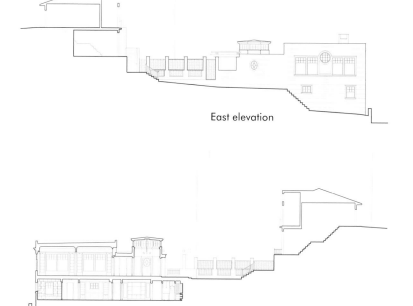

East elevation

North-south section

0 5 10   20 ft

The Museum Center at the Mark Twain House

Hartford, Connecticut
2000–2003

Left top: View from
northwest.

Left bottom: Terrace.

Right: Entry stair.

The Mark Twain House (Edward
Tuckerman Potter, 1874) is a masterful
architectural portrait of one of America's
greatest writers. Our Museum Center adds
ticketing, orientation, a lecture hall, and
exhibition galleries, all linked by a winding stepped ramp that leads visitors up
from parking to the top of the twenty-five-
foot bluff where a café opens to a terrace
overlooking the house and its grounds.
The center is the first museum building
to achieve U.S. Green Building Council
LEED certification.

Right top:
Stepped ramp.

Right bottom:
Left: Ticketing desk.
Right: Great
hall looking to
orientation hall.

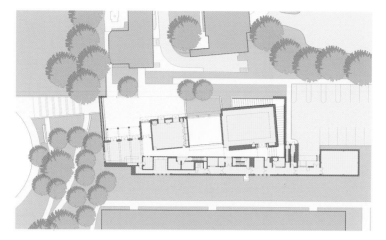

Second floor plan

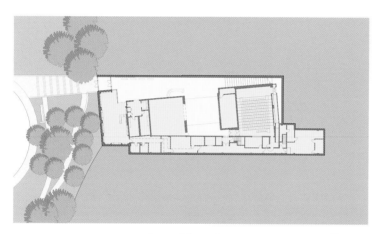

Ground floor plan

0 15 30   60 ft

Site plan

0 32 64   128 ft

AN UNEASY CONSCIENCE IS A HAIR IN THE MOUTH

THERE IS NO SADDER THING THAN A YOUNG PESSIMIST EXCEPT AN OLD OPTIMIST

AND DON'T DIE IN THE MEANTIME

Robinson and Merhige Courthouse

Richmond, Virginia
2001–2008

Sitting at the boundary between Richmond's historic commercial core, now being reinvented as a performing arts district, and the Capitol Square district, the new Federal Courthouse takes its place among other important civic buildings lining Broad Street. The 325,000-square-foot building's signature footprint forms a bent or bowed slab, intended to function as a corner post to the Capitol Square district, which its south-facing outer radius will overlook. The curving footprint of the courthouse provides a garden-like setting for two adjacent historic churches, St. Peter's (1835, 1854) and St. Paul's (Thomas S. Stewart, 1845), located to the south. On the north, cradled in the building's inner radius, a 100-foot-high atrium turns a less formal face to the commercial district. At night, the illuminated atrium and landscaped areas provide a dramatic backdrop for the developing performing arts district.

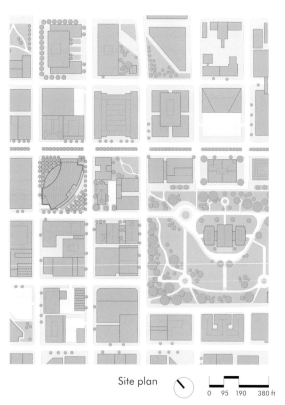

Site plan

0 95 190 380 ft

Top: View from Broad
and Seventh Streets.

Bottom left: Detail at
south facade.

Bottom right: Broad
Street facade.

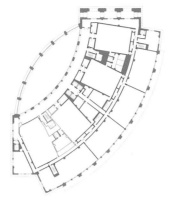

Sixth floor plan

Second floor plan

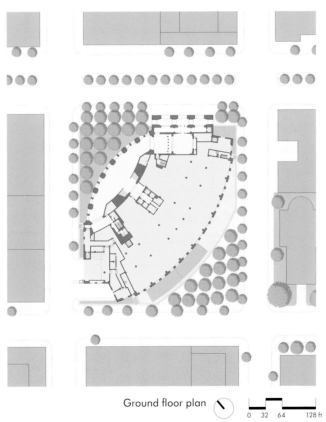

Ground floor plan

0   32   64   128 ft

Below: Special
proceedings courtroom.

House at Seaside

Seaside, Florida
2001–2006

Balancing vernacular and high-style classicism, this compact villa establishes its own identity with superimposed orders on the street facade and an unorthodox beachfront gable carried on a single Ionic column.

Below: South facade from the beach.

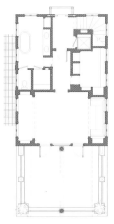

Third floor plan

Second floor plan

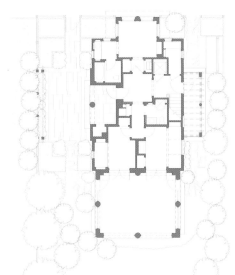

Ground floor plan

0 4 8   16 ft

Left top: Living room.

Left middle: Ground-floor bedroom looking to sleeping porch.

Left bottom: Living room porch.

Right: Sleeping porch.

Torre Almirante

Rio de Janeiro, Brazil
2001–2004

Torre Almirante's curving transparent corner tower, which announces the main entry below, flares upward to create a beacon illuminated by continuously changing light displays from concealed LED fixtures. Above the main entry, three stacked two-story winter gardens, providing unique meeting spaces for tenants, further animate the corner. A double-height open-air loggia at the base integrates the building into downtown Rio's system of continuous pedestrian arcades. Behind it, the 20-foot-tall sweeping backlit onyx lobby wall provides a welcome glow visible through full-height glass walls.

Asked in 2006 to renovate the Castelo Building next door, built in 1933, we inserted a lobby and updated the arcade with detailing that carried forward the original grillwork pattern.

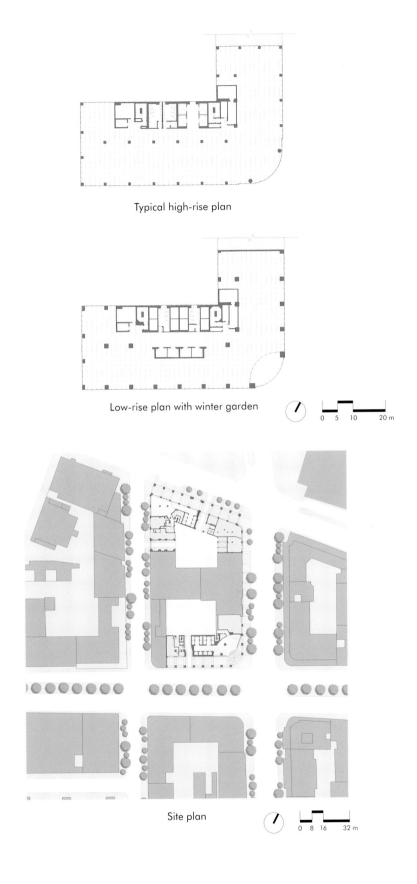

Typical high-rise plan

Low-rise plan with winter garden

0   5   10   20 m

Site plan

0   8   16   32 m

Jacksonville
Public Library

Jacksonville, Florida
2001–2005

A highly efficient, state-of-the-art facility with intimate and grand rooms, garden courtyards, conference areas, cafes, and the like, the building is designed to attract the community in all its diversity and, by virtue of its exterior forms and interior spaces, to become a destination without peer in the city.

A monumental stair rising through the building passes a second-floor courtyard, where a fountain and plantings create an oasis shared by readers and staff, and culminates at the grand reading room, 100 feet square and rising 46 feet to a handkerchief-vaulted ceiling, bathed in natural light from clerestory windows and balconied windows overlooking Hemming Plaza.

Right top: View from
Laura and Monroe
Streets.

Right bottom: Screen
wall at second-floor
courtyard.

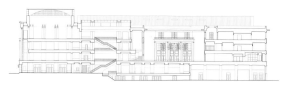

East-west section

Fourth floor plan

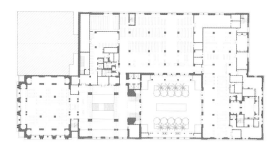

Second floor plan

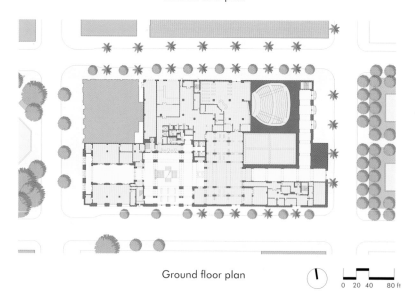

Ground floor plan

Left: Double-height
reading area.

Left: Children's activity
room.

Right top: Children's
room.

Right bottom: Teens'
room.

Top: Grand reading
room with mural by
Al Held.

Bottom: Ansbacher
map room.

Right: Atrium.

The Plaza at PPL Center

Allentown
Pennsylvania
2001–2003

Left top: Hamilton Avenue (south) facade.

Left bottom: View looking east past the Tower at PPL Center (Helmle, Corbett & Harrison, 1928).

Right: Detail at south facade.

A palazzo-like glazed office building set behind a half-acre south-facing landscaped plaza is a notable exemplar of sustainable design. An atrium brings natural light from the top of the building down through all eight floors while providing a centralized common point of orientation. Two-story south-facing winter gardens extend the typical office floors and help reduce heat gain, as do external sunshades at each floor along the south facade and a vegetated roof. Energy audits for the LEED Gold building's first year of operation confirm that it consumes 40 percent less energy than a typical office building of its size and type though its environmental design features added only 4 percent to its construction cost.

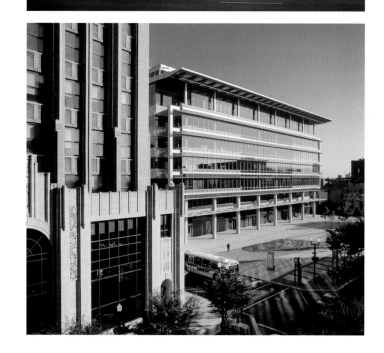

Top left: Atrium.

Top right: Winter
garden.

Bottom left: Terrace
at trading floor.

Bottom right: Atrium.

Eighth floor plan

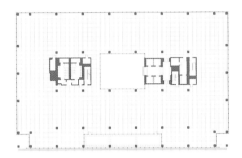

Third floor plan

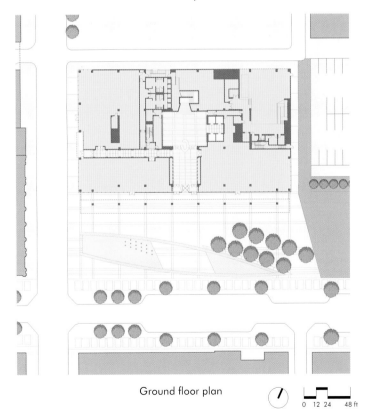

Ground floor plan

0 12 24   48 ft

The Residences at the Ritz-Carlton, Dallas

Dallas, Texas
2001–2007; phase II
completion 2009

Below: Entrance to the residences.

Right: View looking north.

Two buff-colored brick and limestone towers—a cruciform tower providing for a luxury hotel and apartments and additional apartments in the second—connected by a skybridge, are detailed in a simplified Regency style. Four-story townhouses on Olive Street help the towers sit comfortably alongside the adjacent residential neighborhood.

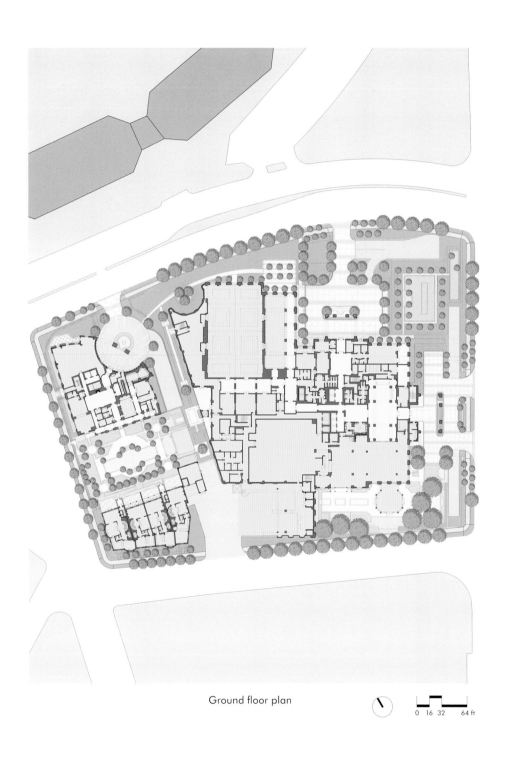

Ground floor plan

0 16 32 64 ft

One St. Thomas
Residences

Toronto, Ontario,
Canada
2001–2008

Left top: View
from south.

Left bottom:
Townhouses on
Charles Street.

Right: Entry on St.
Thomas Street.

This slender, square 29-story tower, rising
through a series of setbacks to a sculptural
penthouse and lantern, combines with
attached townhouses to create a transition
between the highrise residential buildings
of Bay Street and the lowrise structures
of the University of Toronto campus. The
tower's mass is articulated with bay windows, pilasters, cornices, and balconies that
recall grand urban apartment buildings
of the 1920s and 1930s.

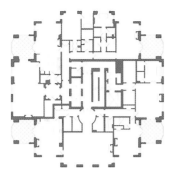

Floor 21

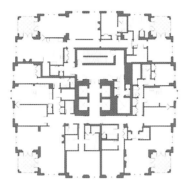

Floor 15

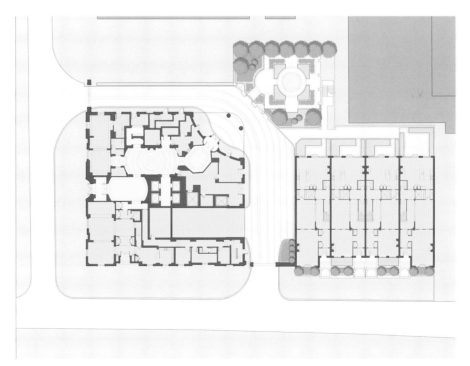

Ground floor plan

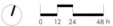

0   12   24   48 ft

Smeal College
of Business

The Pennsylvania State
University
State College, Pennsylvania
2001–2005

Consolidating graduate and undergraduate business programs previously dispersed across the campus, Smeal College
is prominently located at a major campus
entry where it forms part of a new precinct
whose centerpiece is the Meadow, a large
sloping greensward that forms the college's
spacious front yard, shared with the School
of Forestry. A south-facing courtyard offers
the college an outdoor gathering space of
its own.

Two rectilinear wings housing graduate
and undergraduate classrooms are connected by a curved, four-story glass atrium,
serving as a hub of the college's daily life
and as the setting for special gatherings.
A sculptural staircase connecting all levels
offers views to the mountains beyond.

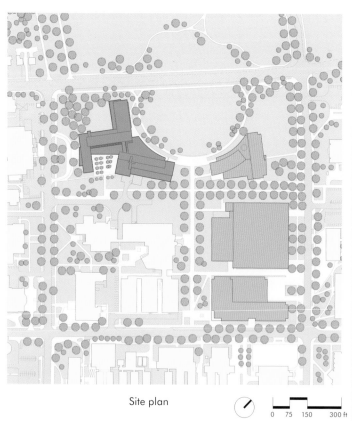

Site plan

0 75 150 300 ft

Left: North facade at
the Meadow.

Top left: Entry on
Shortlidge Road.

Top right: Foyer.

Middle left: Faculty
conference room.

Middle right: North
facade from the
Meadow.

Bottom left: South
courtyard.

Bottom right: Bridge
at atrium.

Third floor plan

Second floor plan

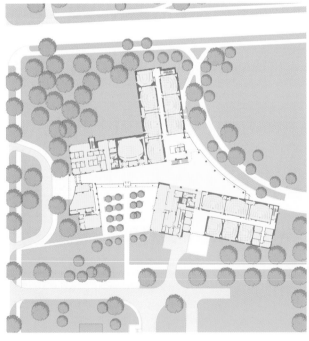

Ground floor plan

0 25 50   100 ft

Joan and Sanford Weill Hall

Gerald R. Ford School
of Public Policy
University of Michigan
Ann Arbor, Michigan
2002–2006

Marking the southern gateway to the university with a tower that houses a monumental stair leading to important public rooms, Weill Hall is organized to encourage a culture of intellectual encounter and exchange, with broad halls and open stairs as well as alcoves and lounges at every corridor intersection. The change in grade across the site allowed for what are effectively two ground floors along the path of travel through the building, with a gateway entrance at the base of the south tower and a more intimate north entry one level above. Picturesque massing and facades of stone-trimmed variegated decorative red brickwork extend the compositional tropes and material palette of such beloved Michigan buildings as the Union and the League, helping to reinforce the university's physical identity.

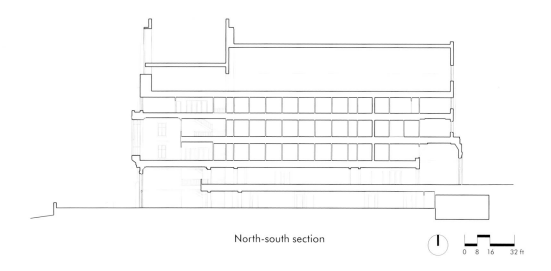

North-south section

0 8 16   32 ft

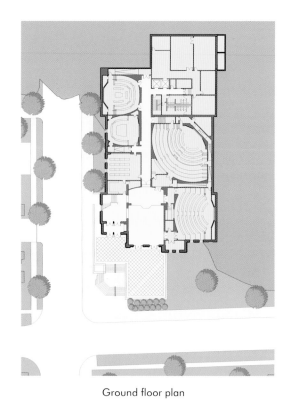

Ground floor plan

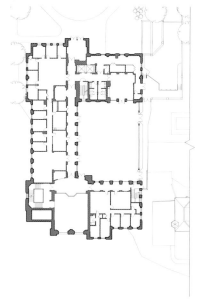

Second floor plan

0 15 30   60 ft

Left: South tower.

Right top: Detail at
west facade.

Right bottom:
North entry.

Top left: Cox alcove.

Bottom left: Second-
floor corridor.

Top right: Towsky
reading room.

Bottom right:
Annenberg auditorium.

Right: Great hall.

North Quad Residential and Academic Complex

University of Michigan
Ann Arbor, Michigan
2006–2010

North Quad represents a new university initiative to combine living, learning, and academic support in one building. Located on a full block anchoring the northwest corner of the main campus, with massing and forms based on the very special blend of Collegiate Gothic and Arts & Crafts that uniquely identify the Ann Arbor campus, North Quad carries forward the strategy we followed in designing Weill Hall (2006), the southern gateway to the main campus. There we looked to the examples of earlier campus architects Emil Lorch, Pond & Pond, and Albert Kahn to create a rich tapestry of deep red brick, stone, and slate, and to shape arcades of flattened arches, grand engaged colonnades, and a landmark tower.

Arranged around interconnected courtyards, with welcoming plazas at the northwest and southeast corners of the block to open up the quad to its surroundings, North Quad preserves the facade of the Carnegie Library on Huron Street as part of a composition that rises in a counterclockwise spiral to a boldly shaped tower terminating the axis of South Thayer Street, where it is visible from as far away as the Diag and constitutes a new icon on the campus skyline.

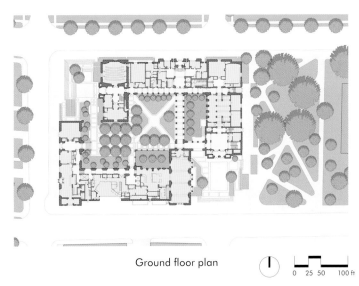
Ground floor plan

0 25 50 100 ft

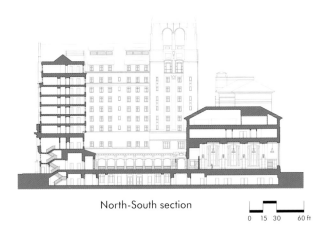
North-South section

0 15 30 60 ft

Site plan

0 18 36 72 ft

Weinberg Building

Sheppard Pratt Hospital
Baltimore, Maryland
2002–2005

Sheppard Pratt Hospital (1861–1895) was designed by Calvert Vaux to meet the needs of mental patients who were confined there for a very long time, if not their entire lives. Mental health care has evolved over the years so that with medication and other treatment methods the typical patient stay is much shorter, more like that of a hospital than an asylum. The Weinberg Building doubles the size of the hospital, enabling the historic buildings to be renovated over time. It acknowledges Vaux's Gothic without direct mimicry while also incorporating the historic power plant and carriage building. Secure outdoor spaces, essential to patient care, are developed as a series of garden rooms.

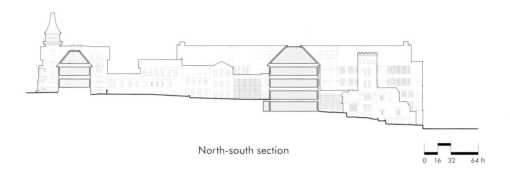

North-south section

0 16 32   64 ft

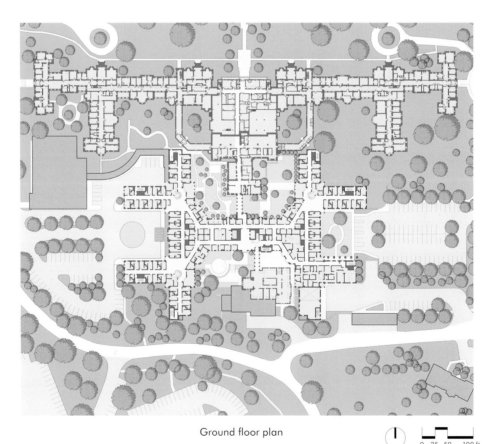

Ground floor plan

0 25 50   100 ft

Left: View looking northwest to original tower.

Right top: Garden court.

Right middle: Link between earlier addition and new building.

Right bottom: North courtyard.

Baker Library | Bloomberg Center

Harvard Business School
Boston, Massachusetts
2002–2005

To transform Baker Library (McKim, Mead & White, 1927), the focal point of the Harvard Business School campus, from a terminus to a crossroads, the building's dead-end stack wings were replaced by a new block accommodating rooms for group study, faculty offices, seminar rooms, and archival storage, thereby opening the building to the south and permitting the business school to address its future development as part of Harvard's expansion into Allston. The U-shaped plan of the expanded library wraps around a top-lit stair that forms a dramatic seam between old and new. As part of the project, with the collaboration of Finegold Alexander + Associates, the facades and important interior rooms of the original Baker building were restored.

Below: Restored
Stamps reading
room.

Below: Restored Stamps reading room.

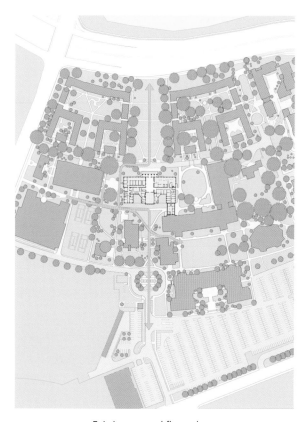

Existing ground floor plan

New ground floor plan

0 25 50   100 ft

Top: South facade,
June 2003.

Middle: South facade,
August 2003.

Bottom: New south
facade.

285

Left top: Seminar room.

Left middle: De Gaspé Beaubien reading room.

Left bottom: The Exchange.

Right: Skylit stair hall.

House on
Lake Michigan

Located on one of the few remaining
undivided estate lots in a northern suburb
of Chicago, this house, inspired by the
free eclecticism of early-twentieth-century
Chicago architects such as Howard Van
Doren Shaw and David Adler, combines
English and American elements into a linear
composition that respects existing plantings
and prioritizes lake views to the east.

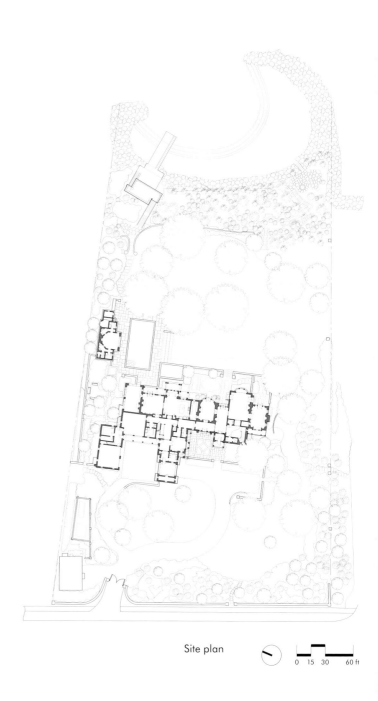

Site plan

0   15   30   60 ft

Left top: Entry court.

Left bottom: View
from Lake Michigan

Right top: Pool house.

Right middle: North
garden looking to
pool terrace.

Right bottom: Sun
deck at boat house.

Below: Dining room.

Residence
in Los Angeles

This stone-clad slate-roofed house engages
the landscape with a sequence of walled
and open courtyards. The mass of the
house is articulated into discrete and
semi-independent pavilions, which, in turn,
provide the architectural focal points for
the outdoor spaces.

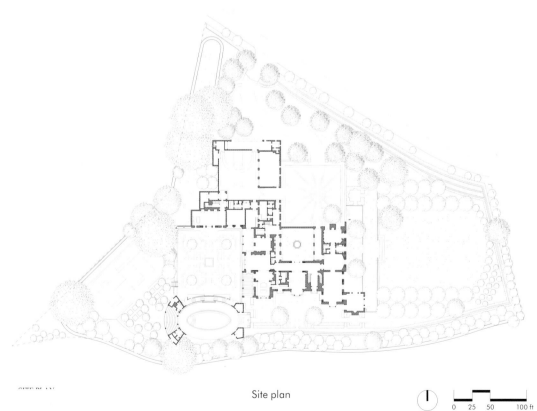

Site plan

Left: East facade.

Right top: Entry to motor court.

Right middle: Detail at east facade.

Right bottom: Courtyard.

Left: Entry arcade.

Right top: Living
room.

Right middle: Family
dining room.

Right bottom: Family
room.

Southeast Federal Center

Washington, D.C.
2002–

Our office contributed to Forest City Washington's selected development proposal for the Washington Navy Yard Annex, facing the Anacostia River. The existing street network is kept substantially intact and five existing buildings will be saved and adaptively re-used as part of what is intended to become a vibrant neighborhood of commercial offices and residences above ground-level retail, with a waterfront park and an anchoring cultural institution.

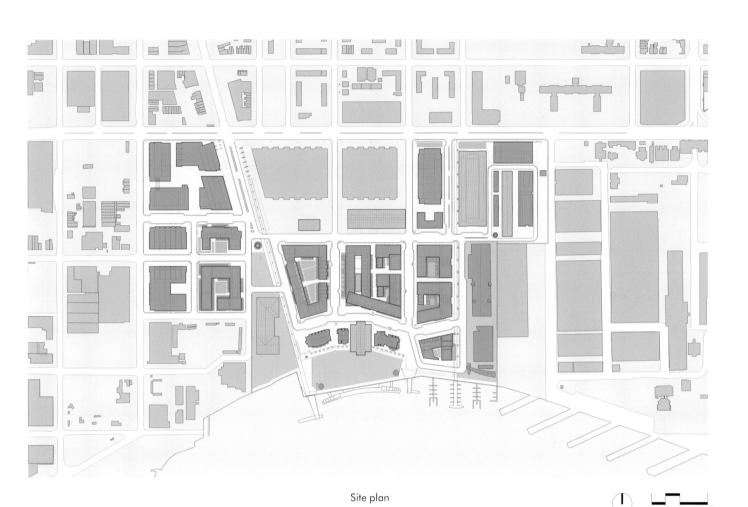

Site plan

0 75 150   300 ft

Bottom left:
Water Street.

Bottom right:
Esplanade.

Apartment on Fifth Avenue

New York, New York
2002–2003

Top: Kitchen looking to guest bedroom.

Bottom: Living room.

This apartment was designed for a couple who returned to the city from a nearby suburb after the last of their children left for college, and who wished to bring the warmth of their previous home, and a summer home which we designed, into a rather bland postwar apartment blessed with spectacular views of Central Park.

Floor plan

0 5 10   20 ft

Rafael Díaz-Balart Hall

Florida International
University College of Law
Miami, Florida
2002–2006

Left top: Main entry
(east) facade.

Left middle: South
facade.

Right: Library tower.

Home to the newly established College of
Law, Rafael Díaz-Balart Hall terminates
a major but still incomplete axis of the
university, the Avenue of the Professions.
A three-story-high entry portico leads to a
monumental lobby off of which the various
programmatic divisions are distributed.
Two landscaped courtyards aerate the plan,
allowing natural light to enter most of the
interior. The grandly proportioned reading
room opens to a broad balcony overlooking
the evolving campus.

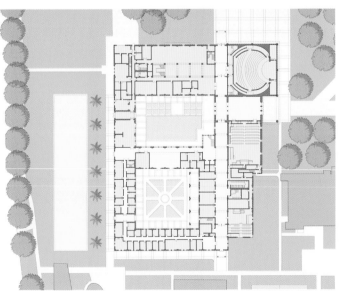

Ground floor plan

0 24 48   96 ft

Left: Corridor.

Top left: Lobby.

Bottom left: North courtyard.

Top right: Reading area in library.

Bottom right: Grand reading room.

American Revolution Center at Valley Forge

Valley Forge,
Pennsylvania
Project, 2002–2008

The American Revolution Center at Valley Forge, the first comprehensive presentation of the Revolutionary War, including the events and ideas that led up to the conflict and its consequences through history and for our future, is folded into the historic landscape and approached along a curved path. On arrival, visitors are greeted by a dramatic glass wall revealing a soaring hall that provides panoramic views to the Valley Forge National Historical Park and the region. The exhibition spaces are faired into the slope. Pennsylvania bluestone, hardwoods, and a vegetated roof contribute to the building's environmentally responsible design. In addition to the museum, the campus, designed in collaboration with Balmori Associates, provides for a study and conference center with guest rooms for scholars and other visitors, a trailhead stop for hiking and biking trails, and outdoor exhibits that present the lessons of the sustainable landscape.

Site plan

0 250 500 1000 ft

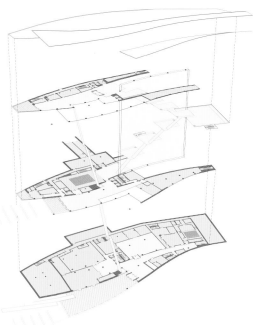

Axonometric

Below: South facade.

West Village Townhouse

New York, New York
2002–2009

Left: Restored street facade.

Right: Renovated garden facade.

Built in 1847 and subdivided into apartments over time, this townhouse was restored to a single-family residence for a young couple who valued its history and location but desired a contemporary interior suited to the needs of a growing family. In the first phase, 2002–2006, shown here, a basement-level, double-height room faces south to the garden, retaining the composition of the Victorian-era tea porch overlooked by the parlor floor above. In the second phase, the upper floors will accommodate bedrooms and a whimsical turret at the children's play area presiding over the skylighted stair.

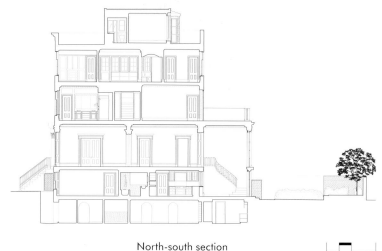

North-south section

0   4   8   16 ft

Left top: Garden.

Left middle: Bedroom.

Left bottom: Media room.

Right: Dining room.

Ocean Course Clubhouse

Kiawah Island
South Carolina
2002–2007

Replacing a temporary clubhouse constructed along with the Pete Dye golf course (1989), the Ocean Course Clubhouse stretches its low profile along the dunes, with deep porches to shade the interior from the Carolina sun.

Ground floor plan

0 31 62 124 ft

Left top: View from driving range.

Left middle: View across Willett Pond.

Left bottom: Dining wing.

Right: Bar porch.

The Gramercy at Metropolitan Park

Arlington, Virginia
2002–2008

As the first phase of our master plan for a 16-acre site in the Pentagon City area, the Gramercy provides 399 apartments and tenant amenities as well as retail space in a building that recalls traditional apartment-house design in Washington.

Below: View from
Fifteenth and South
Fern Streets.

Left top: Shops along
South Fern Street.

Left bottom: Entrance
to courtyard at
Fifteenth Street.

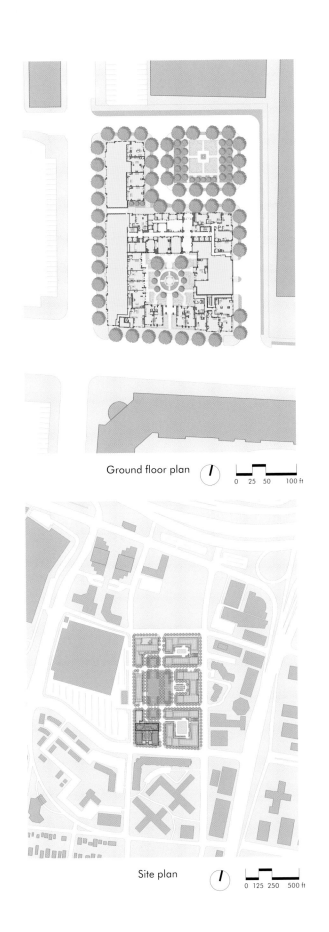

Ground floor plan 0 25 50 100 ft

Site plan 0 125 250 500 ft

Top: Courtyard.

Bottom: Rooftop
pool terrace.

Top: Lobby.

Middle: Rental office.

Bottom: Internet café.

Fulton Corridor
Master Plan

New York, New York
Project, 2002–2005

Top: Shopfronts.

Middle: Fulton Market.

Bottom: View looking west to Royal Insurance Building at Gold Street.

As part of the mandate to renew and revitalize Lower Manhattan in the wake of 9/11/2001, our study of Fulton Street, the area's only river-to-river crosstown street, identified potential improvements that would spur private investment, including a new transit hub at Broadway, a market hall at Nassau Street, and a new park near the South Street Seaport.

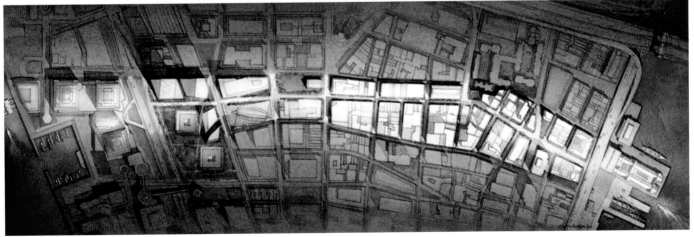

The McNeil Center for Early American Studies

University of Pennsylvania
Philadelphia, Pennsylvania
2003–2005

Top: North facade.

Situated on one of the most prominent remaining open sites on the Penn campus, the McNeil Center conveys its scholarly purpose through its architectural expression while satisfying the university's mandate that each new building reflect the time of its construction. To this end, it is a simple Flemish-bond brick building with the massing and scale of an early nineteenth-century villa and severe details inspired by careful consideration of both federal-style architecture and the work of Louis I. Kahn.

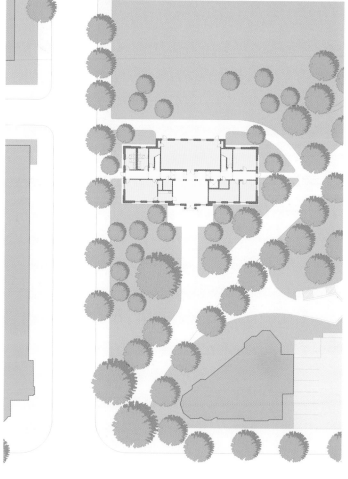

Ground floor plan

0 8 16   32 ft

Top: Lecture room
looking to reception
room.

Middle: Lecture room.

Bottom: Library.

The Clarendon

Boston, Massachusetts
2003–2010

This 32-story, 400,000-square-foot residential tower provides ground-level retail, below-grade parking, 177 rental apartments, and 103 condominiums on a prominent Back Bay site diagonally across from the prismatic John Hancock Tower (I. M. Pei & Partners, 1976). The bold massing of stacked red brick cubes articulated by two-story glazed recesses yields a dynamic skyline presence that reflects traditional Boston architecture but in a compositionally dynamic way.

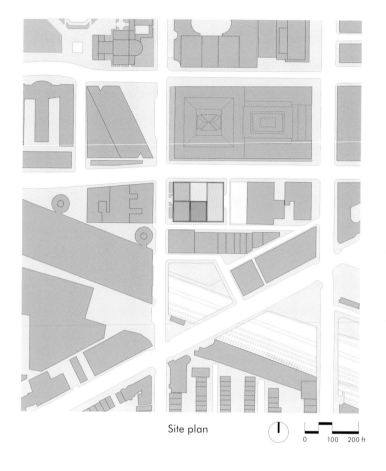

Site plan

0   100   200 ft

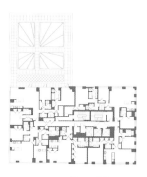

Floor 18

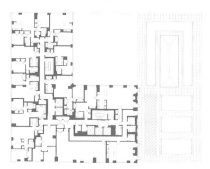

Floor 6

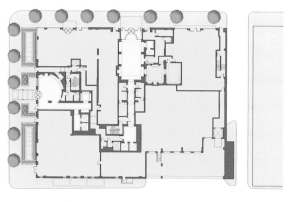
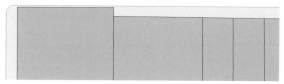

Ground floor plan

0   25 50   100 ft

337

Product Design

Carpets for Bentley Prince Street reflect an understated modernity with an echo of classical references. Our chairs and tables for David Edward grew out of the need to furnish our own library and academic buildings. Tiles for Crossville reconceive mosaic floor patterns and architectural decoration of the classical tradition. Garden ornaments for Haddonstone are designed to help define outdoor rooms in an architectural way. Architectural surfaces inspire our light fixtures for Lightolier.

Top: Bibliothèque
lounge chair for
David Edward.

Bottom: Forsyth
carpet for Bentley
Prince Street.

Top: Olympian urn for
Haddonstone.

Bottom: Cambridge
lounge chair for David
Edward and Crystal
pendant for Lightolier.

Cramer Hill and Pennsauken Waterfront Redevelopment Plans

Camden and
Pennsauken,
New Jersey
Project, 2003–2005

Large-scale redevelopment plans for neighborhoods in two adjacent but very different municipalities on the Delaware River employ related strategies. The plan for the Cramer Hill section of Camden reinforces the existing street grid to help upgrade an underutilized, environmentally degraded neighborhood of rundown housing; the plan for Pennsauken, to the north, proposes to redevelop neglected industrial sites as a string of transit-oriented waterfront villages.

Site plan

0 350 700 1400 ft

Top: View along
Twenty-seventh Street.

Middle: Riverfront
esplanade.

Bottom: View from
Cooper Street Bridge.

Residence at Repulse Bay

Hong Kong, China
2003–2011

Commanding spectacular views over the Hong Kong Golf Club to the deep-water bay and the hills beyond, this villa is bookended by landscaped courtyards to the north and south and organized by an enfilade of principal rooms opening to the west.

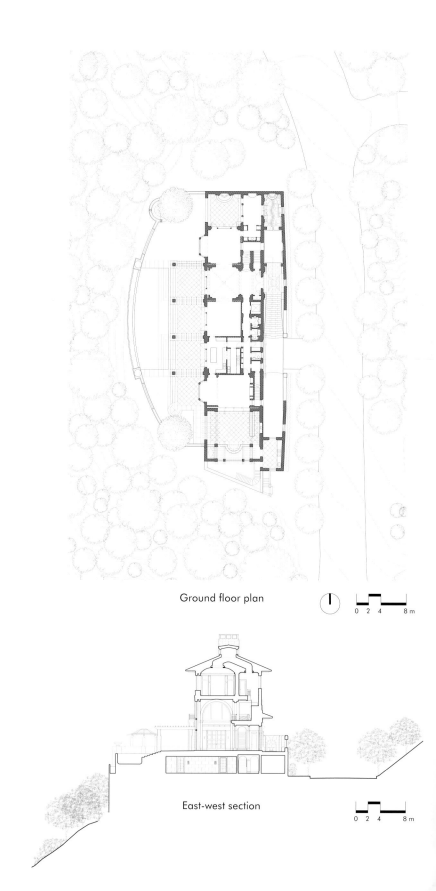

Ground floor plan

0 2 4   8 m

East-west section

0 2 4   8 m

10 Rittenhouse Square

Philadelphia, Pennsylvania
2003–2009

Located on the north edge of Philadelphia's Rittenhouse Square, this 33-story red brick and limestone apartment house recalls early twentieth-century multi-story buildings in Philadelphia. Nearly all of the residences feature high ceilings, large bay windows, and balconies or terraces. Three historic facades that together occupy the building's entire Walnut Street frontage are preserved and restored as part of this project.

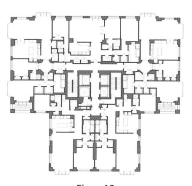

Floor 12

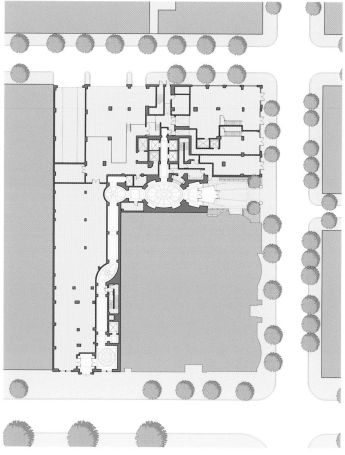

Ground floor plan

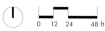

0   12   24   48 ft

Top: South facade
under construction.

Middle: Eighteenth
Street entrance.

Bottom: Residence
living room.

Top: South facade
from Rittenhouse
Square.

Middle: Second-floor
courtyard.

Bottom: Residence
terrace.

Excellence Charter School of Bedford-Stuyvesant

Brooklyn, New York
2003–2006

James W. Naughton's 1880 gauged red brick and brownstone Public School 70, in the Bedford-Stuyvesant section of Brooklyn, was abandoned after a major fire in the late 1970s. The building was left exposed to the elements until the Robin Hood Foundation took it on as the new home for the Excellence Charter School. Our design restores the principal facades, adding a new wing to the east.

Inside the former shell of Naughton's building, carefully restored classrooms, with high ceilings and tall windows, are combined with new spaces, including skylit windowed reading nooks that replace non-code-compliant stairwells. A club-like library, lit by borrowed natural light, forms the heart of the building. Additions at the rear provide for science classrooms, a cafeteria, and a 480-seat auditorium and the roof of the expanded building revives a long-abandoned New York tradition of rooftop athletic facilities.

Top: View looking
southeast, 2003.

Bottom: View looking
southeast, 2006.

Below: Aerial view
looking southeast.

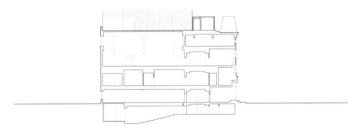

East-west section

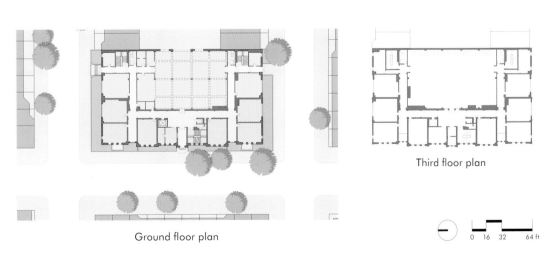

Ground floor plan

Third floor plan

0   16   32   64 ft

GrandMarc at Westberry Place

For the first major project in the rebirth of West Berry Street at the edge of the Texas Christian University campus, an ambitious program of modest housing units intended for students, retail, and parking was accommodated on a single-block site with distinct components of differing character. The Bowie Street building takes its cues from the campus, which it faces; the Berry Street building adapts the particular dialect of the Mediterranean revival characteristic of many Fort Worth neighborhoods.

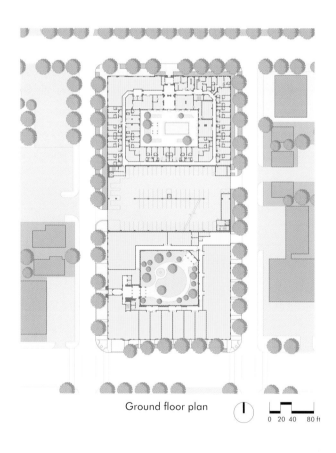

Ground floor plan

0 20 40   80 ft

Calabasas Civic Center

Calabasas, California
2003–2008

Below left: View
looking south.

Calabasas, located in the northwest corner of Los Angeles County, was incorporated in 1992, and city offices and the library were located in rented space for more than a decade. The Civic Center, the new city's first opportunity to express its ideals of community and environmental stewardship, is situated on a gently sloping site, near arid hills that are a gateway to the Santa Monica Mountains. A library and city hall designed in the Mediterranean style are sited informally to shape a variety of outdoor spaces, including an olive grove, a civic plaza, and an amphitheater.

Below: Public plaza looking north, with City Hall (left) and Library (right).

Left: Library entrance.

Right top: City Hall.

Right middle: City Hall arcade.

Right bottom: Library arcade looking to City Hall.

Right top: City
council chamber.

Right middle:
City Hall balcony.

Right bottom:
Library great hall.

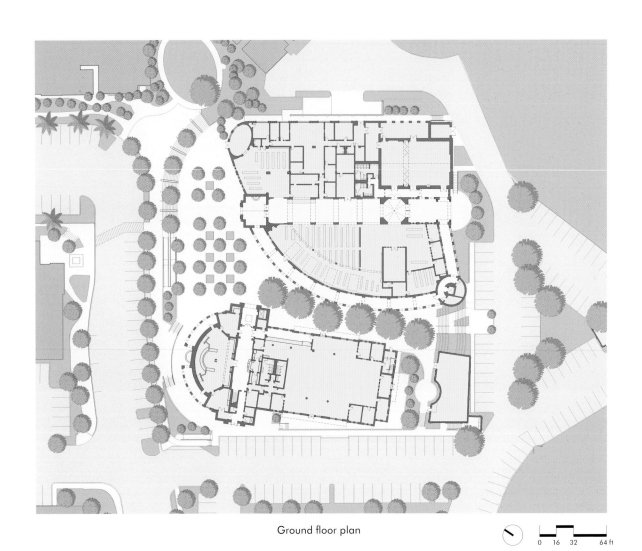

Ground floor plan

0   16   32   64 ft

Medical Office Building at Celebration Health

Celebration, Florida
2003–2007

Top: Celebration Health (1998).

Middle: East facade.

Bottom: Lobby.

Five years after the completion of our firm's Celebration Health (1998), we were asked to add a medical office building to the complex. Balancing the more elaborate fitness wing that it faces across an informal entry court, the new structure carries forward the stucco and red-tile roof vocabulary of the original hospital complex.

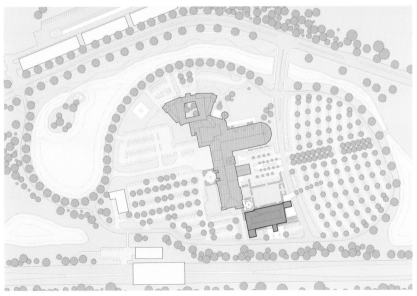

Site plan

0 75 150 300 ft

Highgrove

Stamford, Connecticut
2003–2010

Top: Forest Street
(south) facade.

Bottom: View looking
east along Forest
Street.

Highgrove stands at the edge of the downtown core where it meets a neighborhood
of single-family houses. The mass of the
building is articulated with small-scale
elements: the red brick tower is punctuated by both inset and projecting balconies;
three-story maisonette residences offer
Forest Street a friendly composition of
intimate gardens and front porches.

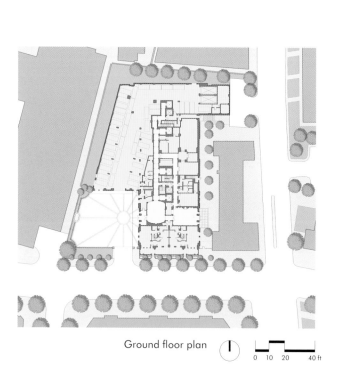

Ground floor plan

0 10 20   40 ft

Top: View looking west along Forest Street.

Bottom left: Lobby.

Bottom right: Pool court.

House on
Buzzards Bay

Right: Entry porch.

At the tip of a peninsula that extends two-and-a-half miles into Buzzards Bay, with incomparable views in three directions, a guest house and a principal residence perched high on a rise present bold, picturesque profiles to the sea.

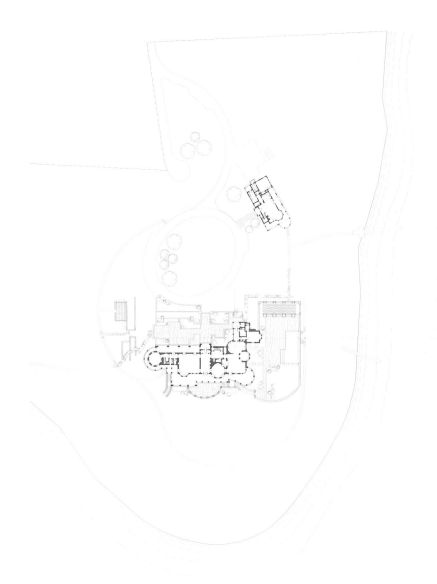

Site plan

0   20   40   80 ft

Left: West tower.

Top: South porch.

Left bottom: Pool
terrace looking to
east facade.

Right bottom: Guest
house.

369

Left top: Entry hall.

Left middle:
Pool cabana.

Left bottom:
Living room.

Right: West stair
looking to library.

Residence at One Central Park

New York, New York
2003–2006

Top: Foyer looking to dining room.

Bottom: Great room.

A Philadelphia couple's desire for a cozy, modern New York City pied-à-terre offered a unique opportunity to work with the interior designers Agnes Bourne and Dennis Miller to reconfigure an apartment in the north tower of One Central Park with internal walls that curve to embrace panoramic views of Central Park, the Hudson River, and the surrounding Manhattan skyline. A pearwood wall in the living room serves as a counterpoint to intricately detailed Asian-inspired folding panels painted by artist Robert Kushner.

Floor plan

0 3 6   12 ft

Lakewood
Public Library

Lakewood, Ohio
2003–2008

Continuing Lakewood's tradition of classical civic buildings, our addition to the
Lakewood Public Library, incorporating
an existing building that was extensively
renovated as part of our work, is entered
under a monumental porch facing Detroit
Avenue and via a less elaborate entry porch
from the parking lot at the rear. At the
building's center, a skylit lobby serves as an
orientation point, and a cross-hall leads via
a grand stair to the grand reading room on
the second floor, bathed in filtered natural
light coming from hidden skylights.

Below: Grand reading room with a mural by Richard Haas.

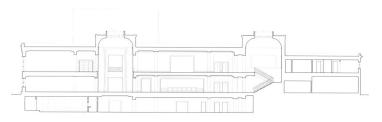

East-west section

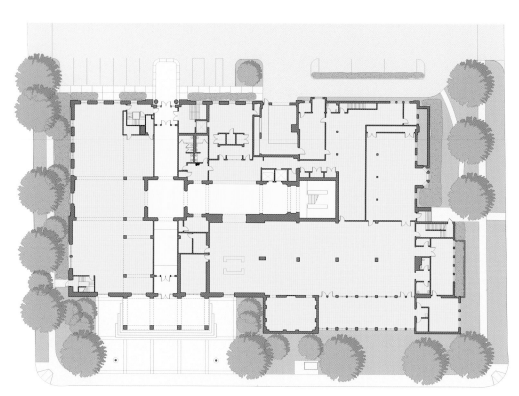

Ground floor plan

0   16   32 ft

CIRCULATION

Left: Lobby.

Top left: Children's activity room.

Bottom left: Children's reading room.

Top right: Grand reading room looking to lobby.

Bottom right: North gallery.

Student and Academic Services Buildings

University of North Carolina
at Chapel Hill
Chapel Hill, North Carolina
2004–2007

Providing a new home for a variety of student services previously dispersed around the campus, two three-story buildings are disposed along an important pedestrian path linking the central campus with outlying residential and recreational neighborhoods. Sheathed in red brick, with oversized wood windows and metal roofs, the buildings recall in particular the architecture of A. J. Davis (1803–1892), an early, and crucial, contributor to the university's architecture.

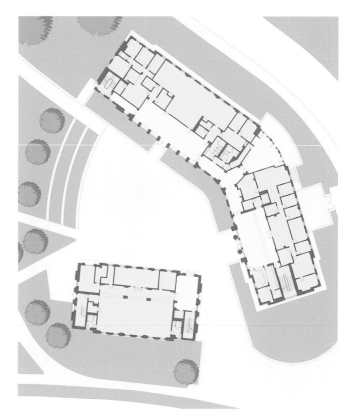

Ground floor plan

0 10 20 40 ft

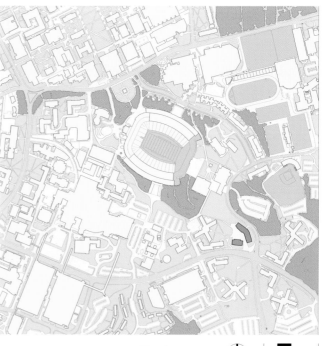

Site plan

0 75 150 300 ft

Top: Detail.

Bottom left: Courtyard
looking east.

Bottom right: South
facade of north
building.

Right: North
building lobby.

Kenan Stadium
Expansion

University of North Carolina
at Chapel Hill
Chapel Hill, North Carolina
2008–

Below: Existing entry.

Surrounded by forest, Kenan Stadium's setting is unequaled among large-scale university sports venues. Over time, however, progressive enlargements have not all been sympathetic to the original, designed by Arthur Cleveland Nash in 1926. Our newly planned expansion, wrapping tall brick arcades around much-needed restrooms and concession spaces at the concourse level and an academic training center above, was developed in collaboration with Heery International of Atlanta and Chapel Hill's Corley Redfoot Zack to help reintegrate the facility with the adjacent historic core campus.

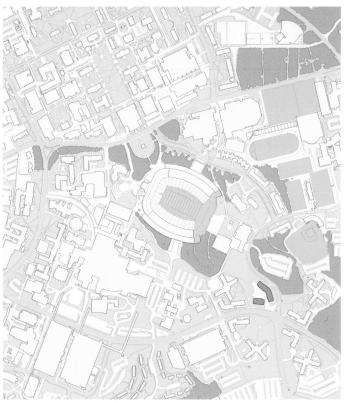

Site plan

0 50 100   200 ft

House at
Bluewater Hill

Below: Entry.

Perched on an extraordinary site three
hundred feet above Compo Beach, this
house orients principal rooms and
porches to views of Long Island Sound
and Sherwood Island. The L-shaped plan
embraces an existing swimming pool. A
gently sloping family lawn and garden were
created to the south. Large windows and
doors bring the views inside, and fireplaces
anchor the living, dining, and family rooms,
which are organized around a large central
stair hall.

Sky-blue stained shingles, leaded hand-
blown glass, and white-painted shutters and
window boxes enhance the casual seaside
feel of the house, while picturesque gables
and dormers at the gambrel roof reduce its
apparent mass.

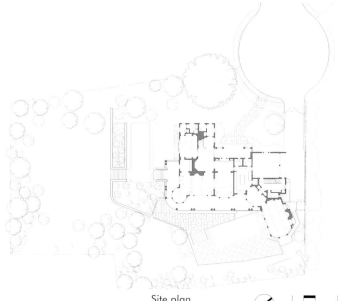

Site plan

0 10 20   40 ft

Below: Family room.

One Crescent Drive

Philadelphia Navy Yard
Philadelphia, Pennsylvania
2004–2005

The first new building realized as part of our previously published master plan for the Philadelphia Navy Yard (2002) is also the first speculative multitenant office building to achieve LEED Platinum certification. Built with a premium of less than 2 percent over the developer's typical construction budget for similar non-LEED certified office buildings, it makes a compelling business case for sustainable design.

Facing the park with a curved glass facade, its other facades are clad in precast panels whose deep red color and ashlar jointing pattern pick up the sandstone and terra cotta palette of the Navy Yard's historic buildings. Inside, a triangular balcony-ringed atrium brings natural light deep into the center of the office floors.

Top: North facade
from Crescent Park.

Bottom, from left:
View from
Crescent Park.
North entry.
View from southwest.

Left: Atrium.

Right: Aerial view
looking southeast.

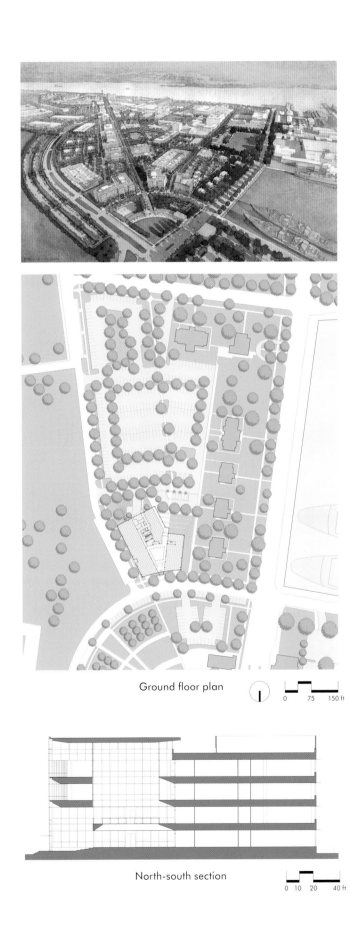

Ground floor plan

0   75   150 ft

North-south section

0 10   20   40 ft

55 West

Las Vegas, Nevada
Competition, 2004

Our proposal combines the excitement of
hotels, casino, entertainment, and destination shopping with a new quiet residential
neighborhood intended for year-round
residents.

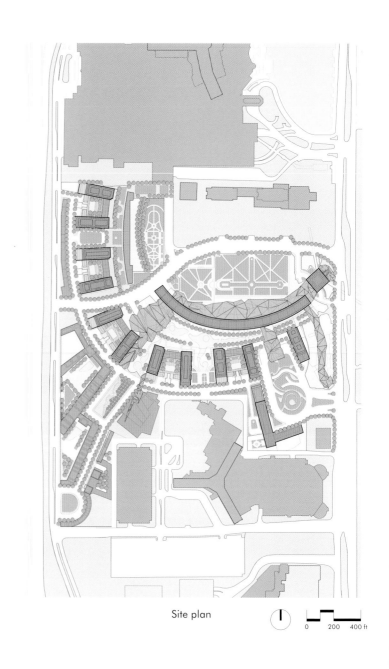

Site plan

0   200   400 ft

Top: Entry.

Bottom left: Guest drop-off.

Bottom right: Indoor shopping street.

St. Regis Hotel

Bal Harbor, Florida
Competition, 2004

Top: Garden court.

Our proposal adapted the classical big-city character of the St. Regis flag to the casual beach resort feel of Bal Harbor. An antidote to the simplistic towers that dominate the coastline north of South Beach, Miami, our hotel tower and condominium tower each embrace a series of sunny pool terraces and sheltered garden courts.

Site plan

0 75 150   300 ft

Fifteen Central Park West

New York, New York
2004–2008

Right: View from
Central Park.

Central Park West comprises an almost
continuous palisade of mid-height apartment buildings punctuated by four
twin-towered icons that establish it as an
internationally acknowledged archetype
of Manhattan and of modernity. Fifteen
Central Park West consists of two buildings: a nineteen-story apartment house
on the park reinforcing the palisade, and,
relating to the four towers, a soaring thirty-
five-story tower behind, separated by a
garden and motor court but connected at
street level by a domed elliptical pavilion.
In contrast to the dark reflective glass of
recent buildings around Columbus Circle,
Fifteen Central Park West is clad in limestone, traditionally the material of choice
for New York's most important buildings;
no material takes the light more beautifully.

Site plan

0 50 100 200 ft

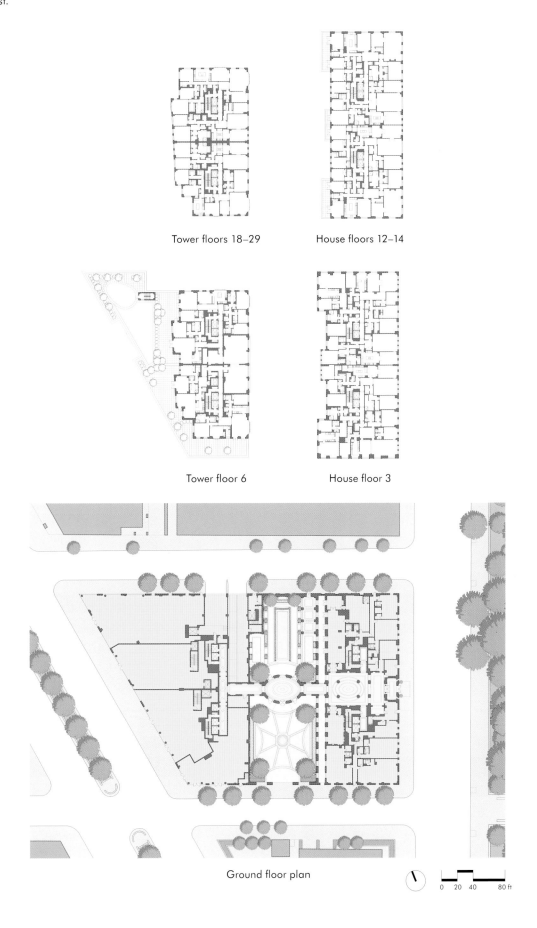

Tower floors 18–29   House floors 12–14

Tower floor 6   House floor 3

Ground floor plan

0   20 40   80 ft

Left: Garden court.

Right: View from West Sixty-second Street to entry pavilion.

Left top: Lobby.

Left bottom: Library.

Right: Entry pavilion.

Overleaf: Skyline
view from northwest.

Wasserstein Hall, Caspersen Student Center, and Clinical Wing

Harvard Law School
Cambridge, Massachusetts
2004–2011

Our plan for the reorganization and expansion of Harvard Law School's seventeen-building campus led to the decision to build a new U-shaped building composed of three wings: the Caspersen Student Center to the south connecting to Harkness Commons (Walter Gropius, 1951); Wasserstein Hall, set along Massachusetts Avenue, housing classrooms and a conference center; and a wing accommodating legal clinics to the north along Everett Street. Limestone facades with large, deeply-recessed windows and arched entrance porches take cues from the many strands of the Law School's architectural legacy, especially the Romanesque-inspired architecture of its founding building, Austin Hall (H. H. Richardson, 1881), and the monumental classicism of Langdell Hall (Shepley, Rutan & Coolidge, 1906; Coolidge, Shepley, Bulfinch & Abbott, 1928).

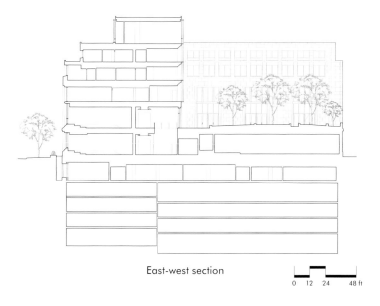

East-west section

0 12 24   48 ft

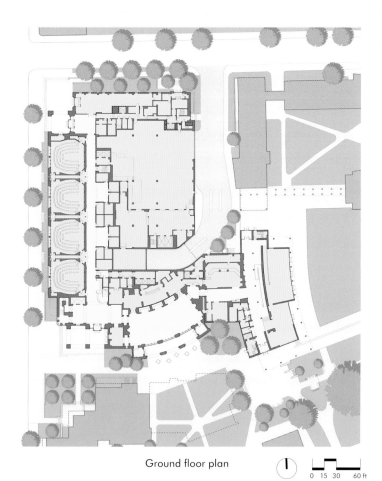

Ground floor plan

0 15 30   60 ft

Top: Aerial view
looking north.

Middle: Southwest
entry at Massachusetts
Avenue.

Bottom: Second-floor
gallery in Wasserstein
Hall.

Top: View of Caspersen
Student Center from
Holmes Field.

Middle: View
looking south along
Massachusetts Avenue.

Bottom: 90-seat
classroom.

Farmer Hall

Richard T. Farmer
School of Business
Miami University
Oxford, Ohio
2004–2009

Farmer Hall occupies a prominent site at the heart of the campus, facing historic Cook Field and adjacent to the confluence of the three main roads by which visitors arrive in the rural town of Oxford. The building is organized in three wings to form a new quadrangle opening to the south, anchored by a stand of mature trees including a majestic sweet gum dating approximately to the university's founding in 1809. Simple colonial-Georgian facades of red brick, painted trim, and slate roofs carry forward the architectural identity of the University's historic campus.

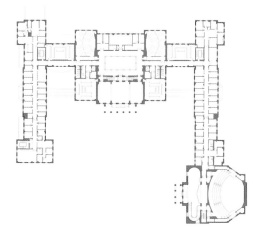

Second floor plan

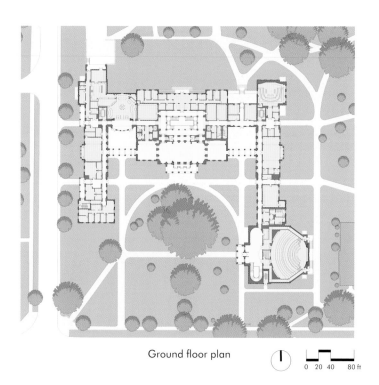

Ground floor plan

0 20 40 80 ft

Top: Entry courtyard.

Bottom left: Entrance to auditorium under construction.

Bottom right: The Commons under construction.

Residence in Highland Park

Highland Park, Illinois
2004–2009

This playfully massed house on an irregular lot greets the bend of a quiet street with a bow-front gable and to the north embraces a wooded ravine. The house is clad in shingles with hunter green trim; its field-stone water table becomes walls that define gardens designed by Douglas Hoerr.

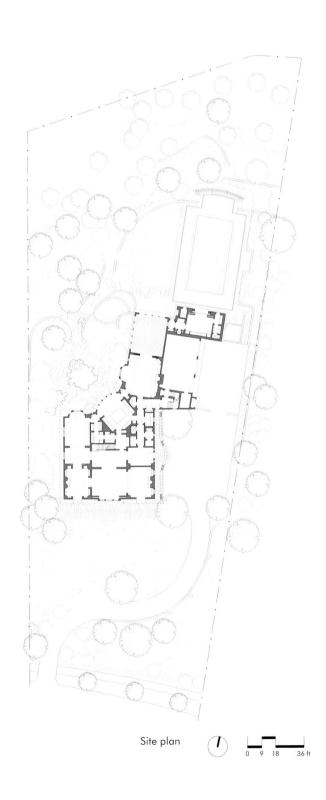

Site plan

Left top: Living room.

Left middle: West gallery looking to dining room.

Left bottom: Library.

Right: Pool terrace.

Sunstone

Quogue, New York
2004–2006

After fifteen happy years, the original owners of this house we designed sold it to a
younger couple with two small children and
an extended family. It was a pleasure to
be invited back to add a playroom and guest
rooms and to update the kitchen and sun-
room, and to work with Scott Salvator, the
new owners' interior designer, who updated
the interiors in a way that is sympathetic
to the original scheme by Albert Hadley.

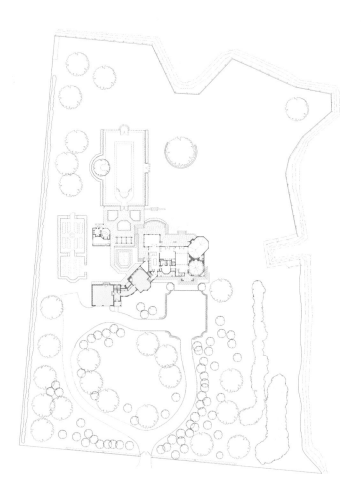

Site plan

0 20 40   80 ft

Top: View looking north.

Bottom, from left:
Garage wing.
Pebble garden.
Cutting garden.

Museum for African Art

Museum Mile
New York, New York
2004–2010

Top: View looking south along Fifth Avenue.

Bottom: Fifth Avenue entrance.

Intended not only as a place for art but also as a gathering place, this first new museum building on New York's Museum Mile since Frank Lloyd Wright's Guggenheim Museum (1959) cradles a plaza on Fifth Avenue at 110th Street, facing the northeast corner of Central Park. The Museum sits as part of 1280 Fifth Avenue, a 19-story residential tower for which we designed the facades.

The strong character of the museum's trapezoidal windows set into pre-cast concrete panels suggests in an abstract way woven patterns often used at many scales in African art and architecture. The 45-foot-high lobby sheltered by a single curving expanse of etimoe wood, leads to a grand stair enclosed in a circular lantern-like copper-colored perforated-metal drum with diamond-shaped apertures. In addition to galleries, the building also includes a 230-seat auditorium, a café, and on the third floor a roof terrace offering dramatic views west over Central Park.

Top left: Roof garden.

Top right: Gift shop.

Middle left: Theater lobby.

Middle right: Event space.

Bottom left: Lobby looking to Central Park.

Bottom right: Theater.

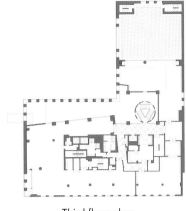

Third floor plan

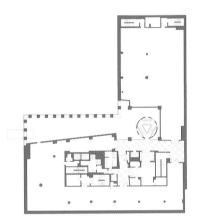

Second floor plan

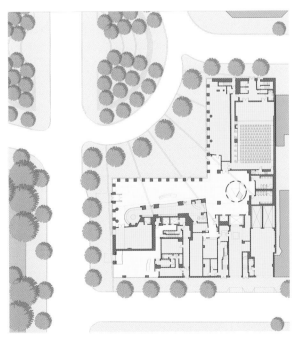

Ground floor plan

0 12 24   48 ft

Site plan: Museum Mile

0   150 300 ft

International
Quilt Study Center
and Museum

University of Nebraska, Lincoln
Lincoln, Nebraska
2004–2008

Right: View from
Holdrege Street.

Overleaf: View
looking southeast with
the sculpture *Reverie*
by Linda Fleming.

The Quilt Center provides a dramatic
setting for the study, conservation, and
exhibition of extensive collections of
historical and contemporary quilts from
around the world. The compact three-
story brick building incorporates galleries,
conservation laboratories, and offices.
Facing a garden designed by Hargreaves
Associates, a reception hall is enveloped by
a glassy bowed facade "stitched together"
to suggest the intricate patterns of quilting.
A carefully orchestrated journey leads
visitors through layers of fritted glass
and metal-mesh screens that help the eye
make the adjustment from the bright
Nebraska sunlight to the controlled light
of the galleries.

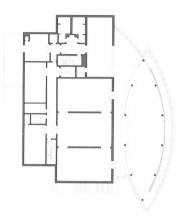

Second floor plan

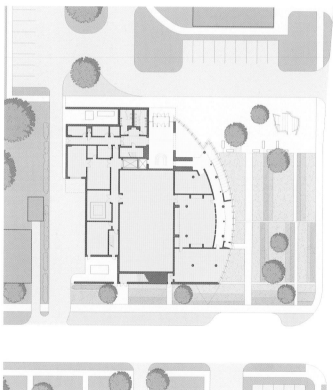

Ground floor plan

0   12   24   48 ft

Top: View from
Thirty-third Street.

Bottom: Details at
east facade.

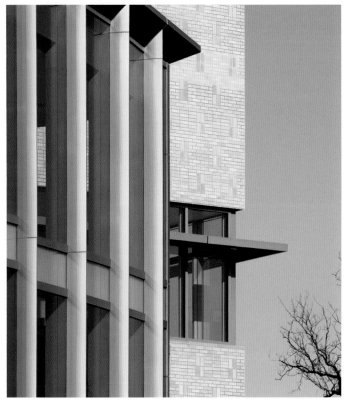

Left: Reception hall.

Top: Reception hall.

Bottom left:
North gallery.

Bottom right:
Conservation
laboratory.

The Century

Bottom left:
Construction view.

Top right: Garden.

Middle right: Lobby.

Bottom right:
Residence living
room.

Set in a four-acre garden designed by
Pamela Burton that provides an oasis
from Century City's buzz, this 42-story,
140-residence tower evokes the stylish
modernism of 1930s Hollywood in its
streamlined elliptical massing and
details. The diagonal siting of the tower
provides open vistas between neighboring
buildings to the ocean, mountains, and
the surrounding cityscape.

Floors 19–26

Floor 2

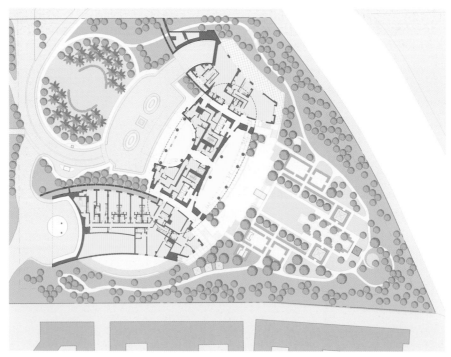

Ground floor plan

0 16 32   64 ft

Writers' Penthouse

New York, New York
2004–2006

A ramshackle rooftop shed has been given
new life as a book-lined aerie. A north-
facing writing room providing a layout
table and desks with views to Midtown
is separated by an elliptical service tower
from a sitting room that opens to a
bamboo-screened south-facing terrace
overlooking the city and the harbor.

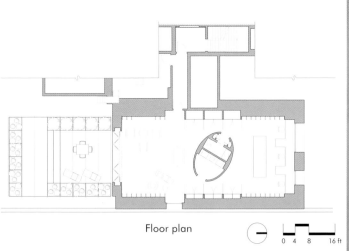

Floor plan

0 4 8   16 ft

Left top: Writing room.

Left middle: Terrace.

Left bottom: Kitchen looking to writing room.

Right: Reading room.

The Mansion
on Peachtree

Atlanta, Georgia
2005–2008

Left top: Skyline view
looking south.

Left bottom: Entry
to the residences on
Stratford Road.

Right: View from
Peachtree Street.

The Mansion on Peachtree combines a top-level hotel and condominium residences in a slender eight-sided tower rising from between two landscaped courtyards on an important urban site. A restaurant pavilion with sidewalk seating opens directly to Peachtree Street. A second restaurant, an enclosed pool, banquet facilities, a spa, and a fitness center overlook a terraced garden leading down to private villas. The 42-story classically inspired light-colored limestone and cast stone tower rises to a dramatic conclusion of full-floor penthouses with setback terraces.

Right top: Entry to
motor court from
Stratford Road.

Right bottom: Hotel
entry.

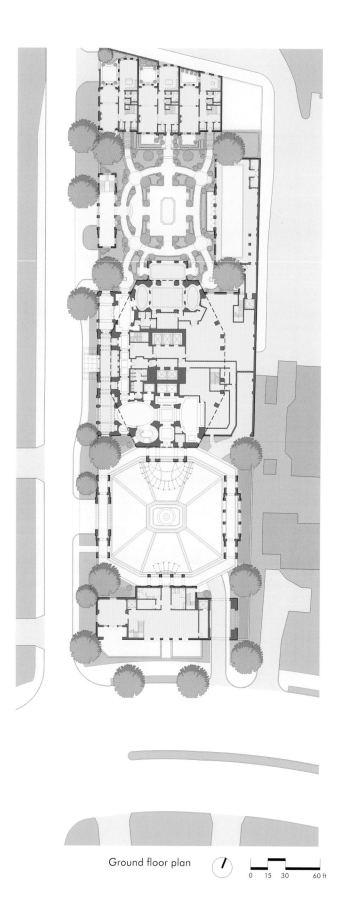

Ground floor plan

0 15 30 60 ft

Below: Garden court
looking to villas.

Park Center for Business and Sustainable Enterprise

Ithaca College School
of Business
Ithaca, New York
2005–2008

Showcasing Ithaca College's commitment
to environmental responsibility by achiev-
ing a LEED Platinum rating, the Park
Center is a layered mass that wraps around
a four-story atrium and a dramatic stair
that bring direct and borrowed daylight to
classrooms, study rooms, and offices. The
building's rubblestone base, garden terraces,
and green roof engage with local landscape
and building traditions.

Site plan

0 75 150 300 ft

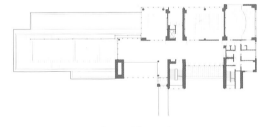

Second floor plan

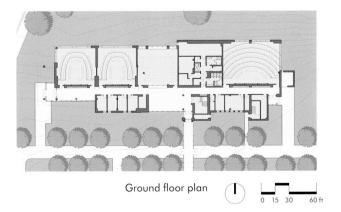

Ground floor plan

0 15 30 60 ft

Left top: Atrium
looking to moot
board room.

Left bottom:
Atrium bridge.

Right: Atrium.

Greenspun Hall

Greenspun College of Urban Affairs
University of Nevada, Las Vegas
Las Vegas, Nevada
2005–2008

Announcing the university's presence with a billboard-like tower commanding a prominent corner where the southern boundary of the campus meets the city that has grown up around it, Greenspun Hall reflects the modernist vocabulary of UNLV's existing buildings, all built since the 1950s. Providing 120,000 gross square feet of classrooms, labs, departmental suites, faculty offices, and radio and television broadcasting facilities, the building relies on time-tested strategies to encourage collegiality: program functions are grouped around a common courtyard; broad stairways and hallways with alcoves facilitate informal interaction. The broadcasting facilities, which require controlled light, high ceilings, and same-floor adjacencies, are located in the ground-floor plinth beneath the building's most dramatic feature, an elevated courtyard shaded by a pergola of photovoltaic panels carried on sixty-foot-high galvanized steel columns.

Greenspun Hall is expected to achieve LEED Platinum certification.

Left top: View looking
southeast.

Left bottom: View
looking southwest.

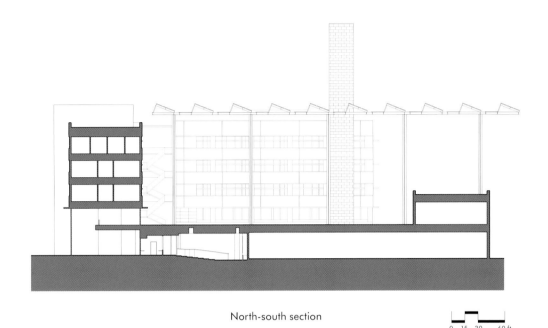

North-south section

0 15 30   60 ft

Ground floor plan

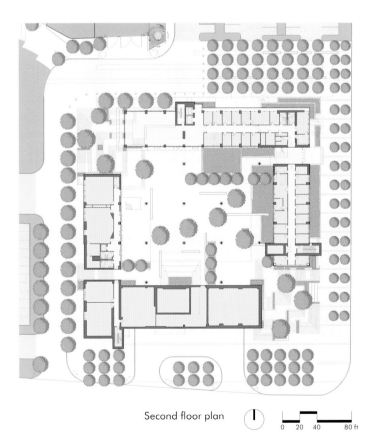

Second floor plan

0   20   40   80 ft

Flinn Hall and Edelman Hall

The Hotchkiss School
Lakeville, Connecticut
2005–2007

During the early-twentieth century, Hotchkiss was realized as a Georgian-style campus by architects Bruce Price, Cass Gilbert, and Delano and Aldrich. During the 1960s, the school strayed from this tradition. Our design for Flinn and Edelman Halls returns Hotchkiss to its architectural roots, with two student residences, each accommodating thirty students and four faculty families in three-story buildings, embracing a new quadrangle. Fine brick details complement double-hung shuttered windows and inviting classical entry porticos to enliven the simple massing of each residence hall.

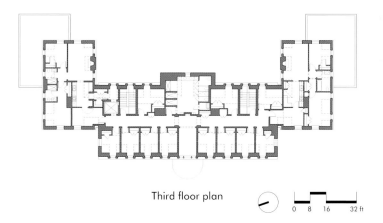

Third floor plan

0 8 16 32 ft

Ground floor plan

0 12 24 48 ft

Below: North facade
of Flinn Hall.

Top: West facade of
Edelman Hall.

Bottom: Flinn Hall
(left) and Edelmann
Hall (right) from new
quadrangle.

Top: View from Flinn Hall to Edelman Hall.

Middle: North facade of Flinn Hall.

Bottom: Faculty wing at Edelman Hall.

Left top: Student commons.

Left middle: Faculty apartment.

Left bottom: Faculty apartment porch.

Right: Garden gate.

Residences on
South Flagler Drive

West Palm Beach, Florida
Project, 2005

A pair of residential buildings—a midrise apartment block and a campanile-evoking tower that rises to twin spires—was designed to give pride of place to an historic church (F. W. Blandford, 1928).

Site plan

0 50 100   200 ft

Front Street District

Hartford, Connecticut
2005–2010

Shops and parking will occupy two key city blocks between the historic Wadsworth Atheneum and the new Connecticut Convention Center.

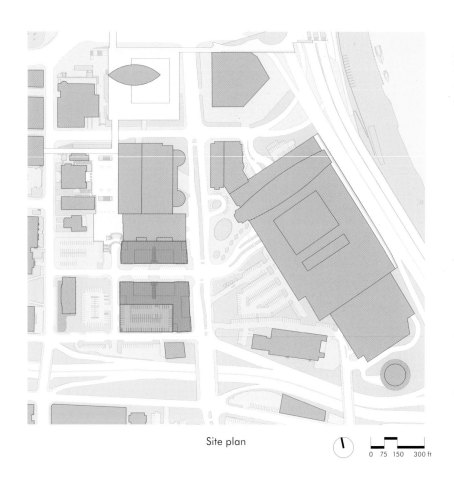

Site plan

0 75 150   300 ft

Del Sur Village

San Diego, California
2005

Top: Residential court.

Middle: Town center.

Bottom: Pedestrian alley.

Located on 135 acres close to the towns of Del Mar and Rancho Santa Fe, Del Sur Village will support a fine-grain mix of urban uses: residences, shops, offices, parks, and recreation. The residential core of the project, immediately to the west of Main Street, is organized by topographically influenced radial avenues, alleys, pedestrian mews, and parking courts that run parallel to the increasing grade, crossed by narrow lanes and stairways that provide for pedestrian movement uphill to Highpoint Park.

Site plan

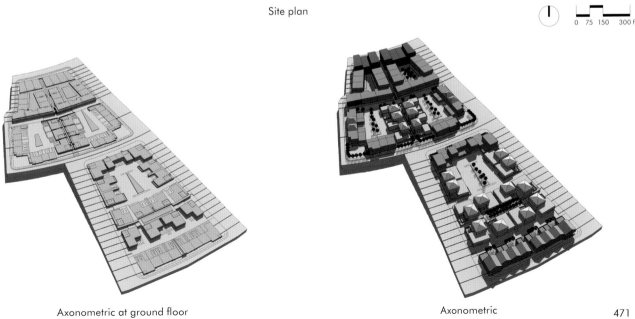

Axonometric at ground floor

Axonometric

471

Bavaro Hall

Curry School of Education
University of Virginia
Charlottesville, Virginia
2005–2010

Located on a steeply sloped site on Emmet Street, at the western perimeter of the University of Virginia's historic Central Grounds, Bavaro Hall doubles the size of the Curry School of Education, currently housed in Ruffner Hall, an unremarkable 1970s building, and in clinics scattered in rented quarters. Simple massing and traditional detailing—red brick and limestone facades with painted wood trim, six-over-six double-hung windows, and a metal standing-seam roof—are in keeping with the architectural traditions first established at the Lawn by Thomas Jefferson. Though stylistically opposed, Bavaro Hall works together with Ruffner to define a central landscaped courtyard framed between two open-air colonnades linking the two buildings, creating a campus within a campus for the Curry School.

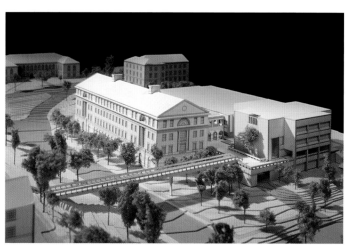

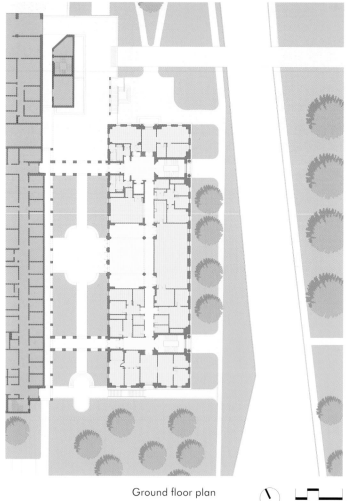

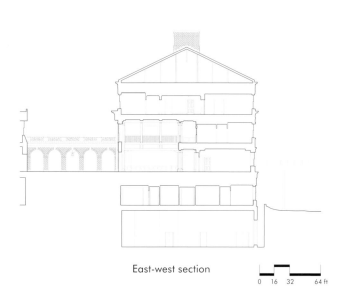

East-west section

0   16   32   64 ft

Ground floor plan

0 20 40   80 ft

Improvements at Abraham Goodman House

Kaufman Center
New York, New York
2005–2008

Top: Original building in 1978.

Bottom: West Sixty-seventh Street (south) facade, 2008.

The Kaufman Center, designed by architects Johansen and Bhavnani and completed in 1978, is a significant example of the Brutalist architectural style. Located one block from Lincoln Center, the center is an important arts and educational institution comprising three component parts: Merkin Concert Hall, a 650-seat performance space; the Lucy Moses School of Music; and the Special Music School, a New York City Public School for musically gifted children. Our work at Kaufman Center fulfilled three objectives: it strengthened the public image of Abraham Goodman House with restoration and sympathetic renovation of its unique facade; it enhanced entry and circulation by enlarging the Merkin Hall lobby; and it improved the appearance and modernized the technical capabilities of Merkin Hall while preserving its much-admired acoustical qualities.

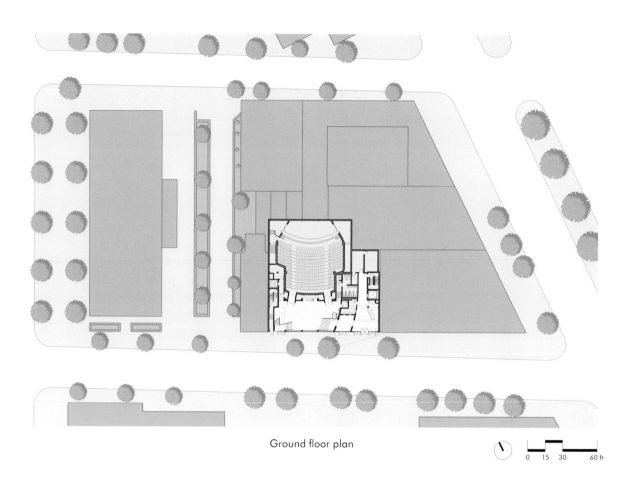

Right top: Orchestra-level lobby.

Right middle: Balcony-level lobby.

Right bottom: Merkin Hall.

Ground floor plan

0   15   30   60 ft

North Instructional Building and Library

Bronx Community College
Bronx, New York
2005–2012

Atop a bluff overlooking the Harlem River in the Bronx, the campus of Bronx Community College was originally planned by Stanford White in 1892 to serve as a new campus for New York University. White's plan was only partially realized with his grandly classical domed Gould Memorial Library (1899) and the arcing open colonnade of the Hall of Fame (1912) at the head of a quadrangle and two classroom buildings. In 1956 Marcel Breuer created a second master plan for the campus and completed a number of buildings in the modernist style.

When N Y U abandoned the campus in 1973, it became home to Bronx Community College, which in 2006 commissioned us to prepare a third campus plan, proposing a combination of historic preservation, adaptive reuse, and new construction, beginning with a 98,600-square-foot three-story building on the north side of the main quadrangle. Situated adjacent to Gould Library, our design returns to the classicism of Stanford White, using a vocabulary of buff-colored Roman brick and light gray cast-stone trim. Inside, ground-floor classrooms are organized along an east-west corridor continuing the axis of the Hall of Fame. A monumental stair on the north-south axis captures spectacular views to Upper Manhattan across the river as it climbs to the library, with a double row of barrel vaults supported by slender columns evoking those used by Henri Labrouste in his St. Genevieve Library in Paris (1851).

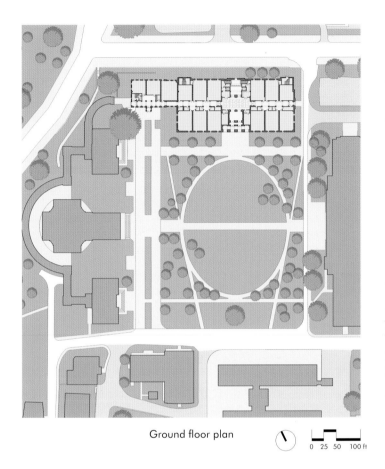

Ground floor plan

0 25 50 100 ft

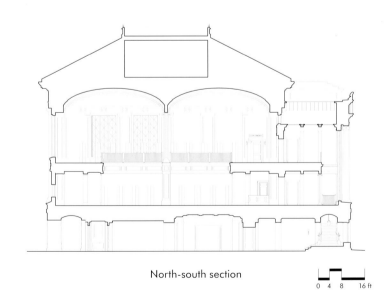

North-south section

0 4 8 16 ft

Top: View from Gould
Memorial Library.

Bottom left: Aerial
view looking north.

Bottom right:
Information commons.

The Brompton

New York, New York
2005–2009

This 20-story residential building carries forward the character of traditional Upper East Side apartment houses that we re-established at the Chatham (2001). Cast stone window bays, quoins, piers, and finials endow the red brick mass with a sense of verticality. The principal entrance is town-house-scaled, leading past two garden courts to the elevators deep within the block.

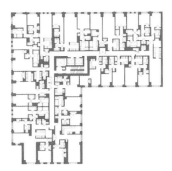

Floor 15

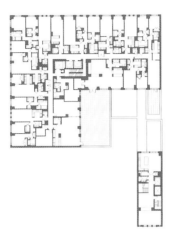

Floor 2

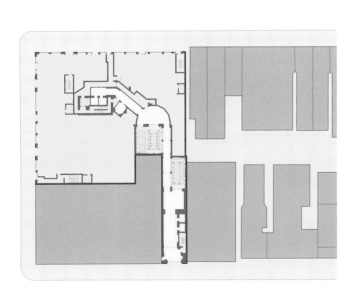

Ground floor plan

0   25   50 ft

Barnett Residential Life Center

Florida Southern College
Lakeland, Florida
2005–2009
Wesley Hall:
Completed 2008
Nicholas Hall:
Completed 2009

Bottom left: View
looking west along
Lake Hollingsworth
Drive.

The campus of Florida Southern College boasts the largest grouping of Frank Lloyd Wright buildings in the world. Replacing ill-conceived facilities that had separated Wright's campus from the Lake Hollingsworth, the Barnett Center consists of two new residence halls that complement Wright's legacy and honor his intentions in a contemporary way.

Extending Wright's geometry, the Barnett Center replaces buildings that ran parallel to the shoreline with four-story Y-shaped buildings set on a diagonal, reestablishing view corridors from the center of campus to the lake and providing every student room a water view. Deep roof overhangs and canopies provide shelter from the intense sun and rain. The palette of cast stone, stucco, and clapboard follows the spirit of the Wright buildings but does not mimic them.

Site plan

0   200   400 ft

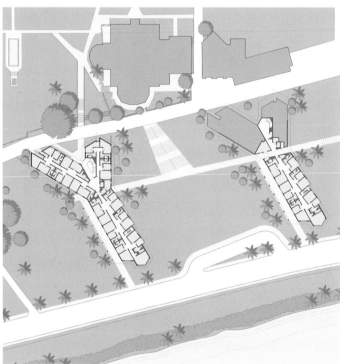

Floor plans

0 15 30   60 ft

486

Top: North entry.

Bottom left: View
from southeast.

Bottom right:
View from Lake
Hollingsworth.

Top left: Third-floor
lounge.

Bottom left: Bedroom.

Top right: West
walkway.

Bottom right: Third-
floor lounge.

Right: Detail
at east facade.

Christoverson
Humanities Building

Florida Southern College
Lakeland, Florida
2006–2010

The Christoverson Humanities Building reflects Florida Southern's desire to create a lakefront gateway to campus, as well as to increase the space for humanities instruction and faculty. A dramatic, welcoming roof greets the approaching visitor across a plaza intended for student use between classes. Beneath the sweeping roof, a grandly proportioned lounge surrounded by classrooms on the piano nobile and ringed by faculty offices on a mezzanine will encourage interaction between students and faculty.

Site plan

0   200   400 ft

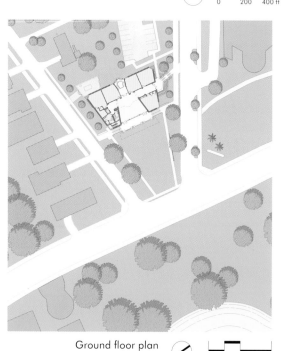

Ground floor plan

0   32   64   128 ft

492

Long Wharf

Saint John, New
Brunswick, Canada
2005–

A bold step in the redevelopment of a
8.2-hectare site, historically used for light
industry and bulk storage, and now a pas-
senger cruise ship docking facility, Long
Wharf will become home to a three-story,
240,000-square-foot corporate office
building set behind a public plaza within
landscaped grounds. At the entrance, a
three-story, light-flooded winter garden
will connect a ground-floor auditorium
and gallery with the building lobby, which
is elevated to overlook Uptown Saint
John. Two four-story south-facing atri-
ums nested within the building will bring
light and views deep into the office floors,
with indoor gardens and common spaces
deployed along primary internal circulation paths. High performance, low-E
coated glazing will optimize daylight while
moderating thermal gain. Connected via
pedestrian bridge to Uptown, the plaza
will be filled with activities for cruise ship
passengers, including a local market and
tour operations, when ships are berthed; at
other times it will be part of a harborfront
promenade.

Site plan

0 15 30   60 m

Top: View from pedestrian bridge.

Bottom: Aerial view looking northeast.

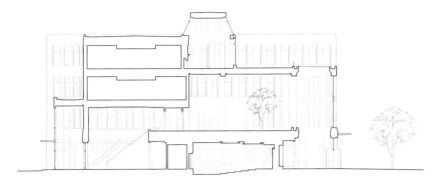

North-south section at main entrance

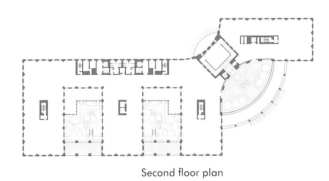

Second floor plan

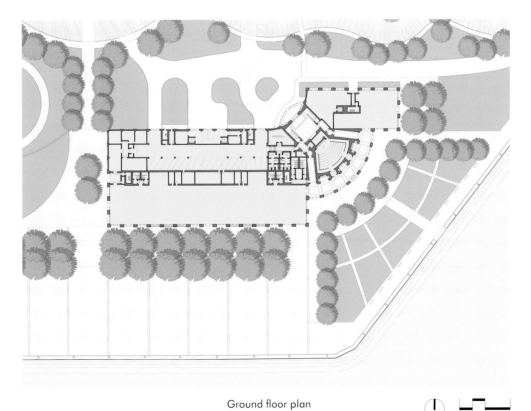

Ground floor plan

0 5 10   20 m

Miller Hall

The Mason School of Business
The College of William and Mary
Williamsburg, Virginia
2005–2009

Top: Construction
view of entry on
Campus Drive.

Bottom: Brinkley
Commons atrium.

Miller Hall, the new 160,000-square-foot
home of the Mason School of Business,
carries forward the red brick vocabulary of
William and Mary's traditional architecture with an H-plan building that marks
a gateway between the existing campus,
the Colgate Darden gardens, and the Lake
Matoaka amphitheater.

A skylit central stair hall accommodates
a broad stair leading up to a major function room on the second floor, where the
school's administrative offices are also
located; the third floor accommodates
faculty offices.

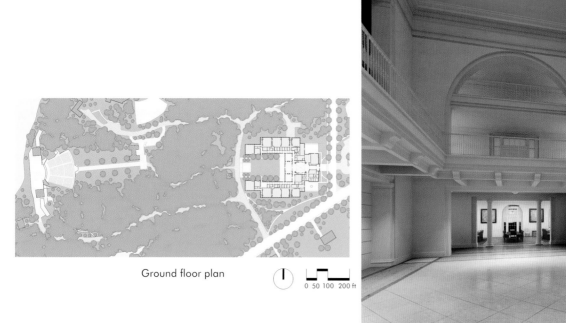

Ground floor plan

0 50 100 200 ft

Resorts at Hvar

Hvar, Croatia
Project, 2006

Our master plan for hotels and residential buildings on Hvar, in the Adriatic Sea off the coast of Croatia, is intended to reinvigorate the island as a vacation destination while maintaining the traditional texture and character of the place. Six resorts—including three-star hotels and a five-star hotel and condominium complex, with settings ranging from a small-scale infill waterfront site to an open landscape overlooking a bay—are each given a unique identity, but all are rooted in the local architectural and cultural heritage.

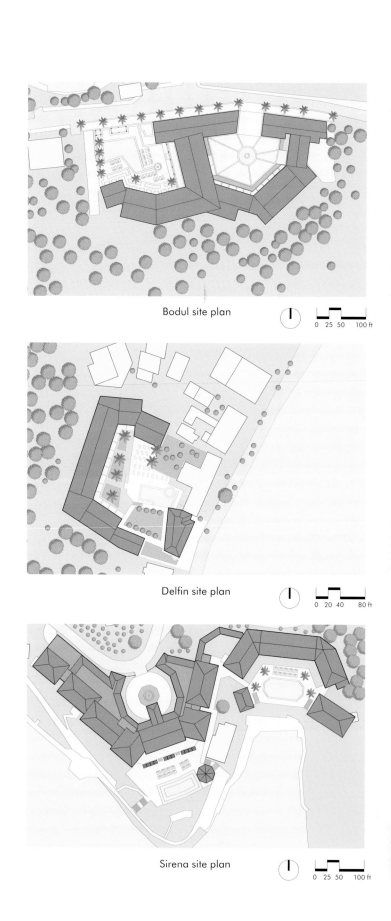

Bodul site plan   0 25 50 100 ft

Delfin site plan   0 20 40 80 ft

Sirena site plan   0 25 50 100 ft

Our Lady of Mercy Chapel

Salve Regina University
Newport, Rhode Island
2006–2010

The campus of Salve Regina University is located in the heart of Newport's renowned "summer cottage" district and includes important historic houses, such as Ochre Court (Richard Morris Hunt, 1881), which today serves as the school's main administration building. Our firm designed Salve's Rodgers Recreation Center (2000) and was invited back to design a chapel nestled among the buildings of Vinland, the former Catherine Lorillard Wolfe estate, (Peabody & Stearns, 1883). An important part of our brief was to display to advantage the generous donation of John La Farge stained-glass windows that were originally installed in a chapel at the Caldwell house (1890).

Combining local stone in the tradition of New England country churches with shingle style details, the chapel establishes an axial relationship with Ochre Court, recasting it and the buildings of the Vinland estate into a cohesive academic group.

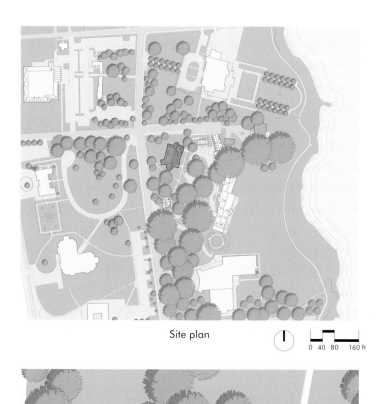

Site plan

0 40 80 160 ft

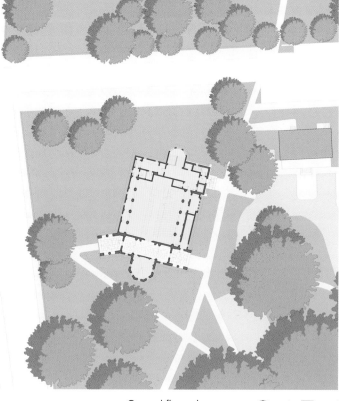

Ground floor plan

0 10 20 40 ft

The Harrison

New York, New York
2006–2009

Top: Entrance
on West Seventy-
sixth Street

Bottom: Lobby.

Consisting of two towers—the 14-story north tower facing Amsterdam Avenue and the 19-story south tower on West Seventy-sixth Street—connected by a single lobby entered from West Seventy-sixth Street, the Harrison recalls the Richardsonian Romanesque style that flourished on Manhattan's West Side when the neighborhood was first developed in the 1880s. A two-story red sandstone base supports a red brick superstructure articulated with French balconies and colored friezes. At the top of both towers distinctive faceted volumes create unique rooms for some of the units.

Left: Tenth-floor
terrace of the north
tower looking west
to the south tower.

Floors 10–11

Floor 4

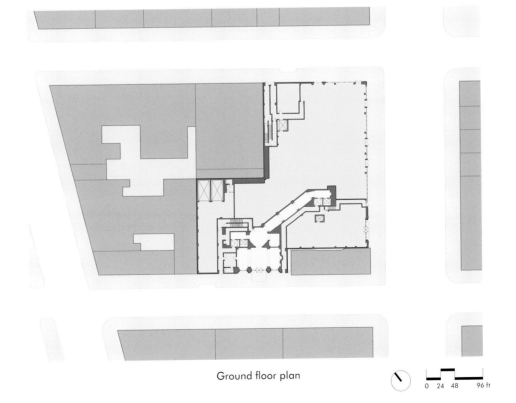

Ground floor plan

0 24 48   96 ft

100 Montgomery Street

San Francisco, California
2006–2009

Asked to update a marble-clad office building in downtown San Francisco designed by Wilbur Peugh that had been plagued by its fragile curtainwall system since completion in 1955, we respected the original character of the facades by overcladding the failing stone with crystallized glass panels that capture the color and sheen of the original. The signature component of the renovation is a new lobby, defined by a dramatic elliptical wall of structural glass carved into the building at the prominent corner of Montgomery and Sutter Streets.

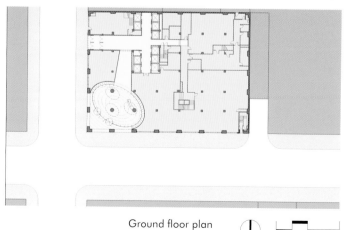

Ground floor plan

0   16   32   64 ft

Villanova Heights

Riverdale, The Bronx
New York
2006–

Bottom: The Dutch
Colonial house.

Set on the highest elevation in the Bronx, these houses, each of which provides accommodations at the high end of residential construction while addressing the realities of production building, offer views north to Van Cortlandt Park and south to the Manhattan skyline. Each house is a unique design drawing on the traditional architectural vocabularies that give Riverdale and adjacent Fieldston their distinct charm.

The first two houses were completed in the spring of 2009.

 Site plan

Top: Aerial view
looking northeast.

Bottom left: The Arts
& Crafts house.

Bottom right: The
Shingle Style house.

The French Norman house.

Left top: Entry (east) facade.

Left middle: Pool terrace looking to north facade.

Left bottom: South facade from West 250th Street.

Right: Garden (north) facade.

Ground floor plan

0 10 20 40 ft

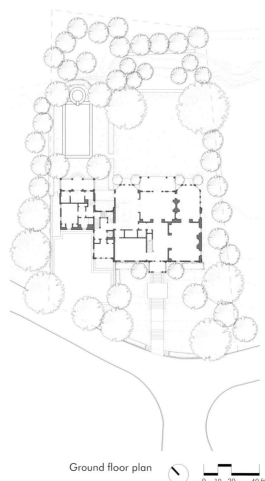

Ground floor plan

0 10 20 40 ft

The Colonial Revival house.

Left top: Garden (north) facade.

Right top: Entry (south) facade from West 250th Street.

Right middle: Pool terrace looking to pool pavilion.

Right bottom: Pergola.

Superior Ink

New York, New York
2006–2009

Superior Ink combines a 67-apartment, 15-story building on West Street in New York's West Village with seven townhouses on Bethune Street. The tower faces the Hudson River with large expanses of glass framed and detailed to reflect nearby late nineteenth- and early-twentieth-century factory and warehouse buildings. Each classically inspired red brick townhouse presents a unique front to Bethune Street, carrying forward the heterogeneous fabric of the West Village.

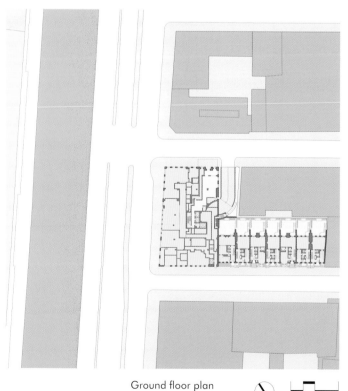

Ground floor plan

0 20 40   80 ft

Below: Townhouses on Bethune Street.

Overleaf: Skyline view from Hudson River.

West Village
Townhouse
Living Perfected

212.488.06
something   or.com
SUPERIOR INK

Berwyn Residences

Berwyn, Pennsylvania
Project, 2006

This residential community in walking
distance of the Daylesford commuter rail
station looks to earlier garden suburbs
by organizing apartment houses and
attached townhouses around a shop-lined
square and a village green, and single-
family houses facing an adjacent residential
neighborhood.

Site plan

0 50 100 200 ft

Ritz-Carlton Hotel and Residences

Almaty, Kazakhstan
2006–

Almaty is a cosmopolitan city of 1.2 million people located at the foot of the Tian Shan Mountains on the southern border of Kazakhstan. The 120-meter-by-200-meter city grid, laid out with a north-south grain, culminates at the government complex at the southern end of the city.

On Furmanova Avenue—a broad, tree-lined north-south boulevard that runs through the city's most prestigious residential neighborhoods and is home to many of the city's elegant shops—four eight- and nine-story apartment houses are arranged to either side of three motor courts across two city blocks. Shops line the ground floor of each building along the avenue, and each building encloses a central court; the upper floors, set back to provide terraces for the penthouses, form a distinctive profile. A fifteen-story hotel at the north end of the site has its own entrance facing Kunaev Park across Tulebaeva Avenue to the east.

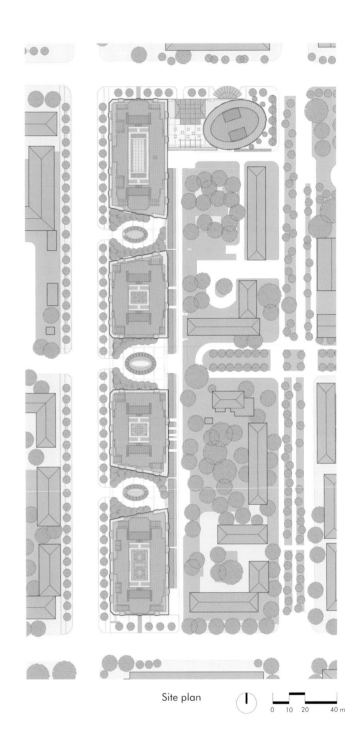

Site plan

0 10 20   40 m

Top: View looking
southeast.

Bottom left:
Residential lobby.

Bottom right:
Residence dining
room.

Top: Residence living
room.

Bottom: Pool.

Ritz-Carlton Hotel and Residences

Astana, Kazakhstan
Project, 2007

Astana, capital of the Republic of Kazakhstan, is being developed following a 2000 master plan by the Japanese architect Kisho Kurokawa who, inspired by L'Enfant's plan for Washington, DC, called for principal government buildings organized around a central mall. Our 60-story Ritz-Carlton hotel and residences—to be the new capital's tallest building—is sited just off the mall. A grand glazed winter court will open to meeting and ball rooms, as well as shops. The building rises to a glazed crown that will sparkle in the sunlight by day and glow like a lantern by night.

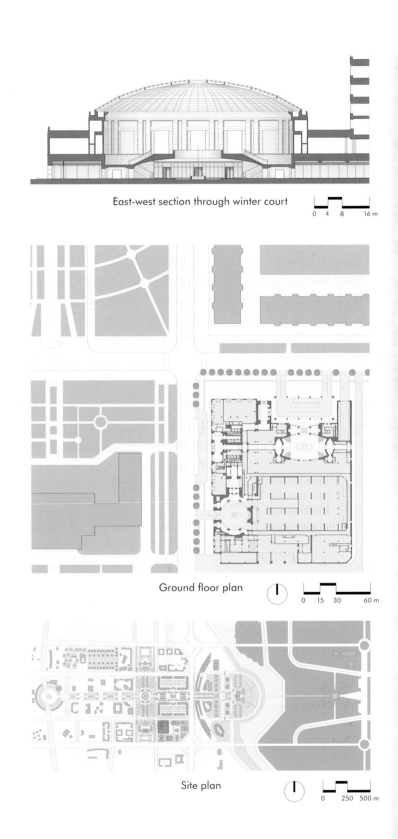

East-west section through winter court

0 4 8   16 m

Ground floor plan

0 15 30   60 m

Site plan

0   250 500 m

Left: View looking southeast.

Right, top to bottom:
Aerial view looking north.
North facade at winter court.
West facade at hotel entry.

Residence in Saint John

Saint John, New
Brunswick, Canada
2006–2007

Our renovation of a mid-nineteenth-century Italianate home respects the original architectural details, remedies previous insensitive alterations, and updates the interiors, infusing them with bright colors to combat the gray northern light and to bring a sense of the surrounding gardens into the house year-round. Finishes and fabrics are English in inspiration, selected to highlight and not upstage an important collection of Canadian art.

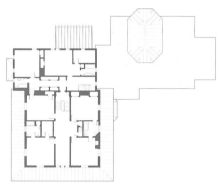

Second floor plan

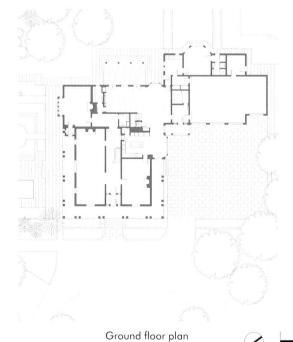

Ground floor plan

0 8 16   32 ft

Below: Garden
(north) facade.

Left: Pergola at
family room.

Right top:
Widow's walk.

Right middle:
Stair hall.

Right bottom:
Library.

Venus Rock

Paphos, Cyprus
2006–

Inspired by traditional Mediterranean towns that seem to grow out of the landscape, a twenty-first-century resort village is woven into the hills and valleys, and oriented to vistas and breezes, to establish its own sense of place.

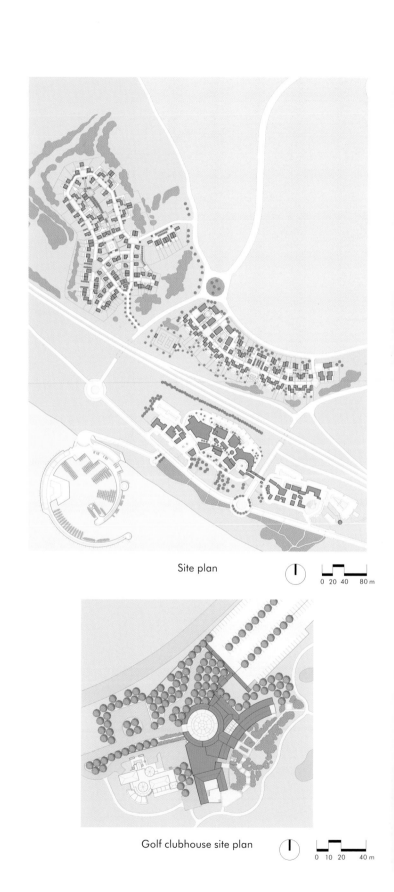

Site plan

0 20 40 80 m

Golf clubhouse site plan

0 10 20 40 m

Greenberg
Conference Center

Yale University
New Haven, Connecticut
2006–2009

The Greenberg Conference Center, providing executive meeting facilities for Yale's Office of International Affairs, which holds seminars and conferences that attract distinguished guests from all over the world, is linked by a glazed arcade to the historic Betts House (Henry Austin and David R. Brown, 1868, restored 2002). The conference center is sited in keeping with the historic pattern of Prospect Street, where large residences—many now converted to institutional uses—are set back to occupy the high point of their lots. The new building is rotated eastward away from the street to allow Betts House to maintain its visual prominence but carries forward some of the earlier building's scrollwork details and its palette of mauve stucco walls scored to simulate dressed stone over a brown ashlar masonry base.

The design of the Greenberg Center deliberately suggests the character of Yale's James Gamble Rogers's Gothic campus, especially in its interior, where wood paneling and timberwork ceilings are employed in the public spaces.

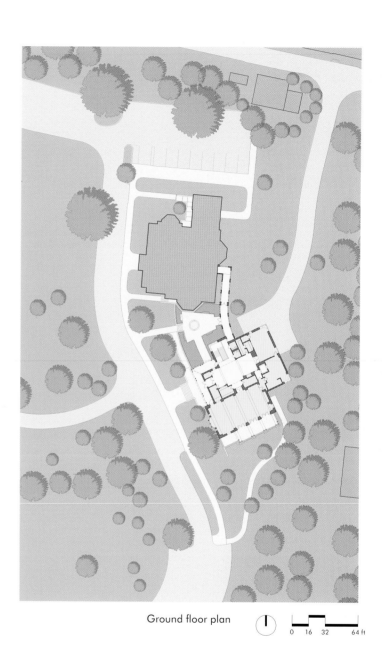

Ground floor plan

0   16   32   64 ft

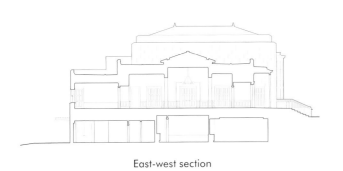

East-west section

North-south section

0 6 12   24 ft

Left: Entry looking to Betts House and tower of the Divinity School.

Right top: View from south.

Right middle: Classroom.

Right bottom: Dining room.

Mas Fleuri

Nestled under a canopy of native umbrella pines and capturing panoramic views of the Mediterranean and the coast of Eze to the east, this house of stucco, local limestone, wrought iron, and red roof tiles offers a fresh interpretation of the timeless villa tradition of the Côte d'Azur.

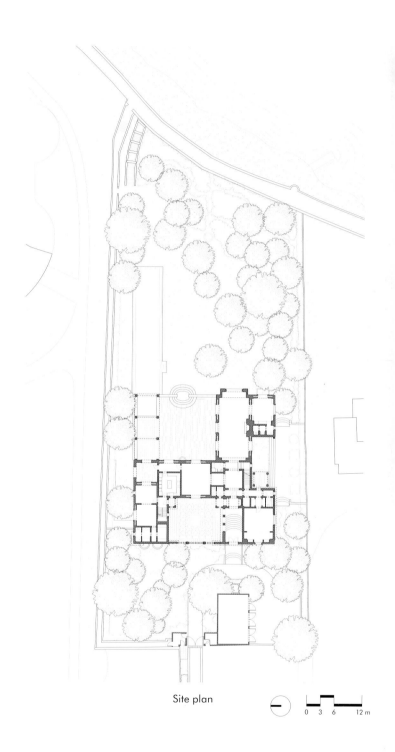

Site plan

0 3 6 12 m

Shir Hadash Center for Jewish Life

German Colony
Jerusalem, Israel
Project, 2007

To keep the apparent building mass in scale with nearby residences, two of the 17,000-square-foot building's five stories are below street level on a sloping mid-block site. The sanctuary is designed for Orthodox worship with men and women separated by a mechitzah. Each side is served by its own stair; each opens onto a generous courtyard facing the street to accommodate overflow worshipers who will still be connected to the service. A vaulted library on the top floor opens onto two exterior balconies overlooking the city of Jerusalem.

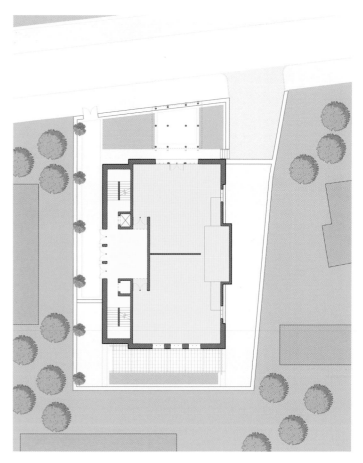

Ground floor plan

0 2 4   8 m

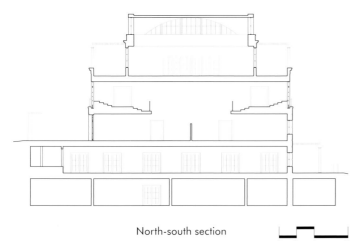

North-south section

0 2 4   8 m

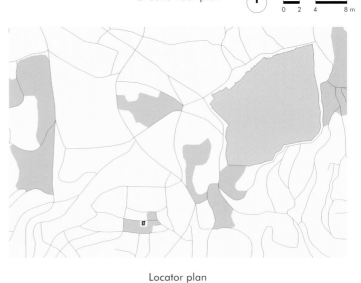

Locator plan

Residences at
Albany Marina

New Providence,
The Bahamas
2006–

Two residential buildings inspired by
Bahamian classicism are intended as part
of a new marina village master-planned
by Duany Plater-Zyberk & Company: one
acts as a gateway to the marina, with the
memorable profile of its narrow south
facade greeting visitors arriving by boat;
the other presents a formal palace-like
presence at the head of the harbor set
between two small parks. The two buildings share a palette of stone, stucco,
and wood shutters and pergolas.

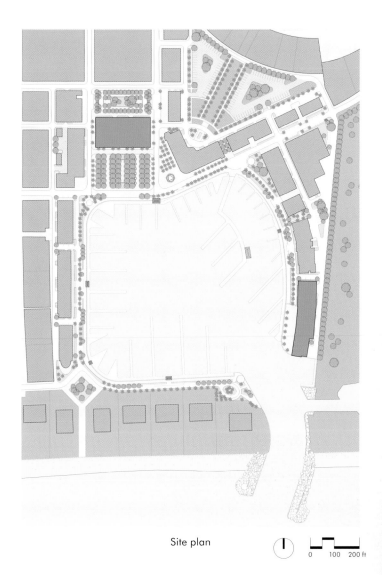

Site plan

0   100   200 ft

Silo Ridge

Amenia, New York
2006–

Top: Aerial view looking southwest.

Middle: Golf villas.

Bottom: Village green.

Silo Ridge is organized in the manner of a traditional town, favoring pockets of density that preserve open green space. A 300-room hotel and other resort functions—including a spa, a banquet hall, and a street of shops—are set on a village green, with a skating pond and a golf clubhouse centered on a smaller square nearby. Winding country lanes lead to more intimate neighborhoods of golf villas and clusters of single-family houses that run along the hillsides, and townhouses with front and rear gardens that face private mews.

Site plan

0   500 1000 ft

Pequot Library

The Pequot Library serves as a community library, a repository of a nationally significant collection of historical documents, and a performance center. The original library was designed in the 1880s by R. H. Robertson in a Romanesque-revival style and has been added onto twice since. In 2000, we proposed an addition that wrapped two wings and a gallery around a new courtyard. This proved too costly. Our second proposal, seen here, harmonizes with the original structure with a palette of stone, red brick, and copper roofing, but its curving mass that adapts to the constraints of the site shows that it is an addition of its time.

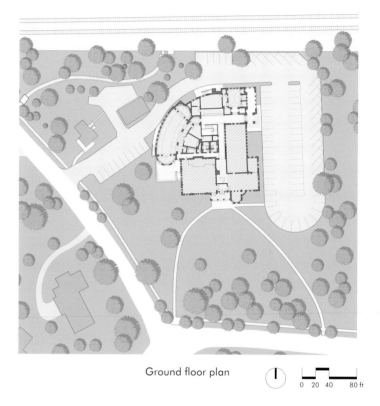

Ground floor plan

0 20 40   80 ft

Top: View to entry looking west.

Bottom left: Children's room.

Bottom right: Aerial view looking northeast.

50 Connaught Road

Central
Hong Kong, China
2007–2010

Right: Connaught
Road (east) facade.

In contrast to Hong Kong's predominant modernist office buildings, our building, recalling classical office towers of the 1920s, is rendered in stone, which takes the light in a way that glass and steel curtain-wall never do. Punched window openings are inset to mitigate glare, so the glass can be clearer than in typical curtainwall buildings. At the top, set-back floors with bay windows take full advantage of the views, while the building's bronze and stone crown is intended as a memorable skyline feature.

Ground floor plan

0   20   40   80 ft

Locator plan

0   40   80   160 ft

Crown Heights High School

Brooklyn, New York
2007–2010

Two charter school organizations, Uncommon Schools and Achievement First, serving 800 students in all, will share this building located on a mid-block site. Facing narrow, residential Pacific Street, a rusticated base, pedimented lobby windows and overscale window surrounds visually connect the building with traditional New York City high schools. To the north, the building takes on the character of an industrial loft in keeping with the commercial character of Atlantic Avenue and its elevated railroad. Terraces and a rooftop playing field offer impressive views to Manhattan.

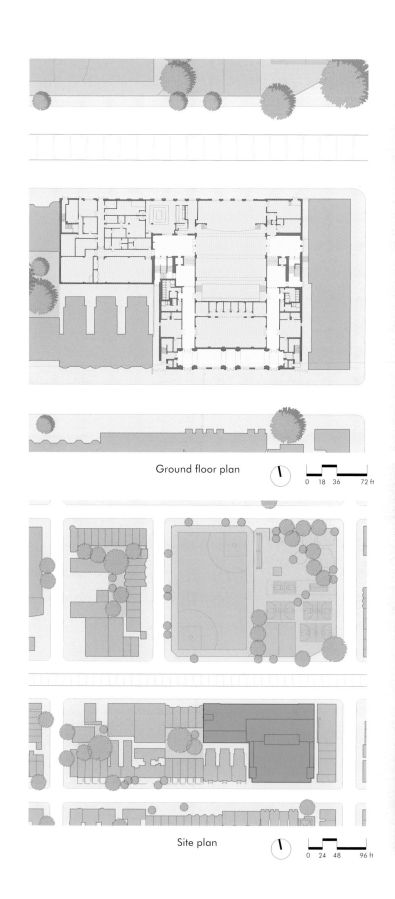

Ground floor plan   0 18 36 72 ft

Site plan   0 24 48 96 ft

Four Seasons Downtown

Hotel and Private
Residences at 30 Park Place
New York, New York
2007–2012

Right: View looking
south along Church
Street.

Sharing a city block with the Woolworth
Building, Cass Gilbert's iconic 1913 skyscraper, and strategically located one block
from the World Trade Center redevelopment site, this slender tower housing a
175-room five-star Four Seasons hotel
and 143 top-end condominium apartments will become an important landmark
among the constellation of towers in Lower
Manhattan. The limestone and cast stone
shaft rises to a dramatic skyline profile of
full-floor penthouses and setback terraces.

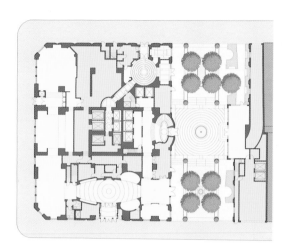

Ground floor plan

0 12 24   48 ft

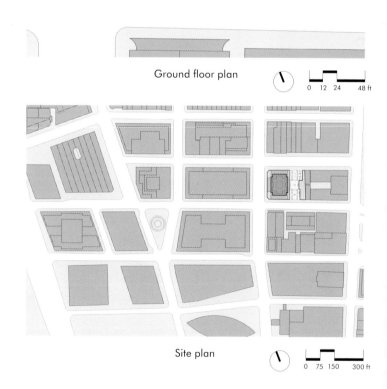

Site plan

0 75 150   300 ft

Floor 2

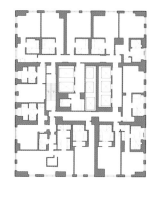

Floors 6–22

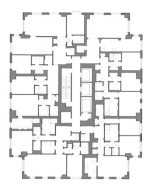

Floors 37–48

0 8 16   32 ft

Left: Skyline view
looking south.

Top left: Hotel lobby.

Middle left: Hotel
lounge.

Bottom left: Hotel
prefunction room.

Top right: Residents'
conservatory.

Middle right:
Residents' dining
room.

Bottom right:
Residential lobby.

Tour Carpe Diem

La Défense
Courbevoie, France
2007–2011

Top: Roof garden

Bottom: View looking
east from the "dalle."

Tour Carpe Diem is an important step forward in the evolution of La Défense toward pedestrian-friendly urbanism and environmentally responsible architecture. The 45,000-square-meter building connects the raised esplanade—the "dalle" that continues the axis of the Champs-Elysées—and the urban fabric of the city of Courbevoie to the north. A landscaped pedestrian street, centered on a linear rain garden and lined with cafés will connect the building's winter garden and lobby with a monumental stair rising from a plaza on the Boulevard Circulaire, where a second front welcomes visitors at what was heretofore very much the back of the site. Faceted facades reflect this dual orientation, catching the ever-changing Parisian light to give the building a strong identity among the towers of La Défense.

Tour Carpe Diem significantly exceeds French regulations for environmentally responsible development. The building's triple-glazed curtain wall incorporates sunshades that respond to the solar orientation of each facade and innovative grilles that provide natural ventilation to reduce dependence on air conditioning. Additional sustainable design strategies include solar water heating, a heat recovery system, and high-performance lighting.

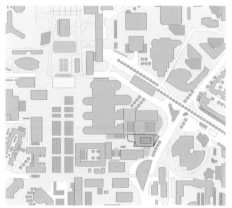

Site plan

0 30 60 120 ft

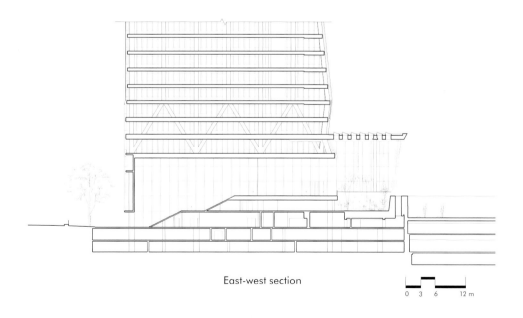

East-west section

0 3 6   12 m

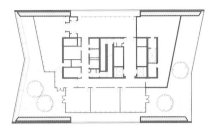

Floor 35

Floor 24

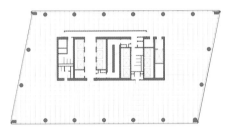

Floor 7

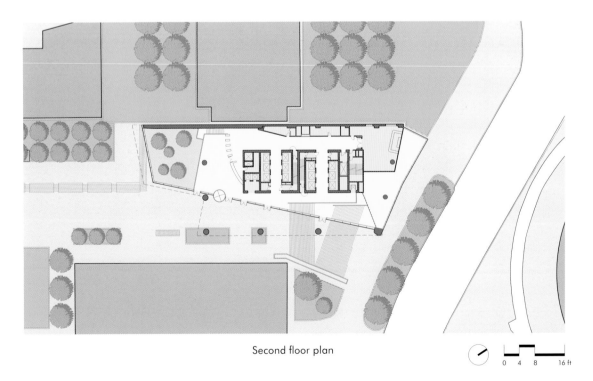

Second floor plan

0 4 8   16 ft

Hancock Technology Center

Marist College
Poughkeepsie, New York
2007–2010

The Hancock Technology Center, housing the School of Computer Science and Mathematics, occupies a prominent site at the heart of the Marist campus, which sits atop a bluff overlooking the Hudson River and its magnificent valley. The Hancock Center carries forward the quiet Gothic architectural tradition established by the Marist Brothers at the turn of the twentieth century, with its rustic stone walls, red brick window surrounds, and limestone detailing.

An L-shaped plan improves the definition of two of the campus's evolving green spaces, the Hudson Meadow and the Quadrangle, each part of a phased sequence of new construction and building replacement that, by removing earlier insensitive development, will enable the campus to take full advantage of its spectacular site.

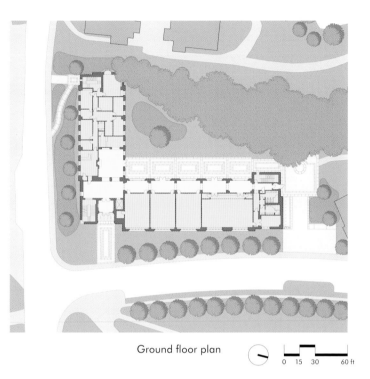

Ground floor plan   0 15 30   60 ft

Site plan   0   250   500 ft

Top: View from campus entry.

Middle left: View from Campus Drive.

Middle right: View from Hudson River.

Bottom left: West terrace.

Bottom right: Lobby looking to student lounge.

McCann Center
Expansion

Marist College
Poughkeepsie, New York
2008–

The second step in a plan to unify
aesthetically disparate facilities into a
coherent athletic precinct complementing
the Hudson River Gothic of the Marist
campus, this stone addition to the
gymnasium will significantly improve
first impressions of the campus for those
arriving from the south.

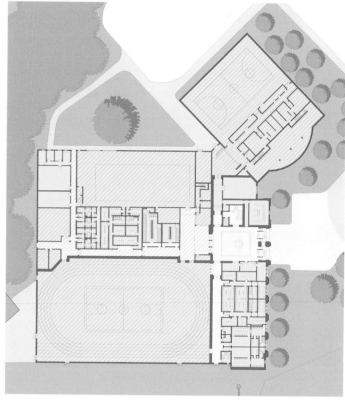

Ground floor plan

0 18 36   72 ft

Tenth Square

Tenth Square, a vibrant mixed-use neighborhood on a gateway site at the edge of downtown New Haven, will have as its centerpiece the new home of the respected Long Wharf Theatre.

New College House

Franklin & Marshall College
Lancaster, Pennsylvania
2008–

Housing nearly 200 students in doubles, suites, and apartments on a site at the northwest edge of campus, New College House carries forward the heritage of architect Charles Z. Klauder's much-loved Georgian master plan and buildings with its simply massed expression of red brick, stone, painted wood trim, and slate roof.

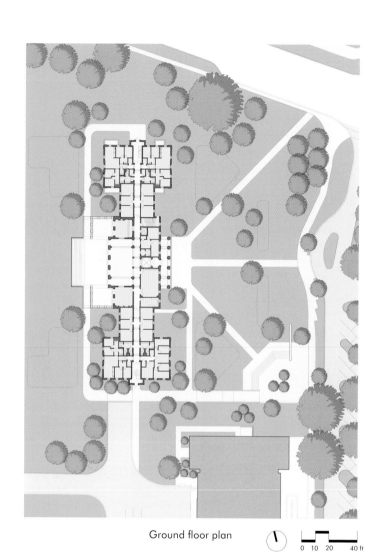

Ground floor plan

0   10   20   40 ft

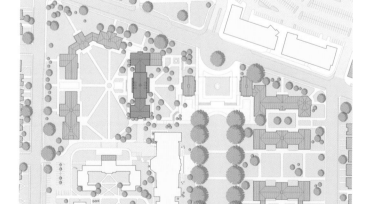

Precinct plan

0   125   250 ft

Caruthers Biotechnology Building

University of Colorado at Boulder
Boulder, Colorado
2008–2011

Bottom: Entry court.

The University of Colorado at Boulder, set in the foothills of the Rockies, was endowed with a character all its own by architect Charles Z. Klauder's 1920 master plan which, inspired by Tuscan hilltop villages, takes full advantage of topography and views. Our master plan for the new, nearby East Campus adapts Klauder's vision to the larger scale that is required for twenty-first-century academic laboratory buildings. Our first building on the new campus, the Caruthers Biotechnology Building, echoes the university's original buildings but substitutes brick for the local sandstone.

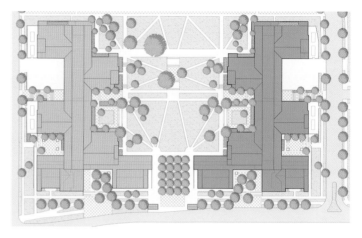

Site plan

0   75   150   300 ft

East Campus plan

0   300   600 ft

Top: View along
Colorado Avenue
looking west.

Bottom left: Bosque at
entry to East Campus.

Bottom right:
Aerial view looking
northeast.

Classical Opera
and Ballet Theater

Astana, Kazakhstan
Competition, 2009

Our proposal confronts the monumental mall of the new capital city with a classically inspired cubical mass of stone and glass. A forecourt embellished with grand cascading fountains, a central reflecting pool, and a broad ceremonial stair sets the stage for arriving theatergoers. The transparent south facade, anchored at each end by limestone pavilions topped with celebratory uplights, further conveys the sense of spectacle. Two grand circular stairs climb to the dramatic lobby and the intimate 1,200-seat theater, flanked by rehearsal rooms, production shops, dressing rooms, chorus rooms, administrative offices, and a 68-room hotel for guest artists. A banquet room and a restaurant set amid roof gardens crown the composition.

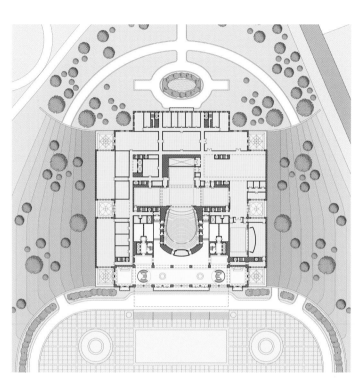

Second floor plan

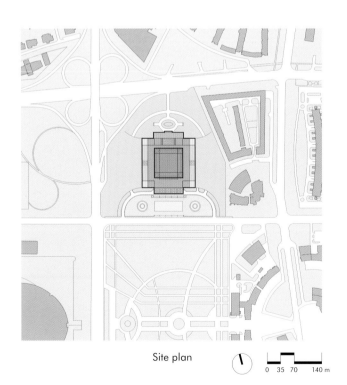

Site plan

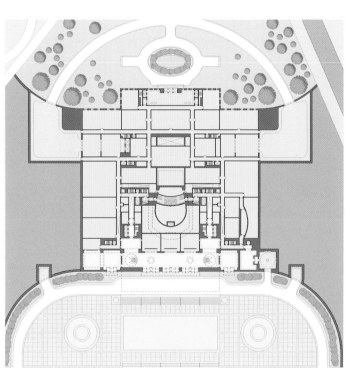

Ground floor plan

George W. Bush Presidential Center

Southern Methodist University
Dallas, Texas
2008–2013

The Presidential Center presents three distinct facades to the adjacent Georgian-style campus. Carrying forward SMU's tradition of Georgian buildings, the simple wall planes are faced with Texas limestone and red brick relieved by rhythmically disposed divided-light windows. On the north, the public entrance to the library and museum stands at the head of a colonnaded court. To the west, the entrance to the Policy Institute is through a portico that concludes the important Binkley Avenue axis of the campus. To the south, the Institute faces university recreational fields, with the Dallas skyline visible in the distance beyond. On the east side, service areas help buffer the Center from the noise of an adjoining freeway. A large central lantern identifies the Center from both the campus and the city.

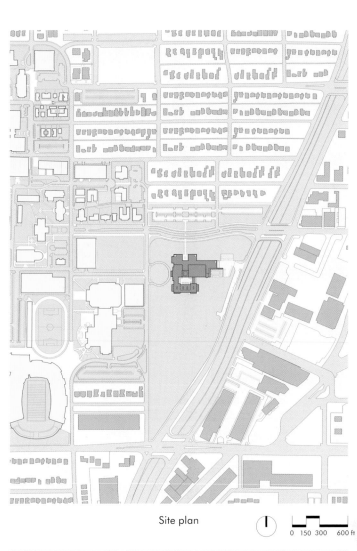

Site plan

0 150 300 600 ft

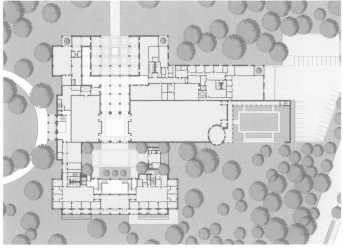

Ground floor plan

0 75 150 ft

Top: Entry to Policy
Institute from Binkley
Avenue.

Bottom: Library
entry court on SMU
Boulevard.

New Residential Colleges

Yale University
New Haven, Connecticut
2008–

Top: Small courtyard
of the north college.

Middle: Main courtyard
of the south college.

Bottom: View from
Prospect Street.

Yale's system of residential colleges, the cornerstone of its undergraduate experience, was established in the 1930s with James Gamble Rogers (1867–1947) providing the design of eight of the original ten to be built. Four of the original colleges are red-brick Georgian. The rest, as well as many other Yale buildings constructed in the 1920s and 1930s, are stone and brick in the Gothic style. All the colleges are organized around variously sized courtyards. The two newest colleges, carrying forward the spirit of Rogers's Gothic, are designed as fraternal twins, similar in size and palette but each enjoying its own identity and organization.

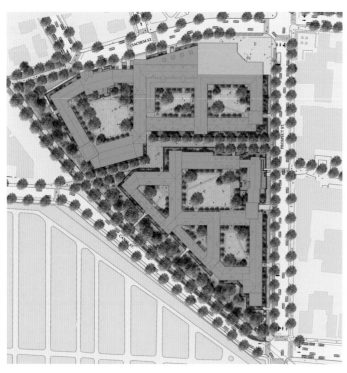

Site plan

Top: Main courtyard
of the north college.

Bottom left: Prospect
Walk.

Bottom right: View
from Farmington
Canal Trail.

579

Additional Projects

Santa Monica UCLA Medical Center / Orthopaedic Hospital Replacement Project
Santa Monica, California, 1997–2011

After the 1994 Northridge earthquake left the bed tower of Santa Monica Hospital with severe structural damage, we were asked to direct a program of demolition and reconstruction to revitalize a beloved neighborhood institution. To brand the new building as part of the UCLA Health Sciences system, our design references the northern Italianate of the historic UCLA campus with a lively combination of brick and cast stone.

55 Railroad Avenue
Greenwich, Connecticut, 2000–2003

In an effort to reposition a visually challenged but strategically located office property, a new cantilevered glass and steel canopy leads to a redesigned lobby, and a sunken concrete plaza is transformed into a garden with outdoor tables and chairs set between a bosque of flowering trees, a raised panel of turf, and an 80-foot-long water wall.

 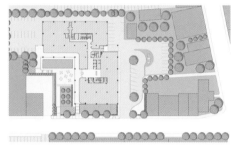

Residence
Atherton, California, 2000

A relaxed use of classical details contrasts with the informality of a shingle-style design in the tradition of such Bay Area architects as Willis Polk and Julia Morgan.

Office Building, Centre du Val d'Europe
Marne-la-Vallée, France, 2000–2004

Marking the entry to the new town of Val d'Europe with a tower and colonnade fronting a roundabout, this six-story stucco and stone office building steps down at its rear to face residential development across a courtyard.

Residence
Bristol, Virginia, 2001

Situated along the crest of a hill of a large country property commanding views to distant mountains, the rough stone and timber structure with its steeply pitched slate roof is rendered picturesque by subtle shifts in fenestration as well as by the informal arrangement of masonry chimneys along its roofscape.

Middle School and Gymnasium
Madison Country Day School
Waunakee, Wisconsin, 2002

Intended as the first phase of our 1999 Master Plan for Madison Country Day School, the new Gymnasium and Middle School Building was to be located adjacent to the existing Lower School, accommodating a large array of functions including a large student commons meant to be the heart of the school, a gymnasium, ten classrooms, and a library, all with a view to the Yahara River.

Cube-is-mmm
Greyston Foundation Benefit and Auction, 2003

An 18-inch high by 8-inch wide cake is composed of three rotated, stacked cubes of alternating white and chocolate cake of graduated sizes, iced in white with silverleaf decoration

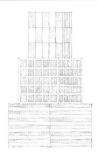

Lyons View Gardens
Knoxville, Tennessee, 2002

A traditional public garden conceived on the model of Filoli outside of San Francisco or Wave Hill in New York for a bluff high above the Tennessee River offering stunning views, Lyons View Gardens was intended as part of the second phase realization of the master plan for Knoxville's Lakeshore Park. The proposal includes two new buildings: a gateway building accommodating administrative space and an event pavilion for private functions.

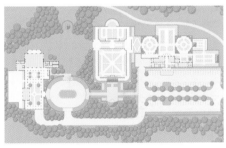

Grumble Knot
Meredith, New Hampshire, 2002–2003

Drawing inspiration from the cottages built in the region in the 1880s, new life has been given to an unremarkable house built in the 1980s on a dramatic site with stunning views of Lake Winnipesaukee and surrounding mountains. New construction flanks the original house providing a tower on the west and a great room on the east, softening the profile of the once boxy house while allowing for a reconfigured plan.

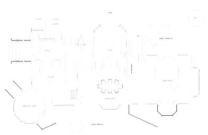

Kensington Manor
Bronxville, New York, 2003

In keeping with neighboring developments from the early twentieth century, four-story Arts and Crafts stucco and stone apartment houses are organized around garden courts in this proposal for a residential community on a prime site adjacent to the Bronxville commuter train station.

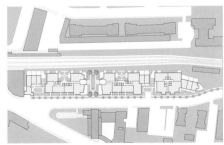

Lakefields
Michigan, 2003–2010

The straightforward plan of this compact rubble-stone and slate-roof lakeside guest house includes a large great room, with arched windows to terraces on three sides, suggesting a glazed loggia poised dramatically above the water.

Residence in Tulsa
Tulsa, Oklahoma, 2003

A classically detailed one-story house was designed to take optimal advantage of its deep suburban lot to create distinct formal and informal outdoor entertaining areas.

 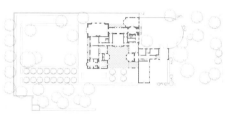

Working Dog's Weekend House
Art for Auction for Puppies Behind Bars, 2003

The life of a guide dog for the blind is a tough one. Like the rest of us, he deserves a weekend retreat, a pup tent in which to unwind.

Birdhouses for the Litchfield Historical Society
2003

Designed for a benefit auction as a pair of pillars flanking a garden path, these fragments of Ionic entablatures with bas relief ornament were set on stylized columns and carefully sized to host nesting pairs of eastern bluebirds.

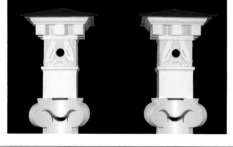 

Street Furniture for JCDecaux North America
2003–2004

Our second line of street furniture for JCDecaux North America is a unified kit of interchangeable parts reinterpreting beloved features of early twentieth-century transportation infrastructure.

The Houses at Greenwich Armory
Greenwich, Connecticut, 2004

Our design converts a 1911 armory into two residences and adds to them seven townhouses staggered behind front gardens while brick walls capped with iron railings hold the street wall. Each townhouse has its own private terrace and garden as well as a service passage located at the rear boundary of the property, and each has direct access to its own enclosed two-bay garage and basement via interior stairs and private elevator.

School of Business and Technology Webster University
Webster Groves, Missouri, 2004–

This L-shaped building will frame the East Quadrangle, a new campus green space that will be the centerpiece of a new precinct at the southeast corner of campus. At the intersection of the two wings, a two-story commons will link the entrance from the quadrangle to the street entrance one level below.

World Expo 2010
Shanghai, China, Competition, 2004
(in association with Frederic Schwartz Architects)

Straddling a bend of the Haungpu River just south of the Bund in central Shanghai, our plan conceived exposition pavilions as landscaped mounds, with a larger glass-covered central pavilion massed as a mountain and a mixed-use tower punctuating the west end of the site.

Residential Development at Reston Town Center
Reston, Virginia, 2004

Two apartment buildings embrace a hierarchy of public, semipublic, and private garden courts conceived as rooms linked to the Town Center's larger network of streets and pedestrian ways. The Moderne-inspired buildings will be faced in a combination of brick, cast stone, and limestone.

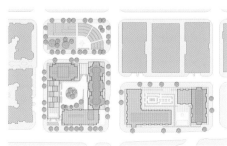

Science and Engineering Quad 2
Stanford University, Palo Alto, California
Competition, 2004

Our proposal for a new quadrangle to accommodate a state-of-the-art high-tech hub extended the western axis of Shepley, Rutan & Coolidge's original quadrangles and linked back to them with walks, arcades, and sandstone and glass buildings that reinterpreted the campus traditions.

East River Park Showboat, NYC 2012 Cultural Olympics
New York, New York, 2004

Anchored off a bend in the East River, offering views to the Brooklyn, Manhattan, and Williamsburg Bridges and the Statue of Liberty, a stage set on a simple barge was to be canopied by a soaring fabric superstructure designed to display projections of the performances below.

Hindsight 20/20
for the exhibition "The Voting Booth" at the Parsons School of Design Gallery, 2004

In the spirit of democracy and inclusiveness, our office held an in-house design competition in response to the call for entries to Parsons School of Design's Voting Booth exhibition. The winning concept, developed by Thomas Morbitzer and Goil Amornvivat, puts the voter in the driver's seat and suggests that the phrase "hindsight is 20/20" is often used unfairly by critics on all sides.

Metropolitan Spice
for the exhibition "Scents of Purpose: Artists Interpret the Spice Box," Contemporary Jewish Museum, San Francisco, 2005

This architecturally proportioned spice box will fit comfortably beside precious candlesticks and Kiddush cups, and remind transplanted New Yorkers—indeed anyone with fond memories of New York—of the iconic skyscrapers of the early twentieth-century skyline.

Westport Weston Family Y
Camp Mahackeno, Westport, Connecticut
2004—

The Westport Weston Family Y proposes move to new facilities at Mahackeno, a 32-acre campus north of town that has been used primarily as a summer camp for over fifty years. The new building will be nestled into the natural terrain at the remote northeast corner of the property adjacent to the Merritt Parkway, preserving the existing camp and the woods, trails, and open space that surround it.

Apartment at Lost Tree Village
Palm Beach, Florida, 2004–2006

A 1970s condominium is reconfigured with secondary spaces disposed to either side of a central gallery that leads to a large living and dining room facing the ocean.

 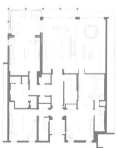

Fudu Mansion
Office Development for Shanghai Fortune
World, Pudong, Shanghai, China
Competition, 2005
(in association with Frederic Schwartz Architects)

Small among Pudong's skyscraping giants, the
215-meter-high, 40-story, 85,000-square-meter Fudu
Mansion was proposed as a dramatic undulation of
light reflective glass, with floor plans formed out of
eight gentle curves to optimize views of the Bund and
the Huangpo River while maximizing the quality of
light in interior spaces and minimizing solar heat gain.

Takanassee Beach
Long Branch, New Jersey, 2005–

On a spectacular site between the Atlantic Ocean and
Lake Takanassee, a small summer colony takes its cues
from seaside Regency precedents such as can be found
at Brighton and Hove in England.

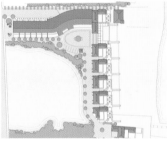

Residential Towers on the New River
Fort Lauderdale, Florida, 2005

Two condominium towers extend the lively residential
and retail neighborhood north of the New River to a
site on the currently underdeveloped
south bank. Vibrant colors, Art Deco detailing, and
spacious balconies give the plan an appropriately
South Florida character.

Center for the Arts, University of Virginia
Charlottesville, Virginia, Competition, 2005

Intended to house two unrelated arts facilities—
a museum and a performance venue—in a single
building located at the key gateway to the university
campus, our proposal calls for a shared lobby, café,
bookstore, loading area, and service spaces in an
articulated building that reflects but does not imitate
the Jeffersonian classicism of the campus.

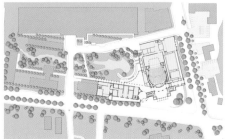

Dunwalke Farm
Far Hills, New Jersey, 2005

A colonial-style house was planned for a working farm as part of a group incorporating a restored stable, an existing garage, and a poolhouse crafted from a storage shed.

Athletics and Events Center, Ithaca College
Ithaca, New York, Competition, 2005

Our scheme for Ithaca College's sprawling athletics program proposed a series of interconnected buildings that reflect the scale of the campus. A lighted turf field doubles as a ceremonial quadrangle, anchored by a glazed hall of fame. The center's grassy roofs, visible from Cayuga Lake, speak to the school's commitment to environmental stewardship.

200 North Riverside Plaza
Chicago, Illinois, Competition, 2005

Our proposal for an office tower over railroad tracks where the three branches of the Chicago River come together combined a lenticular plan with an undulating curtainwall.

 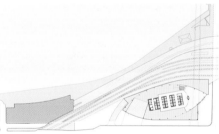

Capital Park
Trenton, New Jersey, Competition, 2006

Our contributions to a competition proposal by landscape architect Diana Balmori were focused on animating and articulating the park with a series of strategically planned architectural interventions: shade canopies, a small restaurant positioned to capitalize on views up and down the river, as well as a retail/café and south-facing plaza adjacent to an existing library facility.

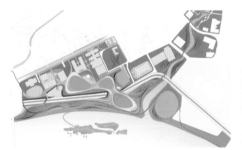 

Pool Pavilion at the Residence on Lily Pond Lane
East Hampton, New York, 2006–2008

Complementing an historic oceanfront house that we renovated for a previous owner, the pavilion can be used year-round. In the summer glazed panels on all four sides can be lowered into the foundation while insect screens roll down with a touch of a button.

 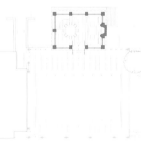

Residence in Watch Hill
Watch Hill, Rhode Island, 2006

We designed this shingle-style house in emulation of the Watch Hill houses that survived the great hurricane of 1938, and those that did not.

Balfour Cosmopolitan Club
Denver, Colorado, 2006

Intended to be a resort-style community just minutes away from downtown Denver and its LoDo entertainment district, the Cosmopolitan Club re-uses Moffat Station, a designated Denver landmark, as its main living room.

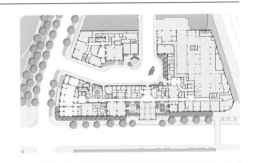

Tuxedo Reserve Welcome Center
Tuxedo, New York, 2004

This shingle-style gatehouse, designed as a sales office to introduce the public to the residential community our office planned in 1997, is intended to serve as a community center in future years.

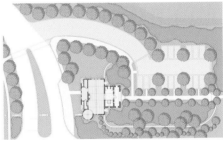

East Hampton Town Hall
East Hampton, New York, 2006–2010

Four historic timber-framed vernacular structures are connected by a glass-and-metal conservatory-style lobby, which allows each to retain its individual integrity while bringing natural light to an internal stair and a suite of offices below grade. Another historic barn will serve as an open-air gateway to the complex from adjacent parking.

Echo Bay
New Rochelle, New York, Project, 2006

A shopping street was proposed as a spine for a new mixed-use neighborhood of apartment houses, loft buildings, and townhouses linking upland development to the waterfront.

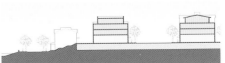

Nelson Fitness Center and Smith Swim Center
Brown University, Providence, Rhode Island
2006–

The Nelson Fitness Center and Smith Swim Center will be located at the center of the Erickson Athletic Complex, connected to the 1970s OMAC gymnasium and, with the Meehan Ice Rink, shaping a new quadrangle that will replace surface parking. A promenade between the fitness center and the swim center will lead from the campus to the sports fields.

Penthouse at One St. Thomas Street
Toronto, Ontario, 2006–2010

Not so much an apartment as a house in the sky atop the residential tower we completed in 2008, this duplex penthouse is organized with the major rooms around the perimeter of the lower floor, and the floor above dedicated to a master suite.

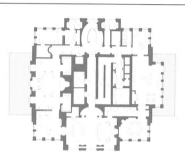

Baisetova Square
Almaty, Kazakhstan, 2006

Six stone-clad apartment houses accommodating 500 units above a retail mall embrace the principal axis that leads to the old parliament building and frame a new civic square on a cross-axis. As at Rockefeller Center in New York, the square is lined with storefronts and enlivened by a public iceskating rink ringed with restaurants one level below.

Kaplankaya
Bozbuk, Turkey, 2006

For a sustainable resort community on a spectacular site on the southwestern coast of Turkey planned by an international roster of architects, our work involved the development of two hill towns.

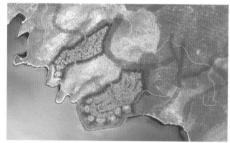

Tole Bi
Almaty, Kazakhstan, 2006

This nine-story apartment house is inspired by early twentieth-century Parisian precedents, with facades articulated by recesses and stacked window bays that rise to a profile of terraces, pergolas, and loggias. Streetfronts are lined with shops; the building's four corners step back to provide access to a skylighted shopping arcade in the center of the block.

Hun-In Village
Seoul, Korea, 2006–

Located in a picturesque, craggy greenbelt only ten minutes from the central business district, Hun-In Village offers an alternative to the high-rise towers typically built to meet the needs of Seoul's affluent class. The plan, providing for 280 apartments and 39 single-family houses, preserves views to the hills beyond the site and integrates a network of hiking trails. A clubhouse, offering dining and recreational amenities, will incorporate a glass-roofed indoor pool.

Chapel Hill Public Library
Chapel Hill, North Carolina, 2006

Doubling the size of a fourteen-year-old library, our addition bookends the existing building with a new public face to the south and a new front door to the north. The loft-like south addition, housing book stacks and reading areas, overlooks Pritchard Park through a louvered window wall. The north addition, faced with glass, brick, wood, and stone, provides a new entrance and much-needed community meeting spaces.

Las Olas
Coral Isles, Florida, 2006–

As with many early twentieth-century Mediterranean Revival houses and the vernacular Andalusian farmsteads that inspired them, this house is composed of simple, discrete volumes juxtaposed to give a picturesque effect. The sinuous plan orients each of the principal rooms toward specific distant views.

Apartment on Park Avenue
New York, New York, 2006–2009

Longtime clients asked us to combine their existing apartment with a neighboring apartment to enhance the entry and create a spacious new master suite.

Apartment on Park Avenue
New York, New York, 2006–2009

Our clients asked us to renovate the traditionally appointed apartment they had lived in for over twenty years to open the plan and streamline the detailing.

Shymbulak Mountain Resort
Medeu Valley, Kazakhstan, 2006

Our plan for a new 150,000-square-meter mountain village is organized around three outdoor spaces: a south-facing skier's plaza opening out to the ski apron with views looking up the mountain; a north-facing village square opening out to the surrounding landscape with views looking down the Medeu Valley to the city of Almaty; and a village walk running east-west, anchored at its ends by a five-star hotel and a gondola terminal.

Leninville
Almaty, Kazakhstan, 2007

Located at the bend of Dostyk, the main road connecting the city of Almaty with the Shymbulak Resort, this project groups an office building, six residential buildings, and a community building symmetrically around a central two-hectare elliptical park.

House in Southampton
Southampton, New York, 2007–2010

This new house, replacing a carriage house our clients had lived in for nearly thirty years, fulfills the wife's dream of a home that will remind her of childhood summers spent on the Côte d'Azur.

House on Edgartown Harbor
Martha's Vineyard, Massachusetts, 2007

The design of a house and outbuildings is in keeping with the neighboring nineteenth-century structures from Edgartown's heyday as a bustling fishing and trading port.

Moon Dance
Park City, Utah, 2007

Moon Dance is a planned community of thirty single-family houses nestled into the Mark O'Meara golf course at Tuhaye, a five-minute walk from the social amenities of our firm's Talisker Club Park. A small park that doubles as a putting green establishes a sense of community amidst the vast landscape.

Harrison MetroCentre
Harrison, New Jersey, 2007–

A mixed-use development consists of fifteen urban
blocks on a 65-acre former industrial site directly
across the Passaic River from Newark's Ironbound
neighborhood on a site bordered by a new riverside
park and the newly constructed minor-league baseball
venue Red Bull Park.

Residence
Almaty, Kazakhstan, 2007

A grand villa on a sloping site with views to the snow-
capped mountains bookends a formal terrace on the
garden side and the motor court in front, where a curving stair rises to a grand formal entrance and a skylit
elliptical hall. The principal rooms give onto terraces
and gardens for gracious large-scale entertaining.

Block "O", Southeast Federal Center
Washington, D.C., 2007

On a block within our master plan for Southeast
Federal Center, two loft-style apartment houses define
a shared courtyard. A variety of windows and terraces
activate the faceted facades and distinguish the rental
slabs from the condominium towers.

Residence
Toronto, Ontario, 2007–

A compact house for a small lot in a dense established
suburban neighborhood is massed informally to
provide most rooms with multiple exposures.

Hudson Point
Esopus, New York, 2007

A 350-unit planned community on 80 acres with
spectacular views over the Hudson River Valley carries
forward a master plan initially developed by Duany
Plater-Zyberk & Company. Prototypes for a variety
of residential types were developed to address the
rolling terrain.

18 Gramercy Park South
New York, New York, 2007–

A reworking of a hotel built for single women (Murgatroyd & Ogden, 1927), located in a New York City landmark district, will create family-sized luxury apartments.

Opera House Residences
Almaty, Kazakhstan, 2007

Located one block from Almaty's Opera House, the residences are grouped around a private central courtyard lined with sixteen maisonettes and entrances to 236 apartments in the twelve-story buildings above. A tree-shaded plaza with a cascading fountain is proposed to replace a much-loved civic open space that has fallen on hard times.

 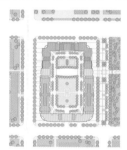

University of Kentucky College of Law
Lexington, Kentucky, 2007

Intended to occupy a prominent site at the heart of the University of Kentucky's historic Lexington campus, where it will present formal fronts both to the greater university campus and to its own internal courtyards, the College of Law carries forward the colonial Georgian architectural vocabulary of the campus with rich red brick, a Kentucky limestone water table, white-painted trim, and slate roofs.

Waterview Cottage
Katama, Martha's Vineyard, Massachusetts
2007–2009

A house originally designed by us as a guest cottage was reconceived and enlarged to accommodate the family's next generation.

Hanwha Jiri Resort
Jirisan National Park, Korea, 2007–

Replacing two outdated hotel buildings located within Korea's Jirisan National Park, this resort is conceived as a rustic national park lodge connected with rugged natural surroundings and attuned to the traditional architecture of the nearby Haum Temple. Visitors cross a fast-running stream, then follow the site entry road upwards through the woods, catching glimpses of the resort silhouetted against the mountainsides.

Miramar Resort
Santa Barbara, California, 2007

Our master plan updates Santa Barbara's renowned Miramar hotel with conference facilities and shops to create a five-star resort village complete with guest cottages.

215 Brazilian Avenue
Palm Beach, Florida, 2007

This three-story limestone and stucco Regency-style boutique hotel is oriented away from the street toward a swimming pool and garden.

House
Cape May, New Jersey, 2007

This house, inspired by Federal period farmhouses of the Mid-Atlantic region, provides the principal rooms with multiple exposures to light and views and offers an interesting progression of spaces from the more formal rooms at the south side of the house to the more casual family rooms to the north. A two-story porch, bracketed by the north and south wings, offers dramatic views towards Delaware Bay.

Gurgaon City Center
Gurgaon, Haryana, India, 2007–

Our master plan calls for a retail center, office buildings, residential buildings, a hotel, and a cultural center set in a 14-acre landscaped oasis from the arid climate and bustling pace of Gurgaon, a satellite city of New Delhi. The first phase is a 685,000-gross-square-foot, 28-story glass-clad office tower.

At Last
Long Branch, New Jersey, 2007–

This limestone and stucco house evokes the neoclassical "cottages" that dotted the New Jersey shore in the early twentieth century. An H-shaped plan with attenuated wings provides each of the principal rooms with views to the Atlantic Ocean.

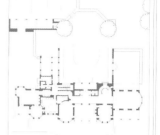

Hotel in Westwood
Los Angeles, California, 2007

The terraced setbacks of this 25-story hotel tower, occupying a triangular block at the corner of Wilshire Boulevard and Gayley Avenue in Los Angeles, negotiate the transition between the high-rise scale of the Wilshire corridor and the residential neighborhood of Westwood.

Barn
Jamestown, Rhode Island, 2007–2009

Perched on a waterfront site, this barn frames a formal lawn for outdoor entertaining. The casual composition, reminiscent of outbuildings on nineteenth-century estate farms, is anchored by a cylindrical stair tower.

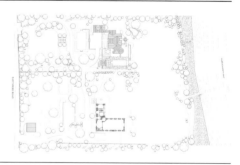

House at Wickapogue
Southampton, New York, 2008–

The L-shaped plan of this house provides an inviting entry garden courtyard, reduces the scale of the house as viewed from the street, and creates two unique garden facades that face south and west.

Strawberry Hill
Victoria Peak, Hong Kong, 2008

On the eastern edge of Victoria Peak, six villas are arrayed in a fan shape to maximize views. A curving drive rises to a loop encircling a common green; each villa enjoys its own entry court, garden, sunning terrace, pool deck, and rooftop terrace with sweeping views across Repulse Bay.

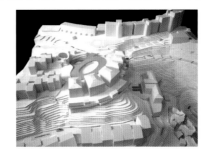 

Hanwha Resort
Seorak, Korea, 2008–

To reposition a sprawling resort that includes two large hotels, a popular family water park, an 18-hole golf course, and an abandoned amusement park, we proposed enhanced landscaping, a new 240-suite hotel, a village center, and the renovation of existing hotel buildings to produce a coherent ensemble inspired by the tradition of great resorts such as the Breakers in Palm Beach.

House in East Hampton
East Hampton, New York, 2008–2010

In renovating a modest house previously owned by a locally prominent watercolorist, we maintained its casual character, reorganized its plan and fenestration, and replaced the existing garage with an abstractly massed guest wing.

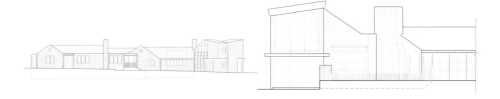

Houses on Lake Geneva
Lake Geneva, Wisconsin, 2008

A spectacular site facing Lake Geneva, a storied playground for prominent Chicago families, offered the opportunity to redevelop property that had been compromised over time.

350 Boylston Street
Boston, Massachusetts, 2009–

This nine-story office block faces Boylston Street with a limestone punched window facade and presents a glassier curtainwall with fritted glass spandrel panels to Arlington Street and the Public Garden across the intersection.

 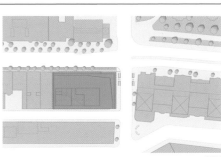

Executive Office
Saint John, New Brunswick, 2009–2010

The office of a chief executive representing the third generation to lead an important family-owned business integrates paneling and other artifacts from the office of the company's founder with new finishes and furnishings.

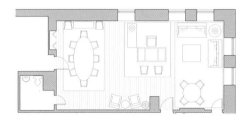

Campus Gates, Marist College
Poughkeepsie, New York, 2009–

The new gates, inspired by gateways of nearby Hudson Valley estates, mark the north and south entrances and provide an appropriate public identity to the college, which over the years had extended its campus on both sides of Route 9.

Pedestrian Crossing, Marist College
Poughkeepsie, New York, 2009–

A tunnel will connect the two halves of the Marist campus separated by heavily-trafficked Route 9. The portals and interior treatment take their inspiration from the adjacent Kieran gatehouse, built in 1865 in picturesque Hudson Valley rubble stone.

Project Credits

Project Credits

Encinal Bluffs Family Compound
Malibu, California

Partner: Roger H. Seifter. Associate Partner: Arthur Chabon. Project Associate: Jacob Morrison. Project Assistants: Hyuna Chung, Thomas Fletcher, Dennis Giobbe, Henry Gunawan, Lenore Passavanti, George Punnoose, Corina Rugeroni, David Solomon, Lynn Wang, Daniel Wolfskehl. Interior Designers: Kenyon Kramer and Jean-Louis Raynaud; Atelier AM. Landscape Designer: Deborah Nevins Associates. Associate Architect: A. Thomas Torres Architects.

Ruth Ryon, "Exec Adds to His Malibu Kingdom," *Los Angeles Times*, May 7, 2000.
Hamish Bowles, "Married to Design," *Vogue*, February 2009, 188-93, 220.

Residence
Kiawah Island, South Carolina

Partner: Roger H. Seifter. Project Associate: Victoria Baran. Project Assistants: Glenn Albrecht, Kelly Greeson, Thomas Hickey. Interior Designer: Gerard D'Andre. Landscape Design Project Manager: Ashley Christopher.

Robert A. M. Stern: Buildings and Projects 1999–2003 (New York: The Monacelli Press, 2003), 194-97.
Robert A. M. Stern: Houses and Gardens (New York: The Monacelli Press, 2005), 364-87.
"South Carolina: High Design by the Seaside," *Architectural Digest*, June 2006, 143.
"First Picks: Architect: Robert A. M. Stern," *Robb Report*, February 2009, 117.

International Storytelling Center
Jonesborough, Tennessee

Partners: Gary L. Brewer, Paul L. Whalen. Project Associates: Jori Erdman, Christine Kelley, Tonia Long, Katherine Oudens. Project Manager: Dana Gulling. Landscape Architect: Andropogon Associates, Ltd. Associate Architect: Ken Ross Architects.

Robert A. M. Stern: Buildings and Projects 1993–1998 (New York: The Monacelli Press, 1998), 308-9.
Lesia Paine-Brooks, "Ground Broken for New Storytelling Facility," *Johnson City Press*, July 1, 1999, 1, 8.
James Brooks, "Storytelling Center Opening Thursday," *Johnson City Press*, June 16, 2002.
Jennifer Lawson, "Storytelling Center Attracts Thousands," *Johnson City Press*, June 16, 2002.
Robert A. M. Stern: Buildings and Projects 1999–2003 (New York: The Monacelli Press, 2003), 560.
Robert A. M. Stern: Buildings and Towns (New York: The Monacelli Press, 2007), 316-21.

Southwest Quadrangle
Georgetown University, Washington, D. C.

Partner: Graham S. Wyatt. Project Designers: Frank de Santis, Jonilla Dorsten, Dana Gulling, Rebecca Laubach, Kevin O'Connor. Project Assistants: Marina Berendeeva, Laura Hinton, Edwin Hofmann, James Johnson, Dewi Jones, Antonio Ng, Sung Ok, James Park, Jong-Hyuck Park, Lenore Passavanti, Christopher Podstawski, Anthony Polito, Corina Rugeroni, Katherine Snow, Karina Tengberg, John Ullman, Michael Wilbur, Yuri Zagorin, Paul Zamek, Sandra Zenk. Landscape Design Associate: Dawn Handler. Landscape Design Assistants: Peter Arato, Norbert Holter, John Merritt, Eric Samuels. Interior Design Senior Associate: John Gilmer. Interior Design Assistant: Paola Velazquez. Landscape Architect: Stephenson & Good. Associate Architect: Einhorn Yaffee Prescott.

David Montgomery, "Georgetown Plans Complex With 800-Bed Dormitory," *The Washington Post*, February 28, 1998, B:5.
"A Natural Rapport," *Georgetown Magazine*, Spring 2001, 18-29.

Robert A. M. Stern: Buildings and Projects 1999–2003 (New York: The Monacelli Press, 2003), 224-27.
Nick Timiraos, "From Hole to Home, Southwest Quad Completed," *The Hoya*, Friday, August 22, 2003.
Rob Anderson and Mike DeBonis, "Our Campus, Our Space," *The Georgetown Voice*, September 11, 2003, 8-9.

Residence in Napa County
Oakville, California

Partner: Roger H. Seifter. Project Managers: Victoria Baran, Robert Epley. Project Assistants: Elise Geiger, Dennis Giobbe. Interior Designer: EJ Interior Design. Landscape Architects: Dennis McGlade, Olin.

Robert A. M. Stern: Buildings and Projects 1993–1998 (New York: The Monacelli Press, 1998), 342-43.

Guild Hall
East Hampton, New York

Partner: Randy M. Correll. Project Senior Associate: Lenore Passavanti. Project Associates : Pamela McGirr, Marc Rehman. Project Manager: Thomas Morbitzer. Project Assistants: Aiyla Balakumar. Interior Design Associate: Shannon Ratcliff. Interior Design Assistant: Marissa Savarese. Landscape Design Project Manager: Ashley Christopher. Landscape Design Project Senior Assistant: Michael Weber.

"Plans to Renovate John Drew," *The East Hampton Star*, June 29, 2006, C:5
Jennifer Landes, "Guild Hall's Grand Unveiling," *The East Hampton Star*, April 7, 2009, C:1.
Andrew Botsford, "Lights Up! John Drew Set to Shine," *East Hampton Press*, April 8, 2009, B:1, 5.
Susan Galardi, "Presenting Guild Hall: The 5-Year, $12 Million Renovation Is Breathtaking," *Dan's Hamptons*, April 10, 2009, 23, 27.
"Guild Hall Is Back!" *The Sag Harbor Express*, April 13, 2009.

Residence
Long Island, New York

Partner: Roger H. Seifter. Project Associate: John Gilmer. Senior Project Assistants: Catherine Popple, David Solomon. Project Assistants: Ricardo Alvarez-Diaz, Christopher Podstawski. Interior Design Associate: John Gilmer. Interior Design Assistants: Kelly Greeson, Georgette Sturam. Interior Designer: David Easton Interiors. Landscape Design Associate: Charlotte M. Frieze. Landscape Designer: Deborah Nevins Associates.

Robert A. M. Stern: Buildings and Projects 1993–1998 (New York: The Monacelli Press, 1998), 344-45.
"The Biggest of the Big," *The East Hampton Star*, February 15, 2001, IV:10.
Robert A. M. Stern: Houses and Gardens (New York: The Monacelli Press, 2005), 412-41.
Margot Adler, "Behind the Ever-Expanding American Dream House," *NPR*, August 10, 2007.

Residence
Palo Alto, California

Partner: Grant F. Marani. Project Senior Associate: Charles Toothill. Project Manager: Tamie Noponen. Project Senior Assistant: Carolyn Foug. Project Assistants: Ricardo Alvarez-Diaz, Christine Kelley, Clemenstien Love. Interior Designer: Fox-Nahem Design. Landscape Architect: Suzman and Cole Design Associates.

Robert A. M. Stern: Buildings and Projects 1993–1998 (New York: The Monacelli Press, 1998), 378-79.
Robert A. M. Stern: Houses and Gardens (New York: The Monacelli Press, 2005), 442-55.

Miami Beach Library
Miami Beach, Florida

Partner: Alexander P. Lamis. Project Associates: Christine Kelley, Salvador Peña-Figueroa. Project Senior Assistants: Tamie Noponen, Rebecca Post, Michael Wilbur. Interior Design Assistants: Sharmell Anderson, Damion Phillips. Landscape Design Associates: Dawn Handler, Marsh Kriplen, Michael Weber. Landscape Design Senior Assistants: Gerrit Goss, Norbert Holter. Associate Architect: Borrelli Partners.

Peter Whoriskey, "Top Firms Vying for the Honor," *Miami Herald,* May 25, 1998, B:1-2.
Richard M. Buck, "Collins Park Cultural Campus Moves Forward," *Impressions (newsletter of the Miami Design Preservation League),* Summer 1998, 1, 3-4.
Beth Dunlop, "Pastels and Preservationists: Miami Beach Navigates the Tension Between Heritage and Contemporary Design," *Architectural Record,* August 1999, 45, 47, 49.
"Robert A. M. Stern Architects with Borrelli & Associates: Regional Library," *Abitare,* May 24, 2000, 157.
Raul Barraneche, "For a Library, Robert Stern Shows His Take on Modernism," *The New York Times,* January 18, 2001, F:3.
"Metro: Miami Beach," *Metropolitan Home,* July / August 2001, 48.
Neisen Kasdin, "Miami Beach: Urban Tropical Deco," *Urban Land,* October 2002, 81.
Robert A. M. Stern: Buildings and Projects 1999–2003 (New York: The Monacelli Press, 2003), 356-57.
G. Stanley Collyer, *Architecture in Practice: Competing Globally in Architecture Competitions* (New York: John Wiley & Sons Ltd., 2004), 152.
Beth Dunlop, "Miami Beach's Newest Library Marries Architecture With Purpose," *The Miami Herald,* April 10, 2005.
Beth Dunlop, "It's Hard to Be a Cool Preservationist," *Oculus,* Spring 2007, 47.
Robert A. M. Stern: Buildings and Towns (New York: The Monacelli Press, 2007), 360-67.
Beth Dunlop, *Miami: Mediterranean Splendor and Deco Dreams* (New York: Rizzoli International Publications, 2007), 222, 226-27.
Witold Rybczynski, "Borrowed Time: How Do You Build a Public Library in the Age of Google?" *Slate,* February 27, 2008.

Peter Jay Sharp Boathouse
Swindler Cove Park, Upper Manhattan, New York, New York

Project Associate Partner: Armand LeGardeur. Project Assistant: Audrey Rae. Design carried forward by Armand LeGardeur Architects.

Jonathan Mandell, "Always Divine, Now Garbage Has Made Her a Saint," *The New York Times,* November 17, 1999, H:10.
"Art Commission Awards: Eight Honored for Excellence in Design," *The New York Times,* February 27, 2000, 11:1.
Kira L. Gould, "Art Commission Honors Outstanding City Projects," *Oculus,* April 2000, 17.
"Design That Makes a Difference," *Metropolitan Home,* March-April, 2001, 86.
Peter Hellman, "On Harlem River, Hope Floats," *The New York Times,* Thursday, October 30, 2003, F:1, 9.
Robert A. M. Stern: Buildings and Projects 1999–2003 (New York: The Monacelli Press, 2003), 386-87.
David Sokol, "Take the A . . . Scull," *Oculus,* Summer 2004, 23.
Kathryn Matthews, "On the Town: Taking the Initiative," *Town & Country,* April 2007, 65.
Robert A. M. Stern: Buildings and Towns (New York: The Monacelli Press, 2007), 534-41.
James S. Russell, "Bette Midler Whacks Weeds, Taps 50 Cent to Turn New York Green," *Bloomberg,* June 25, 2009.

Clearwater Public Library
Clearwater, Florida

Partner: Alexander P. Lamis. Project Associates: Salvador Peña-Figueroa, Kim Yap, Paul Zembsch. Interior Design Assistant: Sharmell Anderson. Associate Architect: Harvard Jolly Clees Toppe Architects.

G.G. Rigsby, "Building a Better Image," *St. Petersburg Times,* January 17, 1999.
G.G. Rigsby, "Clearwater, Architect Urges Yes Vote on Redevelopment Plan," *Business Journal,* July 5, 2000.
Lesley Collins, "Clearwater Unveils Plans for Library," *Tampa Tribune,* May 5, 2001, 5.
Christina Headrick, "Library's Design Looks to Past, Future," *Clearwater Times,* May 6, 2001, 1, 10.
"Graceful Shape of New Library Defies Critics," *St. Petersburg Times,* December 26, 2002.
Robert A. M. Stern: Buildings and Projects 1999–2003 (New York: The Monacelli Press, 2003), 388-89.
Chris Tisch, "A Four-Floor Living Room for the Public," *St. Petersburg Times,* May 2, 2004.
"Spectacular New Library Serves on Many Levels," *St. Petersburg Times,* May 4, 2004.
Beth Dunlop, "Designed by the Book," *The Miami Herald,* April 10, 2005, M:3.
Robert A. M. Stern: Buildings and Towns (New York: The Monacelli Press, 2007), 386-93.
Witold Rybczynski, "Borrowed Time: How Do You Build a Public Library in the Age of Google?" *Slate,* February 27, 2008.

Perkins Visitor Center
Wave Hill, Riverdale, The Bronx, New York

Partner: Gary L. Brewer, Alexander P. Lamis. Project Senior Associate: Julie Nymann. Project Associates: Lenore Passavanti, Salvador Peña-Figueroa. Project Managers: Edmund Leveckis, James Park. Project Assistant: Anthony Goldsby, Interior Design Associate: Ken Stuckenschneider. Landscape Design Associate: Marsh Kriplen.

"For Wave Hill, a $4 Million Visitor Center," *The New York Times,* June 3, 2001, 11:1.
Robert A. M. Stern: Buildings and Projects 1999–2003 (New York: The Monacelli Press, 2003), 390-91.
A.L. Gordon, "Out and About: Wave Hill" *The New York Sun,* May 26, 2004, 22.
"Maira Kalman Mural Unveiled," *Wave Hill News,* Summer 2004, 1,10.
"New and Improved Visitor Center Showcased at Wave Hill," *Riverdale Review,* July 21, 2004.
"Best of 2004, Award of Merit – Renovation: Wave Hill Visitor and Horticultural Center," *New York Construction,* December 2004, 127.
Robert A. M. Stern: Buildings and Towns (New York: The Monacelli Press, 2007), 378-85.

Informatics and Communications Technology Complex
Indiana University / Purdue University, Indianapolis, Indiana

Partners: Kevin M. Smith, Graham S. Wyatt. Project Senior Associate: Dennis Sagiev. Project Assistants: Marina Berendeeva, Meredith Colon, Jeremy Edmunds, Anselm Fusco, Ole Sondresen. Landscape Architect: Oehme, van Sweden & Associates. Associate Architect: Ratio Architects.

A.J. Schneider, "IUPUI Tech Building to Serve as Gateway," *Indianapolis Business Journal,* June 4, 2000, 19.

House in Tidewater Virginia

Partner: Roger H. Seifter. Project Manager: Thomas Hickey. Project Assistants: Alexander Butler, Thomas Garland, Derek Willis. Interior Design Project Manager: Georgette Sturam. Landscape Architect: Ann P. Stokes Landscape Architects.

Robert A. M. Stern: Buildings and Projects 1999–2003 (New York: The Monacelli Press, 2003), 402-3.
Robert A. M. Stern: Houses and Gardens (New York: The Monacelli Press, 2005), 532-63.

Sterling Glen of Roslyn Senior Living Residence
Roslyn, New York

Partner: Paul L. Whalen. Project Senior Associate: Hernán Chebar. Project Associate: Kevin O'Connor. Project Assistants: Jason Hwang, Qu Kim. Interior Designer: Culpepper McAuliffe & Meaders. Landscape Architect: Mathews Nielsen Landscape Architects. Associate Architect: SLCE Architects.

Joe Scotchie, "Public Hearing on Housing Plan," *Roslyn News,* June 24, 1999, 1, 7.
Robert A. M. Stern: Buildings and Projects 1999–2003 (New York: The Monacelli Press, 2003), 406-7.

C.J. Hughes, "A Passion for Living With the Past," *The New York Times*, March 5, 2006, II:9.

Michael J. Brown, Jr., "Sterling Glen's Contributions," *The Roslyn News*, February 9, 2007.

Cara S. Trager, "Habitats: Sterling Glen of Roslyn," *Newsday*, December 1, 2007, B:8.

Zubiarte Retail and Leisure Complex
Bilbao, Spain

Partners: Sargent C. Gardiner, Paul L. Whalen. Project Associate: Johnny Cruz. Project Manager: Nancy Thiel. Project Senior Assistants: Adam Anuszkiewicz, Jason Hwang, Michael McClure, Mike Soriano, Miriam Torres-Marcos. Project Assistants: Veronica Caminos, Gregory Horgan, Yusung Hwang, Andrei Martin, Corina Rugeroni, Jeff Straesser, Richard Wachter, Lindsay Weiss. Landscape Architect: Balmori Associates. Associate Architects: IDOM, LKS Ingenieria.

Whitney Gould, "From Spain, a Model of Rebuilding With Vision," *Milwaukee Journal Sentinel*, April 23, 2000.

José Mari Reviriego, "Abandoibarra abrira su centro comercial en 2003 y primara el ocio y la moda," *El Correo*, February 20, 2001, 2-3.

Xabier Ga Arguello, "El centro comercial de Abandoibarra sera inaugurado la primavera del año 2003," *Bizkaia*, May 3, 2001, 24.

José Mari Reviriego, "Nuestra parcela es mejor que la del Guggenheim," *El Correo*, May 3, 2001, 3.

Robert A. M. Stern: Buildings and Projects 1999–2003 (New York: The Monacelli Press, 2003), 408-9.

José Mari Reviriego, "El edificio será un punto de encuentro en Bilbao," *El Correo*, January 8, 2004, C:5.

Mikel Segovia, "Será un nuevo 'cuadro' para Bilbao," *El Mundo*, January 8, 2004, 14.

Alberto Uriona, "Robert Stern quiere que el centro comercial de Abandoibarra sea un nuevo símbolo de Bilbao," *El País Vasco*, January 8, 2004, 1, 4.

"Stern vista los obras del centro comercial y de ocio Zubiarte," *Expansión*, January, 8, 2004, 1.

María José Tomé, "El arquitecto Stern supervisa Zubiarte," *El Correo*, June 2, 2004, 1, 3.

Denny Lee, "Bilbao Ten Years Later," *The New York Times*, September 23, 2007, Travel:1, 8.

Robert A. M. Stern: Buildings and Towns (New York: The Monacelli Press, 2007), 404-13.

Residence in California

Partner: Randy M. Correll. Project Manager: Veronica Caminos. Project Senior Assistant: Youngmin Woo. Project Assistants: Christiane Gallois, Yusung Hwang, Nicolas Oudin. Interior Designers: Brown Buckley, Brian J. McCarthy. Landscape Design Project Manager: Ashley Christopher, Landscape Design Senior Assistant: Michael Weber. Landscape Design Assistant: Christina Belton.

Robert A. M. Stern: Buildings and Projects 1999–2003 (New York: The Monacelli Press, 2003), 420-21.

Robert A. M. Stern: Houses and Gardens (New York: The Monacelli Press, 2005), 592-629.

Residence at West Tisbury
Martha's Vineyard, Massachusetts

Partners: Randy M. Correll, Roger H. Seifter. Project Associate: Catherine Popple. Senior Project Assistants: Josh Bull, Thomas Morbitzer. Project Assistant: Christopher McIntire. Squash Barn Interior Designer: John Gilmer. Interior Designer: Bunny Williams. Landscape Architect: Rodney Robinson.

Robert A. M. Stern: Buildings and Projects 1999–2003 (New York: The Monacelli Press, 2003), 424-25.

Musiskwartier
Arnhem, The Netherlands

Partners: Daniel Lobitz, Paul L. Whalen. Project Senior Associate: Joel Mendelson. Project Assistants: Can Tiryaki, Richard Wachter. Associate Architect: INBO B.V.

Robert A. M. Stern: Buildings and Projects 1999–2003 (New York: The Monacelli Press, 2003), 426-27.

Meghan Drueding, "Stern Abroad," *Residential Architect*, August 2003, 20.

"CNU Announces 2006 Charter Award Honorees," *CNU (newsletter of the Congress for the New Urbanism)*, April 3, 2006.

Marco Bouman, "De Architect," *De Gelderlander*, August 19, 2006.

Brian Baker, "Meeting the Density Challenge," *Urban Land*, November / December 2006, 86-89.

Van Verleden tot Heden, *Musiskwartier* (Utrecht: Stichting Monuscript, 2006).

Robert A. M. Stern, "Garden City Suburbs," *Wharton Real Estate Review*, Fall 2007, 84-93.

Robert A. M. Stern: Buildings and Towns (New York: The Monacelli Press, 2007), 494-501.

Folly and Pool Cottage in Sonoma
Glen Ellen, California

Partner: Grant F. Marani. Project Manager: Mark Pledger. Project Senior Assistant: Rebecca Post. Project Assistants: Catherine Dayal, Elise Geiger, Qu Kim. Interior Designer: Agnes Bourne. Landscape Architects: Suzman and Cole Design Associates, Ron Herman Landscape Architect.

Aging and Allied Health Building and Gill Heart Institute
University of Kentucky Medical Center, Lexington, Kentucky

Partners: Grant F. Marani, Graham S. Wyatt. Project Associate: Douglas Wright. Project Assistant: Frank de Santis. Associate Architects: Chrisman Miller Woodford, FKP.

Robert A. M. Stern: Buildings and Projects 1999–2003 (New York: The Monacelli Press, 2003), 348-49.

Residence in Edgartown
Martha's Vineyard, Massachusetts

Partner: Randy M. Correll. Project Manager: Dan Teske. Interior Designer: G2. Landscape Architect: Chris Horiuchi.

Robert A. M. Stern: Buildings and Projects 1999–2003 (New York: The Monacelli Press, 2003), 458-59.

Robert A. M. Stern: Houses and Gardens (New York: The Monacelli Press, 2005), 490-507.

Joseph Giovannini, "Fulfilling Its Promise: An Expanded and Reimagined Retreat on Martha's Vineyard Gets a New Lease on Life," *Architectural Digest*, February 2007, cover, 130-39, 202.

Residence
Salt Spring Island, British Columbia

Partner: Grant F. Marani. Project Senior Associates: Lenore Passavanti, Charles Toothill. Project Associate: Douglas Wright. Project Assistants: Marcus Carter, Elise Geiger, Eric Hofmann, Jason Hwang, Jong-Hyuck Park, Kimberly Raspanti, Daniel Wolfskehl. Interior Design Senior Assistant: Kelly Greeson. Interior Design Assistants: Amie Haugh, Joy Tucci. Interior Designer: John Gilmer Architecture and Interior Design. Associate Architect: Steven Zibin Architect.

Robert A. M. Stern: Buildings and Projects 1999–2003 (New York: The Monacelli Press, 2003), 460-61.

Robert A. M. Stern: Houses and Gardens (New York: The Monacelli Press, 2005), 564-91.

Mildred Schmertz, "New Outlook on the Shingle Style: Paying Homage to Craftsmanship in British Columbia," *Architectural Digest*, October 2007, 312-20.

Talisker Club Park
Park City, Utah

Partners: Daniel Lobitz, Paul L. Whalen. Project Associate: Rosalind Tsang. Project Manager: Nancy Thiel. Project Senior Assistants: Bina Bhattacharyya, Gaylin Bowie, Johnny Cruz, Sargent C. Gardiner, Joel Mendelson, Julie Nymann. Project Assistants: David Abecassis, Merced Baumer, Laura Boutwell, Lauren Cahill, Sarah Frank, Russell Grant, Stuart Johnson, Jill Lagowski, Miguel Lasala, David MacPhail, Matthew Meehan, Rebecca Morgan, William Perez, Corina Rugeroni, Jeremy Shannon, Elizabeth Trafton, John Tulloch, Holly Zeiler. Landscape Design Project Manager: Michael Weber. Landscape Design Assistants:

Daniel Evans, Kevin Hasselwander, Mark Rodriguez. Interior Designer: Paul Duesing Partners. Associate Landscape Architect and Associate Architect: IBI Group.

Robert A. M. Stern: Buildings and Projects 1999–2003 (New York: The Monacelli Press, 2003), 566.

Valery Pine Behr, "All-Season Investments," *Western Interiors*, May / June 2005, 11.

Ellen Shakespeare, "The Abundant Life at Tuhaye Park," *Talisker Club Living: Belong*, 2005, 18-19.

Susan Kime, "Breaking Ground," *Robb Report: Vacation Homes*, Fall 2005, 47.

"Breaking Ground: Talisker Club," *The New York Times*, February 9, 2007, F:8.

Jennifer Ceaser, "Magic Mountain: Park City Projects Reach Their Peak," *New York Post*, January 31, 2008, 54.

"Rise Above: The Architecture of Robert A. M. Stern," *Robb Report Vacation Homes*, December 2008 / January 2009, 75.

Samantha Brooks, "Happy Accidents," *Robb Report Vacation Homes*, April / May 2009, 15.

Samantha Brooks, "Vacation Homes: Mountain Resort Community Talisker Club," *Robb Report*, June 2009, 98, 100-1.

Feil Residence Hall
Brooklyn Law School, Brooklyn, New York

Partner: Paul L. Whalen. Project Senior Associates: Hernán Chebar, Julie Nymann. Project Associate: Kevin O'Connor. Project Assistants: Ching-Chyi Yang, Jason Hwang, Kimberly Raspanti, Corina Rugeroni, Oscar Sanchez, Susi Yu. Interior Design Associate: Ken Stuckenschneider. Associate Architect: SLCE Architects.

Tara Bahrampour, "A Native Son to Design for the Law School," *The New York Times*, May 27, 2001, 14:7.

Greg Wilson, "Brooklyn Law School Eyes New Dorm to Ease Crunch," *New York Daily News*, April 14, 2002, 4.

Tara Bahrampour, "Quakers, Unlikely Actors in a Building Squabble," *The New York Times*, May 5, 2002, 14:8.

Errol Louis, "Plan for Law School Dorm Draws Heavy Fire," *The New York Sun*, May 30, 2002, 6.

David W. Dunlap, "In Downtown Brooklyn, Too Tall Suddenly Fits," *The New York Times*, July 4, 2002, B:3.

Robert A. M. Stern: Buildings and Projects 1999–2003 (New York: The Monacelli Press, 2003), 488-89.

Michael Brick, "Plugging a Hole in Brooklyn's Heart," *The New York Times*, January 7, 2004, B:1, 2.

"Residence Hall to Open in 2005," *BLS Law Notes (The Magazine of Brooklyn Law School)*, Fall 2004, 2, 3, 32-34.

"BLS Community Celebrates Feil Hall Dedication," *Brooklyn Law School News*, October 17, 2005.

Robert A. M. Stern: Buildings and Towns (New York: The Monacelli Press, 2007), 442-51.

Comcast Center
Philadelphia, Pennsylvania

Partners: Meghan L. McDermott, Graham S. Wyatt. Project Senior Associate: Don Lee. Project Assistants: Giovanna Albretti, Goil Amornvivat, Daniel Arbelaez, Nicholas Acevedo, Phillippe Bihet, Alexander Butler, Steven Chua, Daniel Cobb, Aristotelis Dimitrakopoulos, Lorenzo Galati, Natalie Goldberg, Afzal Hossain, Carlos Hurtado, Leonid Khanin, Gemma Kim, Tae Kim, Jill Lagowski, Miguel Lasala, Trevor Laubenstein, Seung Jun Lee, Meghan Leininger, Breen Mahony, Thomas Manley, Ernesto Martinez, Jennifer Newsom, Kevin O'Connor, Jack Robbins, Yok Saowasang, Kayzad Shroff, Jeffrey Straesser, Kathryn Stutts, Sue Jin Sung, Brian Taylor, David Vimont, Robie Wood, Wendy Yeung. Interior Designers: Daroff Design, Gensler. Landscape Architect: Olin. Associate Architect: Kendall / Heaton Associates.

"High Rise Rouse," *The Philadelphia Inquirer*, December 21, 2000.

Henry J. Holcomb, "Stern Will Design New Skyscraper," *The Philadelphia Inquirer*, February 18, 2001, C:1, 9.

Henry J. Holcomb, "Developers Court Comcast for a Project of Magnitude," *The Philadelphia Inquirer*, May 3, 2001, C:1, 7.

Henry J. Holcomb, "New Center City Skyscraper 'Will Rise Up in a Quiet Way,'" *The Philadelphia Inquirer*, May 17, 2001, A:1, 4.

Harriet Lessy, "Rouse Plans $390 Million Skyscraper," *Philadelphia Daily News*, May 17, 2001.

John E. Czarnecki, "Stern to Scrape Philly Sky," *Architectural Record*, June 2001, 40.

Dorie Baker, "For American Architects, the Sky Is Still the Limit, Says Stern," *Yale Bulletin & Calendar*, November 9, 2001. 3.

Sasha Issenberg, "Are Skyscrapers Obsolete?" *Philadelphia*, December 2001, 129, 162.

Roxanne Patel, "The House That Rouse Built," *Philadelphia*, December 2001, 126-29, 156, 158-63.

Michael Brick, "A Little Something for the Philadelphia Skyline," *The New York Times*, May 29, 2002, C:6.

Thomas J. Walsh, "New Designs on Philadelphia," *Urban Land*, October 2002, 142-49.

Graham S. Wyatt, "Pennsylvania: Big Ideas," *Pennsylvania Architect*, August 2003, 17-18.

Robert A. M. Stern: Buildings and Projects 1999–2003 (New York: The Monacelli Press, 2003), 496-505.

Henry J. Holcomb, "Liberty Property Trust Reveals a Bolder Design for New Tower," *The Philadelphia Inquirer*, January 22, 2004, A:1, C:1, 3.

Joseph Dennis Kelly II, "Philadelphia Sets a Path Toward Revitalization Through a Redefined Government Role," *Architectural Record*, October 2004, 73-74, 76, 78.

Henry J. Holcomb, "It's a Go for Comcast's Tower," *The Philadelphia Inquirer*, January 4, 2005, A:1, 10.

"Comcast Tower: We're Moving on Up," *The Philadelphia Inquirer*, January 5, 2005, A:14.

Henry J. Holcomb, "A Tall Order: The Comcast Center Ultimately Will Benefit the City, Experts Say," *The Philadelphia Inquirer*, January 6, 2005, C:1, 3.

Inga Saffron, "Not Much to Look at, on the Outside," *The Philadelphia Inquirer*, January 9, 2005, B:1, 5.

Joseph Dennis Kelly II, "Stern's Philadelphia Tower Finally Moving Forward," *Architectural Record*, February 2005, 28.

Richard Conniff, "What Makes a Building Green?" *Environment (The Journal of the Yale School of Forestry & Environmental Studies)*, Spring 2005, 3-11.

Chris Wilson, "Built of 'Steal'," *New York Post*, July 1, 2005, 7.

David W. Dunlap, "Freedom Tower's 'Unique' Corners Found on Other Drawing Boards," *The New York Times*, August 25, 2005, B:3.

Joseph Dennis Kelly II, "Philadelphia Grows Up With a Slew of High-Rise Projects," *Architectural Record*, December 2005, 40.

Inga Saffron, "Of Urinals, Plumbers and a Backseat to N.Y.," *The Philadelphia Inquirer*, March 19, 2006.

"Comcast Center," *Boom: New Architecture in Philadelphia*, June 2006, 40-41.

Georges Binder, ed., *One Hundred and One of the World's Tallest Buildings* (Mulgrave, Australia: The Images Publishing Group, 2006), 186-87.

Henry J. Holcomb, "Topping Off—With Care," *The Philadelphia Inquirer*, June 19, 2007, A:8.

Robert Steuteville, "Green Tower With New Urban Plan Rises in Philly," *New Urban News*, June 2007, 12.

Inga Saffron, "Onward to Elsewhere: Sculptures Dash Across Comcast Lobby, As Will We," *The Philadelphia Inquirer*, November 20, 2007, A:1, 10.

Nadav Malin, "Investing in the Environment: The Financial Industry's Approach to Green Building," *Environmental Building News*, November 2007, 1, 11-19.

Robin Pogrebin, "Building Respect at Yale," *The New York Times*, December 16, 2007, Arts & Leisure:1, 38.

Bob Fernandez, "Walk in the Clouds," *The Philadelphia Inquirer*, April 26, 2008.

Natalie Kostelni, "Rouse Vision Complete in New Tower," *Philadelphia Business Journal*, May 9, 2008.

Inga Saffron, "Comcast's New Tower Blank Slate for the City," *The Philadelphia Inquirer*, June 1, 2008, A:1, 12.

Rick Nichols, "Things Are Looking Up Downstairs," *The Philadelphia Inquirer*, July 10, 2008, F:1, 2.

William Hanley, "Newsmaker: Robert A. M. Stern," *Architectural Record*, August 2008.

C.C. Sullivan, "Sky-High Ratings," *Interior Design*, October 2008, 270-79.

C.C. Sullivan, "Philadelphia Freedom," *Archi-tech*, January / February 2009, cover, 14-19.

Witold Rybczynski, "That Dogma Won't Hunt: Why Are Architects So Obsessed With Schools and Rules?" *Slate*, February 4, 2009.

Suzanne Stephens, "Robert A. M. Stern Architects Raises the Bar With Philadelphia's Comcast Center," *Architectural Record*, May 2009, 168-72, 174-75.

Suzanne Stephens, "Green Strategies for a Public Space," *Architectural Record*, May 2009, 173.

Sara Hart, "Comcast: The World's Largest Tuned Liquid Column Damper," *Architectural Record*, May 2009, 173.

Witold Rybczynski, "How High: Are High Ceilings a Sign of Wretched Architectural Excess or Just Good Taste?" *Slate*, May 28, 2009.

Northrup Hall
Trinity University, San Antonio, Texas

Partner: Alexander P. Lamis. Project Senior Associate: Adam Anuszkiewicz. Project Associates: Enid De Gracia, Thomas Fletcher, Salvador Peña-Figueroa, Diane Burkin. Project Manager: Mike Soriano. Project Assistants: Julia Buse, Ernesto Martinez, Ahmad-ali Sardar-Afkhami. Interior Design Associate: Hyung Kee Lee. Interior Design Assistants: Virginia Cornell, Kathleen Mancini. Landscape Design Project Manager: Ashley Christopher. Associate Architect: Kell Muñoz Architects.

"Buzz," *Architecture*, April 2001, 37.

"Architect Chosen, Contracts Signed, as Plans for New Northrup Progress," *Trinity*, Spring 2001, 7.

Amy Dorsett, "Trinity's Northrup Hall Coming Down," *San Antonio Express-News*, December 21, 2001.

Mike Greenberg, "Aesthetic Turf War?" *San Antonio Express-News*, December 23, 2001.

Stephen Sharpe, "Trinity Razes Ford's Original Building," *Texas Architect*, September / October 2002, 12.

Robert A. M. Stern: Buildings and Projects 1999–2003 (New York: The Monacelli Press, 2003), 514-15.

Mildred F. Schmertz, "A Divine Dialogue," *Architectural Digest*, November 2004, 134, 136, 138.

Vincent B. Canizaro, "Less is More: More is Loss," *Texas Architect*, January / February 2005, cover, 3, 22-25, 57.

"New Campus Architecture," *The Chronicle of Higher Education*, March 25, 2005, B:3, 5-6, 10, 12, 14.

Mary Carolyn Hollers George, "O'Neil Ford at Trinity University," *Texas Architect*, September / October 2005, 26-27.

Robert A. M. Stern: Buildings and Towns (New York: The Monacelli Press, 2007), 394-403.

Residence
East Hampton, New York

Partner: Randy M. Correll. Project Manager: Mark Haladyna. Project Assistants: Marc Rehman, Derek Willis. Interior Designers: Marcie Braga, Jean-Paul Beaujard. Landscape Designer: Stephen Scanniello. Landscape Architect: Diane Devore.

Robert A. M. Stern: Buildings and Projects 1999–2003 (New York: The Monacelli Press, 2003), 516-17.

Gerald Clarke, "East Hampton Illusion," *Architectural Digest*, December 2005, 218-23, 240.

Robert A. M. Stern: Houses and Gardens (New York: The Monacelli Press, 2005), 508-31.

Tribeca Green
Battery Park City, New York, New York

Partner: Paul L. Whalen. Project Associates: Hernán Chebar, Michael D. Jones. Project Associates: Bina Bhattacharyya, Gaylin Bowie. Project Assistants: Qu Kim, Michiko Murao, Corina Rugeroni, Megan St. Denis. Interior Design Associates: Hyung Kee Lee, Ken Stuckenschneider. Landscape Architects: Mathews Nielsen, Michael Van Valkenburgh Associates. Associate Architect: Ismael Leyva Architects.

Robert A. M. Stern: Buildings and Projects 1999–2003 (New York: The Monacelli Press, 2003), 569.

Jayne Merkel, "Architecture in Developer Land," *AD*, January / February 2004, 6-15.

Gunnar Hand, "Downtown Park, Upstate Landscape," *The Architect's Newspaper*, November 2, 2004, 3.

"All Rise," *The Architect's Newspaper*, July 27, 2005, 16.

Robin Pogrebin, "Putting Environmentalism on the Urban Map," *The New York Times*, May 17, 2006, G:7.

Margaret Jaworski, "Developers Making Eco-Friendly a Habit," *Crain's New York Business*, October 9-15, 2006, 41.

Steve Cutler, "Green Buildings," *New York Living*, March 2007, 40-43.

Charles Lockwood, "The Many Shades of Green Living," *New York Living*, March 2007, 34-36.

Robert A. M. Stern: Buildings and Towns (New York: The Monacelli Press, 2007), 476-83.

Dining Hall
The Taft School, Watertown, Connecticut

Partner: Graham S. Wyatt. Project Senior Associates: Jeffery Povero, Jennifer Stone. Project Assistants: Lorenzo Galati, Brendan Lee, Yok Saowasang, Jeremy Shannon. Interior Design Senior Associate: John Gilmer. Interior Design Associate: Ken Stuckenschneider. Interior Design Assistants: Vennie Lau, Joy Tucci. Landscape Design Project Manager: Michael Weber. Landscape Design Assistants: Daniel Evans, Norbert Holter, Sung Ok, Mark Rodriguez.

Julie Reiff, "Serving Up Space at the Heart of the School," *Taft Bulletin*, Summer 2008, cover, 20-25.

Columbus Public Library
Columbus, Georgia

Partner: Alexander P. Lamis. Project Associates: Julie Nymann, Salvador Peña-Figueroa, James Pearson, George Punnoose. Project Assistants: Sara Evans, Anthony Goldsby, Samuel O'Meara. Interior Design Senior Associate: John Gilmer. Interior Design Associates: Hyung Kee Lee, Ken Stuckenschneider. Interior Design Assistants: Sharmell Anderson, Kasumi Hara. Landscape Design Associate: Marsh Kriplen. Landscape Design Project Manager: Michael Weber. Landscape Architect: French and Associates. Associate Architect: Hecht, Burdeshaw, Johnson, Kidd and Clark.

Mark Rice, "Architects Examined," *Columbus Ledger-Enquirer*, August 25, 2000, 1, 2.

Mark Rice, "Architect Is Selected for Columbus Library," *Columbus Ledger-Enquirer*, September 9, 2000.

Mark Rice, "Architect Shares Vision for Library," *Columbus Ledger-Enquirer*, April 22, 2001, A:1.

Mark Rice, "Design Dazzles," *Columbus Ledger-Enquirer*, August 9, 2001.

Holly Yan, "New Library to Have Cool Interior, Dude," *Columbus Ledger-Enquirer*, August 7, 2002, C:4.

Robert A. M. Stern: Buildings and Projects 1999–2003 (New York: The Monacelli Press, 2003), 524-25.

"A Stroll Through the Library," *Columbus Public Library* (a special publication of Columbus and the Valley *magazine*), December 2004, 12-15.

Mark Rice, "Book Opens on New Era," *Columbus Ledger-Enquirer*, January 4, 2005.

Tony Adams, "Columbus Public Library's Official Opening: Grand Reviews," *Columbus Ledger-Enquirer*, January 9, 2005, A:1.

Robert A. M. Stern: Buildings and Towns (New York: The Monacelli Press, 2007), 422-29.

Cottage at Michaelangelo Park
San Francisco, California

Partner: Grant F. Marani. Project Manager: Charles Toothill. Project Assistants: Eric Hofmann, Qu Kim, Pamela McGirr.

The Museum Center at the Mark Twain House
Hartford, Connecticut

Partners: Kevin M. Smith, Graham S. Wyatt. Project Senior Associates: Kurt Glauber, Dennis Sagiev, Jennifer Stone. Project Associates: Enid De Gracia. Assistants: John Ellis, Sam O'Meara, Ole Sondresen, Kim Yap. Interior Designer: Sharmell Anderson. Landscape Architect: Robert M. Toole.

"Finally, Twain at Center Stage," *Hartford Courant*, November 16, 2000.

Gregory B. Hladky, "Yale Dean to Design Mark Twain Center," *New Haven Register*, November 16, 2000, A:3, 6.

Frances Grandy Taylor, "Yale Dean Relishes Twain Architectural Project," *Hartford Courant*, November 17, 2000, 1-3.

Laurie Ledgard, "Worthy of the Almighty and Robert Stern," *Hartford Business Journal*, November 20, 2000, 1, 16.

"Off the Record," *Architectural Record*, February 2001, 32.

Mike Swift, "Architectural Wonders," *Northeast*, March 11, 2001, 1, 5-9, 13.

Stacey Stowe, "Architectural Superstars Tackle Three Hartford Attractions," *The New York Times*, July 29, 2001, 14:7.

Tom Puleo, "A Novel Design," *Hartford Courant*, November 16, 2001, B:1, 2.

Eleanor Charles, "Visitors' Center to Be Built at Mark Twain House," *The New York Times*, January 20, 2002, 11:9.

Steve Grant, "A Hidden Architectural Gem By Design: The New Twain Museum Center Is Built in the Shadow of the House," *Hartford Courant*, October 14, 2003, D:1, 5.

"Where Twain Fans Shall Meet," *Hartford Courant*, September 30, 2003, A:10.

Mike Swift, "Following the Understated, Underground Trail of Mark Twain's New Neighbor," *Hartford Courant*, October 14, 2003, D:1, 5.

Steve Grant, "Mark Twain House Gets a Subtle Addendum," *Hartford Courant*, October 29, 2003.

Michael J. Crosbie, "Welcome Addition," *Hartford Courant*, November 16, 2003, C:4.

Robert A. M. Stern: Buildings and Projects 1999–2003 (New York: The Monacelli Press, 2003), 526-29.

Charles Lockwood, "Green Firsts," *Urban Land*, June 2007, 46-50.

Robert A. M. Stern: Buildings and Towns (New York: The Monacelli Press, 2007), 352-59.

Alison Leigh Cowan, "Rumors of Demise Not So Greatly Exaggerated," *The New York Times*, June 3, 2008, B:1, 4.

Martin Filler, "Rolling Out the Unwelcome Mat for Visitor Centers," *Architectural Record*, March 2009, 33-35.

Robinson and Merhige Courthouse
Richmond, Virginia

Partner: Grant F. Marani. Project Associate: Paul Zembsch. Project Assistants: Giovanna Albretti, Marcus Carter, Jonathan Grzywacz, Jacqueline Ho, Eric Hofmann, Carlos Hurtado, Susannah Jackson, Charles Toothill. Interior Design Associate: Ken Stuckenschneider. Interior Design Assistant: Sharmell Anderson. Landscape Design Associate: Marsh Kriplen. Landscape Design Assistants: Jennifer Berlly, Ashley Christopher, Jacqueline Ho, Caitlyn Lenihan. Landscape Architect: Snead Associates. Associate Architect: HLM Design, Heery International.

Alan Cooper, "Seventh-Broad Site for Courthouse?" *Richmond Times-Dispatch*, October 11, 2001, B:5.

Alan Cooper and Will Jones, "Courthouse to Be Built Downtown," *Richmond Times-Dispatch*, February 16, 2002, B:1, 4.

Tom Campbell, "Courthouse to Fit Setting," *Richmond Times-Dispatch*, November 16, 2002, B:4.

Edwin Slipek, Jr., "Order in the Court," *Style Weekly*, December 4, 2002, 35.

Vision + Voice: Design Excellence In Federal Architecture: Building Legacy (Washington, D.C.: General Services Administration, 2002), 52.

Robert A. M. Stern: Buildings and Projects 1999–2003 (New York: The Monacelli Press, 2003), 530-31.

Philip Langdon, "Three Years after 9/11, Security Mindset Threatens Civic Design," *New Urban News*, September 2004, 1, 3-5.

Edwin Slipek Jr., "A Rare Opportunity for a Grand Civic Space," *Style Weekly*, March 1, 2006.

Edwin Slipek Jr., "Broken Necklace," *Style Weekly*, May 30, 2007, 24.

Function, Form, and Meaning: Design Excellence in Federal Courthouses (Washington, DC: U.S. General Services Administration, 2007), cover, 2, 9, 11.

Tom Campbell, "A Mini-Boom on Broad: Nearly Complete Courthouse First of Three Projects in Works," *Richmond Times-Dispatch*, October 29, 2007, A:1, 6.

Edwin Slipek, Jr., "The Law Is Luxurious," *Style Weekly*, September 3, 2008, 19.

Edwin Slipek, Jr., "Thar She Blows: The New U.S. Courthouse Is Dressed for an Architectural Party on Broad Street, but the Other Guests Didn't Show," *Style Weekly*, December 3, 2008, 23-24.

"Curtain Wall Blast-Proofs Courthouse With Class," *Architectural Products*, December 2008, 72-73.

United States Courthouse, Richmond, Virginia (Washington, D.C.: General Services Administration, 2008).

House
Seaside, Florida

Partner: Gary L. Brewer. Project Manager: Mark Pledger. Project Assistants: Kayin Tse, Kim Yap. Interior Design Associate: Ken Stuckenschneider. Interior Design Assistant: Georgette Sturam. Landscape Design Project Managers: Ashley

Christopher, Mei Wu. Landscape Design Assistant: Jennifer Berlly.

Fred A. Bernstein, "Seaside at 25: Troubles in Paradise," *The New York Times*, December 9, 2005, F:1, 6.

Witold Rybczynski, "Seaside Revisited: A Model Town, 25 Years Later," *Slate*, February 28, 2007.

Hadiya Strasberg, "Windows on the Gulf," *Period Homes*, November 2007, 20-22.

Gerald Clarke, "Making a Splash in Seaside," *Architectural Digest*, April 2008, cover, 154-63, 235.

Rhonda Eleish and Edie van Breems, *Swedish Country Interiors* (Salt Lake City, Utah: Gibbs Smith, 2009), 95-104.

Eve M. Kahn, "Scandinavia on the Panhandle," *Period Homes*, September 2009, cover, 14-16.

Torre Almirante
Rio de Janeiro, Brazil

Partner: Meghan L. McDermott, Graham S. Wyatt. Project Senior Associate: Don Lee. Project Assistants: Giovanna Albretti, Daniel Arbelaez, Jennifer Bernell, Flavia Bueno, Lara Kailian, Leonid Khanin, Ernesto Martinez. Associate Architect: Pontual Arquitetura.

"Off the Record," *Architectural Record*, April 2002, 24.

Robert A. M. Stern: Buildings and Projects 1999–2003 (New York: The Monacelli Press, 2003), 532-35.

Robert A. M. Stern: Buildings and Towns (New York: The Monacelli Press, 2007), 414-21.

Jacksonville Public Library
Jacksonville, Florida

Partner: Alexander P. Lamis. Project Senior Associate: Jeffery Povero. Project Associates: James Pearson, Salvador Peña-Figueroa, George Punnoose, Kim Yap. Project Assistants: Daniel Arbelaez, Jennifer Berlly, Ceren Bingol, Matthew Casey, Thomas Fletcher, Mark Gage, Anthony Goldsby, Jill Lagowski, Joshua Lekwa, Ernesto Martinez, Mark Rodriguez, Mike Soriano, John Tulloch. Interior Design Associates: Hyung Kee Lee, Shannon Ratcliff. Interior Design Assistants: Kasumi Hara, Kathleen Mancini. Landscape Design Associate: Marsh Kriplen. Landscape Design Project Manager: Michael Weber. Landscape Design Senior Assistant: Ashley Christopher. Landscape Architect: Nancy Jenkins-Frye, ASLA. Associate Architect: Rolland, DelValle & Bradley.

P. Douglas Filaroski, "Library Officials Approve 4 Firms to Submit Designs," *The Florida Times-Union*, June 14, 2001, B:1, 8.

P. Douglas Filaroski, "Architects Vie to Design New Jacksonville Library," *The Florida Times-Union*, July 12, 2001.

P. Douglas Filaroski, "Nashville's Novel Idea a Preview for Jacksonville," *The Florida Times-Union*, July 20, 2001, A:1, 13.

P. Douglas Filaroski, "New Library Must Deal With Past," *The Florida Times-Union*, August 4, 2001, B:1, 3.

"Record News," *Architectural Record*, August 2001, 32.

"Jacksonville Public Library Proposals," *The Florida Times-Union*, December 16, 2001.

David Bauerlein, "City's New Main Library Will Have Classical Look," *The Florida Times-Union*, December 19, 2001, A:1, 9.

David Bauerlein, "Stern Library Design Rises to Top: Mayor Accepts Committee's Pick," *The Florida Times-Union*, December 21, 2001.

William A. Leuthold, "Library: Classical Design Is Timeless," *The Florida Times-Union*, December 25, 2001.

G. Stanley Collyer, "Budget Questions in Jacksonville," *Competitions*, Spring 2002, 6-33.

David Bauerlein, "Designers Flesh Out Library Plan," *The Florida Times-Union*, November 24, 2002.

David Bauerlein, "Ground Broken for Main Library," *The Florida Times-Union*, December 17, 2002, A:1, 7.

Robert A. M. Stern: Buildings and Projects 1999–2003 (New York: The Monacelli Press, 2003), 536-41.

Mary Kelli Palka, "Library Staff Gives Sneak Peek," *The Florida Times-Union*, January 29, 2004.

Eve M. Kahn, "Stern's Latest Turn," *Traditional Building*, July/August 2004, 216.

G. Stanley Collyer, *Architecture in Practice: Competing Globally in Architecture Competitions* (New York: John Wiley & Sons, 2004), 152.

Mary Kelli Palka, "A First Peek Inside the Main Library," *The Florida Times-Union*, November 9, 2005, A:1, 7.

Mary Kelli Palka and Tanya Perez-Brennan, "A New Classic: Five Stories of Style," *The Florida Times-Union*, November 9, 2005, C:1, 6.

Mary Kelli Palka, "New Main Library's Big Day Arrives," *The Florida Times-Union*, November 12, 2005, A:1, 9.

"A Cathedral of Books," *The Florida Times-Union*, November 12, 2005, B:6.

Mary Kelli Palka, "A Grand Opening," *The Florida Times-Union*, November 13, 2005, A:1, 14.

Ron Littlepage, "New Main Library Is Great Destination for Children," *The Florida Times-Union*, November 15, 2005.

Dan MacDonald, "Abstractionist's Final Painting Finds a Home at the City's New Downtown Public Library," *The Florida Times-Union*, January 12, 2006.

Mary Kelli Palka, "With Its New Digs and More Books, Main Library Is Now a Destination," *The Florida Times Union*, May 22, 2006.

Martha McDonald, "Book Ends," *Traditional Building*, April 2007, 12-14.

Robert A. M. Stern: Buildings and Towns (New York: The Monacelli Press, 2007), 430-41.

Shannon Mattern, *The New Downtown Library: Designing With Communities* (Minneapolis: University of Minnesota Press, 2007), 21-22.

Witold Rybczynski, "Borrowed Time: How Do You Build a Public Library in the Age of Google?" *Slate*, February 27, 2008.

The Plaza at PPL Center
Allentown, Pennsylvania

Partners: Meghan L. McDermott, Graham S. Wyatt. Project Associates: Fred Berthelot, Breen Mahony, Kevin O'Connor. Assistants: Ching-Chyi Yang, Ernesto Martinez, William Smith, David Vimont, Lindsay Weiss. Interior Design Assistant: Sharmell Anderson. Interior Designer: Spillman Farmer Architects. Landscape Design Project Manager: Marsh Kriplen. Landscape Design Senior Assistant: Michael Weber. Landscape Design Assistants: Christina Belton, Carlos Hurtado. Associate Architect: Kendall / Heaton Associates.

Henry J. Holcomb, "Rouse Office Building is Planned for Allentown," *The Philadelphia Inquirer*, November 15, 2001.

Ann Wlazelek, "Emmaus Grad Built PPL Model," *Morning Call*, November 29, 2001, B:4.

Bob Wittman, "PPL Plaza Design is Clean, Green," *The Morning Call*, September 18, 2002: A1, 4.

Bob Wittman, "Herbs to Blossom Into PPL Roof Garden," *Morning Call*, May 15, 2003, B:3.

Inga Saffron, "Truly Green and Distinctly Urban, Rouse Building Graces Allentown," *The Philadelphia Inquirer*, June 20, 2003, E:1, 4.

Graham S. Wyatt, "Pennsylvania: Big Ideas" *Pennsylvania Architect*, August 2003, 18.

Robert A. M. Stern: Buildings and Projects 1999–2003 (New York: The Monacelli Press, 2003), 542-43.

"It's Grand Being Green," *Recycling Today*, June 2004, 114.

"Building Industry Honors PPL Plaza," *The Express-Times*, June 4, 2004, B:7.

Tony Illia, "Urban Land Institute Awards Superior Development," *Architectural Record*, December 2004, 42.

"Best of the Best: ULI Awards for Excellence Winners Competition," *Urban Land*, November / December 2004, 163.

"Project Deconstruction: The Plaza at PPL Center," *Architectural Products*, January / February 2005, 38-40.

Edmund C. Snodgrass and Lucie L. Snodgrass, *Green Roof Plants: A Resource and Planting Guide*, (Portland, Oregon: Timber Press, 2006), cover, 76-77.

Robert A. M. Stern: Buildings and Towns (New York: The Monacelli Press, 2007), 368-77.

Ron Derven, "Liberty Property Trust: Building the Extraordinary Work Environment," *Development*, Fall 2008, cover, 32-33, 36-37.

The Residences at the Ritz-Carlton, Dallas
Dallas, Texas

Partners: Daniel Lobitz, Paul L. Whalen. Project Senior Associate: Hernán Chebar. Project Associate: Gaylin Bowie. Project Managers: David MacPhail, Nancy Thiel. Project Assistants: Merced Baumer, Kohilam Chandrahasan, Ching-Chyi Yang, Dennis George, Ulises Liceaga, Michiko Murao. Interior Design Associate: Hyung Kee Lee. Interior Design Assistant: Lisa Koch. Interior Designers: Frank Nicholson Incorporated, Hayslip Design Associates. Landscape Architect: The Office of James Burnett. Associate Architect: HKS.

Steve Brown, "Uptown Putting on the Ritz," *The Dallas Morning News*, April 21, 2004, D:1, 8.

Scott Cantrell, "The Ritz-Carlton a Sweet in Plain Wrapper," *The Dallas Morning News*, September 24, 2007.

One St. Thomas Residences
Toronto, Ontario, Canada

Partner: Paul L. Whalen. Project Senior Associate: Hernán Chebar. Project Associate: George Punnoose. Project Assistants: Ching-Chyi Yang, Eric Hofmann, David McPhail, John Tulloch, Richard Wachter. Interior Designer: Gluckstein Design. Landscape Architect: Laura Starr Associates. Associate Architect: Young + Wright Architects.

Christopher Hume, "Stern Stuff," *Toronto Star*, May 4, 2002, P:1, 10.

Therese Bissell, "Then We Take Toronto," *Nuvo*, Spring 2003, 44-46.

Meghan Drueding, "Stern Abroad," *Residential Architect*, August 2003, 21.

Christopher Hume, "A Stern Approach to Modernism," *Toronto Star*, December 6, 2003, P:1, 4.

Robert A. M. Stern: Buildings and Projects 1999–2003 (New York: The Monacelli Press, 2003), 544-45.

John Bentley Mays, "Expensive Hat With Shabby Shoes," *The Globe and Mail*, February 6, 2004.

Alex Bozikovic, "How Toronto Should Be Getting High," *The Globe and Mail*, April 29, 2006.

Kelvin Browne, "Best New Buildings of 2006," *National Post*, December 20, 2006.

Kate Pickert, "Feeling the Stern Effect: Raising the Bar—and Prices—Around the Country," *The Real Deal*, October 2007, 36.

Christopher Hume, "Condo Critic: One St. Thomas," *Toronto Star*, March 22, 2008.

Smeal College of Business
The Pennsylvania State University, State College, Pennsylvania

Partners: Kevin M. Smith, Graham S. Wyatt. Project Senior Associate: Jonas Goldberg. Project Associates: Fred Berthelot, Enid De Gracia, Kevin Fitzgerald, Sue Jin Sung. Project Senior Assistant: Gregory Christopher. Project Assistants: Jennifer Berlly, Alex Butler, Russell Greenberg, Jill Lagowski, Jennifer Newsom, Ryan Rodenberg, Lindsay Weiss. Landscape Architect: Lager Raabe Skafte, Sasaki Associates. Associate Architect: Bower Lewis Thrower Architects.

Graham S. Wyatt, "Pennsylvania: Big Ideas" *Pennsylvania Architect*, August 2003, 18.

David J. Neuman, *Building Type Basics for College and University Facilities* (New York: John Wiley & Sons, 2003), 92-120.

Robert A. M. Stern: Buildings and Projects 1999–2003 (New York: The Monacelli Press, 2003), 546-57.

"Princeton Review: Smeal Offers Best Facilities, Top Ten Faculty," *Smeal College of Business News*, October 10, 2007.

Joan and Sanford Weill Hall
Gerald R. Ford School of Public Policy, University of Michigan, Ann Arbor, Michigan

Partners: Preston J. Gumberich, Graham S. Wyatt. Project Senior Associates: Jeffery Povero, Jennifer Stone. Project Associate: George Punnoose. Project Assistants: Fred Berthelot, Thomas Fletcher, Ryan Rodenberg, Jeremy Shannon, Zong Ji Zhan. Interior Design Associates: Hyung Kee Lee, Ken Stuckenschneider. Interior Design Assistant: Khara Nemitz. Landscape Architect: Ann P. Stokes Landscape Architects. Associate Architect: Albert Kahn Associates.

Geoff Larcom, "New U-M Landmark in the Making," *The Ann Arbor News*, June 29, 2003.

Diane Brown, "Regents Approve Building Design for Ford School," *The University Record*, June 30, 2003.

"Joan and Sanford Weill Give $5 Million for U-M's Ford School of Public Policy Building," *University of Michigan News*, February 18, 2004.

Jared Wadley, "President Ford Celebrates Groundbreaking of New Ford School of Public Policy," *University of Michigan News*, November 12, 2004.

Geoff Larcom, "School of Public Policy Stands as a Tribute to the Fords," *The Ann Arbor News*, December 27, 2006.
"New Campus Architecture," *The Chronicle of Higher Education*, February 23, 2007, B:3-4, 6, 10, 12, 14, 16.
Mary E. Kremposky, "Weill Hall: An Advanced Degree in Craftsmanship," *CAM (Construction Association of Michigan)*, June 2007, cover, 48-54.
Robert A. M. Stern: Buildings and Towns (New York: The Monacelli Press, 2007), 484-93.

North Quad Residential and Academic Complex
University of Michigan, Ann Arbor, Michigan

Partners: Preston J. Gumberich, Graham S. Wyatt. Project Senior Associate: Jeffery Povero. Project Associate: George Punnoose. Project Managers: Sean Foley, Bradley Gay, Celeste Hall. Project Assistants: David Abecassis, Kanu Agrawal, Daniel Arbelaez, Fred Berthelot, Hee-Young Cho, Kathryn Everett, Megan Fullagar, Stephanie Mena, Connie Osborn, William Perez, Yok Saowasang, Dongju Seo, Sue Jin Sung, Michael Tabacinic. Interior Design Assistant: Phillip Chan. Landscape Architect: Pollack Design Associates. Associate Architect: Einhorn Yaffee Prescott.

Farayha Arrine, "North Quad Back to Drawing Board," *Michigan Daily*, April 10, 2006.
Dave Gershman, "North Quad to Get New Look," *The Ann Arbor News*, July 31,2006.
Dave Gershman, "U-M Shows Upgraded Plans for North Quad," *The Ann Arbor News*, December 16, 2006.
Nancy Connell, "Design for North Quad Gets Regents' Nod," *The University Record*, January 10, 2007.
Jessica Vosgerchian, "The Rise and Fall of the Frieze Building," *Michigan Daily*, February 9, 2007.
Austin Dingwall, "An Educated Guess About the Future of Campus Architecture," *Michigan Daily*, November 7, 2007.
James Tobin, "North Quad and Nellie's Books," *Michigan Today*, October 2007.

Weinberg Building
Sheppard Pratt Hospital, Baltimore, Maryland

Partners: Paul L. Whalen. Project Manager: Nancy Thiel. Project Assistants: Ravi D'Cruz, Scott Kruger, David MacPhail, Ben Pell. Landscape Design Associate: Marsh Kriplen. Landscape Design Project Manager: Michael Weber. Associate Architect: HDR.

Gerard Shields, "Sheppard Pratt to Expand and Renovate," *The Baltimore Sun*, March 7, 2002.
Edward Gunts, "He Aims to Please: Stern Will Limit Design Losses at Sheppard Pratt Health," *The Baltimore Sun*, July 29, 2002.
Debra Wood, "Pioneer Spirit: Sheppard Pratt Project Takes Tradition into the 21st Century," *Mid-Atlantic Construction*, December 2004, cover, 3, 8-9, 13.
"Architectural Showcase: Behavioral Health Facility," *Healthcare Design*, September 2006, 86.
Robert A. M. Stern: Buildings and Towns (New York: The Monacelli Press, 2007), 468-75.
Steven S. Sharfstein, Faith B. Dickerson, and John M. Oldham, eds., *Textbook of Hospital Psychiatry* (Washington, DC: American Psychiatric Publishing, 2009), front cover.

Baker Library | Bloomberg Center
Harvard Business School, Boston, Massachusetts

Partners: Alexander P. Lamis, Graham S. Wyatt. Project Associate Partner: Kevin M. Smith. Project Senior Associates: Melissa DelVecchio, Kurt Glauber. Project Associate: Don Johnson. Project Team: Giovanna Albretti, Alexander Butler, Matthew Casey, Enid De Gracia, Sara Evans, Thomas Fletcher, Mark Gage, Mark Haladyna, Edmund Leveckis, Ryan Rodenberg, Thomas Salazar, Mike Soriano, Sue Jin Sung, Brian Taylor, John Tulloch, Lindsay Weiss. Interior Design Associate: Ken Stuckenschneider. Interior Design Assistants: Nadine Holzheimer, Hyung Kee Lee, Khara Nemitz. Landscape Architect: The Halvorson Company. Associate Architect: Finegold Alexander + Associates.

Adriana Boden, "Baker Library: A Renovation in the Making," *The Harbus (The Independent Student Weekly for the Harvard Business School)*, May 5, 2003, 1, 3, 5.

Robert A. M. Stern: Buildings and Projects 1999–2003 (New York: The Monacelli Press, 2003), 571.
Robert Campbell, "Harvard Library Is Back in Business," *The Boston Globe*, November 6, 2005.
Sharon Shinn, "The B-School's New Home," *BizEd*, November / December 2005, 30-32, 35-36.
Meaghan O'Neill, "Library Competition Awards Best Interiors," *Interior Design*, May 19, 2006.
"Interior Worlds: LAMA and IIDA Name the Best Library Interiors of 2006," *American Libraries*, September 2006, 64.
Jayne Merkel, "Hitting the Books," *Architectural Record Review*, October 2006, 7-10, 12, 14.
Norman Oder, "Winners: Academic Libraries," *Library by Design*, Fall 2006, 6.
Robert A. M. Stern: Buildings and Towns (New York: The Monacelli Press, 2007), 452-59.

House on Lake Michigan

Partner: Randy M. Correll. Project Associate: Timothy Deal. Project Assistants: Glenn Albrecht, Haven Knight, Samuel O'Meara, Mark Rodriguez, David Vimont, Holly Zeiler. Interior Designer: Victoria Hagan Interiors. Landscape Architect: Douglas Hoerr Landscape Architecture.

Robert A. M. Stern: Buildings and Projects 1999–2003 (New York: The Monacelli Press, 2003), 571.
Steven M.L. Aronson, "Tapping Tradition: The Splendor of America's Past Is Reborn on Lake Michigan," *Architectural Digest*, October 2009, cover, 100-9.

Residence
Los Angeles, California

Partner: Roger H. Seifter. Project Senior Associate: Victoria Baran. Project Senior Assistant: Christopher McIntire. Project Assistants: Alexander Butler, Susanna Chao, Joshua Coleman, Troy Curry, Timothy Deal, Caroline Graf Statile, Sallie Hambright, Joshua Lekwa, Todd Sullivan. Interior Designer: Thomas Pheasant. Landscape Project Managers: Ashley Christopher, Bibi Gaston. Landscape Design Assistant: Mark Rodriguez.

Robert A. M. Stern: Buildings and Projects 1999–2003 (New York: The Monacelli Press, 2003), 571.

Southeast Federal Center
Washington, D. C.

Partners: Sargent C. Gardiner, Paul L. Whalen. Project Associates: Johnny Cruz, Joel Mendelson. Project Manager: Bryan Hale. Project Assistants: Ravi D'Cruz, Christopher Pizzi. Associate Architects: Communication Arts, Shalom Baranes, SMWM.

Dana Hedgpeth, "Developer Chosen for Southeast Federal Center," *The Washington Post*, January 30, 2004.
Peter Slain, "Curbside," *The Architect's Newspaper*, February 17, 2004, 4.

Apartment on Fifth Avenue
New York, New York

Partner: Randy M. Correll. Project Associate: Pamela McGirr. Interior Design Assistant: Georgette Sturam.

Rafael Díaz-Balart Hall
Florida International University College of Law, Miami, Florida

Partner: Alexander P. Lamis. Project Associates: James Pearson, Salvador Peña-Figueroa, Kim Yap. Project Assistants: Goil Amornvivat, Dryden Razook, Zong Ji Zhan. Interior Designer: Shannon Ratcliff. Associate Architect: Harper Aiken Donahue & Partners.

Andres Viglucci, "Reaching for the Stars," *Miami Herald*, September 17, 2006.
Laura Figueroa, "Political Family Patriarch Díaz-Balart Honored," *Miami Herald*, February 11, 2007.
Beth Dunlop, "A Study in Judicious Design," *Miami Herald*, March 11, 2007, M:5, 13.
Deborah O'Neil, "Raising the Bar," *FIU Magazine*, Spring 2007, 6-10.
Robert A. M. Stern: Buildings and Towns (New York: The Monacelli Press, 2007), 526-33.

American Revolution Center at Valley Forge
Valley Forge, Pennsylvania

Partners: Alexander P. Lamis, Kevin M. Smith. Project Senior Associate: Julie Nymann. Project Associates: Michael D. Jones, Thomas Lewis, Salvador Peña-Figueroa, Kim Yap. Project Assistants: Goil Amornvivat, Seher Aziz, Seth Burney, Deirdre Cerminaro, Mark Gage, Alena Kereshun, Gemma Kim, Qu Kim, Anthony Polito, Tehniyet Masood, Sara Rubenstein, Vanessa Sanchez, Addie Suchorab, Can Tiryaki, Zong Ji Zhan. Landscape Architect: Balmori Associates.

"Buzz," *Architecture*, October 2002, 16.
Herbert Muschamp, "Conjuring Histories at Revolutionary Crucible," *The New York Times*, February 25, 2004, E:1, 4.
"Robert A. M. Stern Unveils Plans for American Revolution Center at Valley Forge," *Architectural Record*, February 25, 2004.
Margaret Foster, "Forging Ahead at Valley Forge," *Preservation*, February 25, 2004.
Inga Saffron, "A Fitting Approach for a History Center," *The Philadelphia Inquirer*, February 27, 2004, E:1, 5.
Nicholas von Hoffman, "Robert A. M. Stern: The Making of a Legend in the World of Architecture," *Architectural Digest*, April 2004, 96, 102, 160.
Joseph Dennis Kelly II, "Stern Designing American Revolution Center," *Architectural Record*, April 2004, 50.
Bay Brown, "On the Boards," *Architecture*, May 2004, 43.
Nancy Petersen, "Revolution Museum Hits Setback," *The Philadelphia Inquirer*, November 3, 2005.
Judith H. Dobrzynski, "Retreat at Valley Forge," *The New York Times*, July 3, 2006, A:15.
Nancy Petersen, "Museum at Valley Forge is On Again," *The Philadelphia Inquirer*, February 14, 2007.
"The American Revolution Center Must Be Built," *(Philadelphia) Times-Herald*, July 22, 2007.
"American Revolution Center: Pick a Spot and Build It," *The Philadelphia Inquirer*, July 18, 2008.
Jeff Gammage, "American Revolution Center Headed for Center City," *The Philadelphia Inquirer*, July 2, 2009.

West Village Townhouse
New York, New York

Partner: Randy M. Correll. Project Associate: Rosa Maria Colina. Project Manager: Caroline Graf Statile. Project Assistants: Matt Casey, Nicholas DeRosa, Michael Dudley, Josh Lekwa, Jeremy Shannon. Landscape Design Project Manager: Ashley Christopher.

Ocean Course Clubhouse
Kiawah Island, South Carolina

Partner: Gary L. Brewer. Project Senior Associate: Jonas Goldberg. Project Associate: Kevin Fitzgerald. Interior Designers: Hirsch Bedner Associates. Landscape Architect: DesignWorks.

Robert Behre, "Ocean Course Clubhouse Above Par, Picturesque," *The Post and Courier*, September 10, 2007.
Stephani L. Miller, "Reinvention's Housing Tour a Hit," *Residential Architect*, December 4, 2007.
Steve Eubanks, "Places in the Heart: Kiawah's Clubhouses," *Kiawah Island Legends*, 2008, 50-61.
"Rise Above: The Architecture of Robert A. M. Stern," *Robb Report Vacation Homes*, December 2008 / January 2009, 75.

The Gramercy at Metropolitan Park
Arlington, Virginia

Partners: Daniel Lobitz, Paul L. Whalen. Project Senior Associate: Hernán Chebar. Project Assistants: Ching-Chyi Yang, Russell Grant, Gemma Kim, Christopher Pizzi. Interior Design Associate: Hyung Kee Lee. Landscape Architect: Lewis Scully Gionet. Associate Architect: WDG.

Kerry A. Sullivan, "High Design," *Units*, October 2007, 40-45.
Susan Straight, "Distinction in Detail, 136 Floor Plans' Worth," *The Washington Post*, May 10, 2008.

Fulton Corridor Master Plan
New York, New York

Partner: Paul L. Whalen. Project Manager: Jack Robbins.

Karrie Jacobs, "Social Engineering on Fulton Street," *Metropolis*, October 2003, 84-92.
David W. Dunlap, "Waiting, Waiting on a Plan for the Fulton Corridor," *The New York Times*, January 20, 2006, B:3.
Eva Hagberg, "The View From the Bridge," *The Architect's Newspaper*, June 8, 2005, 1.
Gunnar Hand, "Fulton Street Plan Chugs Along," *The Architect's Newspaper*, July 13, 2005, 1, 2.

The McNeil Center for Early American Studies
University of Pennsylvania, Philadelphia, Pennsylvania

Partners: Preston J. Gumberich, Graham S. Wyatt. Project Senior Associate: Jeffery Povero. Project Associates: Fred Berthelot, George Punnoose. Project Assistants: Daniel Arbelaez, Jill Lagowski, Jennifer Stone, Jeremy Shannon. Interior Design Associates: Hyung Kee Lee, Shannon Ratcliff. Landscape Architects: Olin.

Inga Saffron, "Old Buildings Lost, but New Residents Gained," *The Philadelphia Inquirer*, January 16, 2006.
Ian Baldwin, "Ugly American Studies Building," *Daily Pennsylvanian*, March 2, 2006.
Inga Saffron, "Good Boom/Bad Boom," *Boom: New Architecture in Philadelphia*, June 2006, 11.
George W. Boudreau, ed., *Early American Studies: An Interdisciplinary Journal*, Spring 2006, cover, v-vi.
Witold Rybczynski, "That Dogma Won't Hunt: Why Are Architects So Obsessed With Schools and Rules?" *Slate*, February 4, 2009.

The Clarendon
Boston, Massachusetts

Partner: Paul L. Whalen. Project Senior Associate: Michael D. Jones. Project Associates: Bina Bhattacharyya, Gaylin Bowie. Project Assistants: Noel Angeles, Goil Amornvivat, Lauren Cahill, Dianne Chia, Johnny Cruz, Ravi D'Cruz, Dax Gardner, Bryan Hale, Stuart Johnson, Adele Lim, Annie Mennes, Samuel Roche, Tad Roemer. Interior Design Associates: Hyung Kee Lee, Ken Stuckenschneider. Interior Design Assistants: Tina Hu, Alys Stephens Protzman, Alexandra Rolland. Landscape Architect: Copley Wolff Design Group. Associate Architects: CBT Architects, Ismael Leyva Architects.

Chris Reidy, "Tower Residences Planned for Back Bay," *The Boston Globe*, July 3, 2004.
Anahad O'Connor, "Cracking Under the Pressure? It's Just the Opposite, for Some," *The New York Times*, September 10, 2004, A:1, 20.
Thomas C. Palmer Jr., "BRA Approves $160m Clarendon Complex," *The Boston Globe*, July 1, 2005.
Steve Cutler, "The New Urbanism: The Flight to the Cities," *New York Living*, April 2008, 33-43.
Catherine Bolgar, "Luxury Homes Fare Well in a Mixed Market," *The Wall Street Journal*, May 10-11, 2008, W:11A.
"Building on His Success," *The Boston Globe*, May 16, 2008.

Product Design

DAVID EDWARD

Partner: Alexander P. Lamis. Senior Associate: Jeffery Povero. Project Manager: Nathaniel Pearson.

Karen D. Singh, "Essential Reading," *Interior Design*, June 2004, 86.
"Traditional Library Values," *Library by Design*, Fall 2005, 20.

BENTLEY PRINCE STREET

Partners: Alexander P. Lamis, Paul L. Whalen. Project Manager: Nathaniel Pearson. Project Assistants: John Boyland, Shannon Ratcliff.

Karen D. Singh, "Essential Reading," *Interior Design*, June 2004, 86.
"Library Inspired," *Architectural Products*, September / October 2004, 16.
"Book Smart," *Architectural Products*, April 2005, 70.

Norman Oder & Ann Kim, "Midnight in the Garden," *Library by Design*, Fall 2005, 38.

Ann Kim, "Tread on Me," *Library by Design*, Fall 2008, 28.

CROSSVILLE

Partner: Alexander P. Lamis. Project Manager: Nathaniel Pearson. Project Assistants: John Boyland, Hyung Kee Lee, Alexandra Rolland.

"Flooring: Crossville," *Interior Design*, July 2007, 180.

"Classic Contemporaries," *Architectural Record*, January 2008, 172.

"Products," *Contract*, March 2008, 38-40.

Karen D. Singh and Jen DeRose, eds., "Step Lively," *Interior Design*, March 2008, 92.

Mollie Magill, "Building Relationships," *Connecticut Cottages & Gardens*, April 2008, 28.

Laura Wallis, "Perfect Ten: *Home* 2008 Kitchen & Bath Awards," *Home*, May 2008, 48, 50-52.

"Architectural-Style Tile," *Architectural Products*, May 2008, 77.

Paige Phelps, "Architect Robert A. M. Stern Brings Designer Eye to Line of Tiles," *The Dallas Morning News*, June 5, 2008.

Mollie Magill, "Building Relationships," *Hamptons Cottages & Gardens*, July 1–15, 2008, 36.

Nigel F. Maynard and Shelly D. Hutchins, "Urbane League," *Residential Architect*, July 2008, 64.

"Winners of the 10th Annual Kitchen and Bath Awards," *Home*, July / August 2008, 19.

"NeoCon Star Turns," *Interior Design*, August 2008, 129-32, 134.

HADDONSTONE

Partner: Alexander P. Lamis. Project Manager: Nathaniel Pearson. Project Assistant: Alvaro Jose Soto. Landscape Design Senior Associate: Michael Weber

Sarah Kinbar, "I Love This: Olympian Line From Haddonstone," *Garden Design*, April 29, 2009.

"Robert A. M. Stern Designs to Offer New Garden Ornaments Made by Haddonstone," *Traditional Building*, May 21, 2009.

"Earthly Delights," *Hamptons Cottages & Gardens*, July 2009, 84.

Clare Martin, "Finding Neo," *Old House Journal*, August 2009, 24.

"Demeter's Delight," *Connecticut Cottages & Gardens*, July / August 2009, 16.

"Understated Urns," *Architectural Record*, August 2009, 114.

"Set in Stone," *Architectural Digest*, September 2009, 156.

"Antennae Roundup," *The World of Interiors*, October 2009, 39.

LIGHTOLIER

Partner: Alexander P. Lamis. Project Manager: Nathaniel Pearson. Project Assistant: Alvaro Jose Soto. Lighting Designer: FMS / Fisher Marantz Stone.

Cramer Hill and Pennsauken Waterfront Redevelopment Plans
Camden and Pennsauken, New Jersey

Partners: Daniel Lobitz, Paul L. Whalen. Project Senior Associate: Joel Mendelson. Project Manager: Saul Hayutin. Project Assistants: Jane Costello, Kleber Salas.

Jill P. Capuzzo, "Camden's Billion-Dollar Gamble," *The New York Times*, June 27, 2004, 14 (New Jersey):1, 8.

Susan Warner, "Visions of Another Trendy Enclave," *The New York Times*, September 26, 2004, 14 (New Jersey):1, 9.

Frank Kummer, "Cherokee Signs Deal to Develop Riverfront," *The Philadelphia Enquirer*, May 25, 2005.

Jim Miara, "Reviving Cities," *Urban Land*, July 2005, 86-87, 90-94.

Kareem Fahim, "Rethinking Revitalization: In Crumbling Camden, New Challenges for a Recovery Plan," *The New York Times*, November 5, 2006, 37-38.

Residence at Repulse Bay
Hong Kong, China

Partner: Grant F. Marani. Project Senior Associate: Charles Toothill. Project Assistant: Kayin Tse. Interior Design Associates: John Boyland, Ken Stuckenschneider. Interior Design Assistant: Georgette Sturam. Landscape Architect: St. Legere Design International, Ltd. Associate Architect: Ronald Lu & Partners Ltd.

10 Rittenhouse Square
Philadelphia, Pennsylvania

Partners: Meghan L. McDermott, Graham S. Wyatt. Project Associate: Breen Mahony. Project Assistants: Daniel Arbelaez, Gregory Christopher, Laura Dunne, Leonid Khanin, Katherine LoBalbo, Miguel Lasala, Ryan Rodenberg, Lindsay Weiss. Interior Design Associate: Ken Stuckenschneider. Interior Design Assistant: Khara Nemitz. Landscape Design Senior Associate: Michael Weber. Landscape Design Project Manager: Ashley Christopher. Landscape Design Assistant: Mark Rodriguez. Associate Architects: Ismael Leyva Architects, Polatnick/Zacharjasz Architects.

Henry Holcomb, "Rittenhouse Square Condo Tower Planned," *The Philadelphia Inquirer*, December 3, 2003, C:1, 7.

Inga Saffron, "Conquering Philadelphia's Fear of Crowds," *The Philadelphia Inquirer*, January 4, 2004, C:1.

"Leyva and Stern Join Forces—Again," *e-Oculus*, January 22, 2004, 7.

Inga Saffron, "Is It Just a Facade?" *The Philadelphia Inquirer*, Sunday, February 1, 2004, D:1, 3.

Alan J. Heavens, "Living High at Rittenhouse," *The Philadelphia Inquirer*, January 2, 2005, K:1, 7.

Joseph Dennis Kelly II, "Philadelphia Grows Up With a Slew of High-Rise Projects," *Architectural Record*, December 2005, 40.

Inga Saffron, "Old Buildings Lost, but New Residents Gained," *The Philadelphia Inquirer*, January 16, 2006.

Jennifer Ceaser, "Give Me Liberty," *New York Post*, March 29, 2007, 54-55.

"League Celebrates Excellence in Preservation," *Preservation Advocate*, Fall 2007, 1-3.

Robert A. M. Stern: Buildings and Towns (New York: The Monacelli Press, 2007), 502-9.

Steve Cutler, "The New Urbanism: The Flight to the Cities," *New York Living*, April 2008, 33-43.

Witold Rybczynski, "That Dogma Won't Hunt: Why Are Architects So Obsessed With Schools and Rules?" *Slate*, February 4, 2009.

Excellence Charter School of Bedford-Stuyvesant
Brooklyn, New York

Partners: Augusta Barone, Graham S. Wyatt. Project Senior Associates: Melissa DelVecchio, Dennis Sagiev. Project Associate: Enid De Gracia. Project Assistants: Goil Amornvivat, Jennifer Berlly, Thomas Fletcher, Nicolas Oudin, Brian Taylor, Russell Vaccaro. Landscape Design Senior Associate: Kendra Taylor. Landscape Design Assistant: Susie Grossman.

Michael Winerip, "New Libraries Make the City's Schools Come Alive," *The New York Times*, February 23, 2005, B:1, 6, 9.

GrandMarc at Westberry Place
Fort Worth, Texas

Partner: Graham S. Wyatt. Project Senior Associates: Jeffery Povero, Jennifer Stone. Project Associates: Fred Berthelot, Kevin Fitzgerald, Sue Jin Sung. Landscape Design Project Manager: Michael Weber. Landscape Design Assistant: Mark Rodriguez.

Anna M. Tinsley, "Berry Street Plan Would Add Business, Beautify Area," *Star-Telegram*, Sunday, November 30, 2003.

"Best of 2006: GrandMark at Westberry Place, Fort Worth," *Texas Construction*, December 2006, 57.

Calabasas Civic Center
Calabasas, California

Partner: Alexander P. Lamis. Project Associates: Salvador Peña-Figueroa, James Pearson. Project Assistants: Roland Sharpe Flores, Jill Lagowski, Thomas Morbitzer, Alex Piggott, Mike Soriano, Kim Yap, Zong Ji Zhan. Interior Designer: Pacific Office Interiors. Landscape Architect: Pamela Burton & Company. Associate Architect: Harley Ellis Devereaux.

Joann Groff, "Calabasas Civic Center Breaks Ground Saturday," *The Acorn*, January 4, 2007.

Angie Valencia-Martinez, "City Is Gunmetal Green: Calabasas Recycles Arms for City Hall," *The Free Library*, September 21, 2007.

Joann Groff, "Home ... at Last: Calabasas Civic Center Is Community's Crown Jewel," *The Acorn*, July 17, 2008.

Medical Office Building at Celebration Health
Celebration, Florida

Partner: Paul L. Whalen. Project Associate: Johnny Cruz. Associate Architect: Hunton Brady.

Highgrove
Stamford, Connecticut

Partner: Paul L. Whalen. Project Senior Associates: Hernán Chebar, Joel Mendelson. Project Manager: Miyun Kang. Landscape Architect: Wesley Stout Associates. Associate Architect: SLCE Architects.

Eleanor Charles, "In Stamford, the Condominium Market Is Sizzling," *The New York Times*, December 14, 2003, 11:7.
Joseph Dobrian, "City Living Trends in the Suburbs," *New York Living*, February 2005, 39-42.
Lisa Prevost, "Lap of Luxury in Downtown Stamford," *The New York Times*, January 15, 2006, 11:13.
Troy McMullen, "Condos With a Name: Available," *The Wall Street Journal*, March 31, 2006, W:1, 8.
"Condos in the Country," *The Real Deal*, September 2007, 158.
Alex Padalka, "Pampered in Stamford," *New York Construction*, January 2008, 35-36.
"The Dean: Architect Robert A. M. Stern Is a Classicist Who Defies Classicism," *New York Spaces*, October 2008, 28.
"The Lure of the High Life," *The Modern Estate*, January / February 2009, 34.
Lisa Prevost, "For Sure-Bet Buildings, Iffy Times," *The New York Times*, July 19, 2009, Real Estate:8.

House on Buzzards Bay
Massachusetts

Partner: Randy M. Correll. Project Manager: Damon Van Horne. Project Assistants: Aaron Boucher, Anthony Furino, Christiane Gallois, Douglas Neri, Marc Rehman. Interior Designer: Anne Mullin Interiors. Landscape Architect: Oehme Van Sweden.

Mildred Schmertz, "Seaside Traditions: Formal Flair for a Rambling Shingle Style House on Buzzards Bay," *Architectural Digest*, October 2008, cover, 208-17, 312.

Residence at One Central Park
New York, New York

Partner: Grant F. Marani. Project Associate: Rosa Maria Colina. Project Assistant: Megan St. Denis. Interior Designers: Agnes Bourne Studio, Dennis Miller Associates.

"Time Warner Center, Manhattan, New York," *New York Living*, February 2008, 24-25.

Lakewood Public Library
Lakewood, Ohio

Partner: Alexander P. Lamis. Project Senior Associate: Julie Nymann. Project Associates: James Pearson, Salvador Peña-Figueroa, Mike Soriano, Kim Yap. Interior Design Assistants: Phillip Chan, Khania Curtis, Khara Nemitz, Leah Taylor, Eric Van Speights. Landscape Senior Associate: Michael Weber. Associate Architect: CBLH Design.

Thomas Ott, "Library Expansion to Reflect Lakewood," *The Plain Dealer*, November 20, 2004, B:2.
Jeff Endress, "Library Announces Citizens' Groundbreaking Ceremony," *The Lakewood Observer*, May 2, 2006, 5.
Steven Litt, "Lakewood's New Library Plan Speaks Volumes," *The Plain Dealer*, May 12, 2006, E:1, 6.
John Elliott, "Building by the Book: Renovation, Addition Provide New Presence at Lakewood Public Library," *Properties*, May 2008, 20, 22-28.

Thealexa Becker, "Robert A. M. Stern Delivers a Gem: Lakewood Public Library Officially Rededicated," *The Lakewood Observer*, June 10, 2008, 1, 10-11.
Steven Litt, "New Lakewood Library Is a Majestic If Chilly Monument to Books," *The Plain Dealer*, August 23, 2008.

Student and Academic Services Buildings
University of North Carolina at Chapel Hill, Chapel Hill, North Carolina

Partners: Kevin M. Smith, Graham S. Wyatt. Project Senior Associate: Melissa DelVecchio. Project Manager: Lara Kailian. Project Associate: Fred Berthelot. Project Assistants: Lina Ayala, Gregory Christopher, Alex Pigott, Sue Jin Sung, Brian Taylor. Interior Design Associate: Shannon Ratcliff. Interior Design Assistant: Michelle Everett. Landscape Architect: Ann P. Stokes Landscape Architect. Associate Architect: Corley Redfoot Zack.

Kenan Stadium Expansion
University of North Carolina at Chapel Hill, Chapel Hill, North Carolina

Partners: Kevin M. Smith, Graham S. Wyatt. Project Manager: George de Brigard. Project Assistants: Anne Barker, Matthew Blumenthal, Melanie Fox, Hussam Jallad, Ian Miller, Rachel Reese.

House at Bluewater Hill
Westport, Connecticut

Partner: Gary L. Brewer. Project Assistant: Maryann Kril. Interior Designer: Jed Johnson Associates. Landscape Design Associate: Michael Weber.

Robert A. M. Stern: Buildings and Projects 1999—2003 (New York: The Monacelli Press, 2003), 565.

One Crescent Drive
Philadelphia Navy Yard, Philadelphia, Pennsylvania

Partners: Meghan L. McDermott, Graham S. Wyatt. Project Associate: Kevin O'Connor. Project Assistants: Carlos Hurtado, Tae Kim, Don Lee, Kathryn Stutts, Brian Taylor, Luis Vasquez, Robie Wood. Landscape Architect: Wells Appel Land Strategies. Associate Architect: Vitetta.

John Grady, "Positioned for Growth," *Urban Land*, July 2005, 88-89, 95-97.
Lisa Chamberlain, "Recycling a Big Urban Navy Yard," *The New York Times*, May 31, 2006, C:8.
Inga Saffron, "Good Boom/Bad Boom," *Boom: New Architecture in Philadelphia*, June 2006, 11.
John Salustri, "Liberty Makes the Biz Case for Green," *Globe St.*, November 8, 2007.
Nadav Malin, "Investing in the Environment: The Financial Industry's Approach to Green Building," *Environmental Building News*, November 2007, 1, 11-19.
Ron Derven, "Liberty Property Trust: Building the Extraordinary Work Environment," *Development*, Fall 2008, cover, 32-33, 36-37.

55 West
Las Vegas, Nevada

Partner: Paul L. Whalen. Associate Partner: Daniel Lobitz. Project Senior Associate: Sargent C. Gardiner. Project Assistants: Lina Ayala, Bina Bhattacharyya, Susanna Chao, Ravi D'Cruz, Elizabeth Eggleston, Seher Erdogan, Natalie Goldberg, Russell Greenberg, Bryan Hale, Gemma Kim, Tin Yiu Lo, William Perez, Leo Stevens, Rob Teeters.

St. Regis Hotel
Bal Harbour, Florida

Partner: Paul L. Whalen. Project Senior Associate: Hernán Chebar. Project Associate: Michael D. Jones.

Fifteen Central Park West
New York, New York

Partners: Michael D. Jones, Paul L. Whalen. Project Senior Associate: Victoria Baran. Project Associates: Mike Soriano, Paul Zembsch. Project Managers: Jie Huang, Jack Robbins. Project Assistants: Kanu Agrawal, Russell Grant, Carlos

Hurtado, Tin Yiu Lo, Rizwana Neem, Rob Teeters, David Winterton. Interior Design Associate: John Boyland. Interior Design Assistants: Jamie Murphy, Alexandra Rolland. Landscape Design Senior Associate: Michael Weber. Landscape Design Senior Assistant: Ashley Christopher. Landscape Design Assistant: Mark Rodriguez. Associate Architect: SLCE Architects.

David W. Dunlap, "Tall and Shorter Towers Set for Mayflower Site," *The New York Times*, August 4, 2005, B:7.

David Patrick Columbia, "The Many Faces of Robert A. M. Stern," *New York Social Diary*, August 24, 2005.

John Freeman Gill, "The Rich are Different. So is a Certain Rock." *The New York Times*, September 26, 2005, 14

Michael Calderone, "Big Euro Machers Will Crash Plaza: Ritzy Pied-à-Terres," *The New York Observer*, October 24, 2005, 13, 15.

Steve Cutler, "A Luxurious New Cornerstone at South End of Central Park," *The Real Deal*, November 2005, 1.

Steve Cutler, "Architect Profile: Robert A. M. Stern," *New York Living*, November 2005, 13-16.

S. Jhoanna Robledo, "The Height of Fashion," *New York*, November 7, 2005.

Motoko Rich, "For Choicest Apartments, Many More Choices," *The New York Times*, November 10, 2005, F:1, 4.

Michael Calderone, "A Drink with Bob Stern," *The New York Observer*, November 28, 2005, 3.

"Estates for Sale," *Architectural Digest*, February 2006, 103.

Steve Cutler, "The Zeckendorfs: A Lasting Legacy," *New York Living*, May 2006, 16-17.

Paul Goldberger, "Edifice Complex," *Bergdorf Goodman*, Resort Holiday issue, 32, 34.

Diane Greer, "Limestone Icon: New Manhattan Tower Fills Out Prime Central Park Site," *New York Construction*, January 2007, cover, 5, 47-49.

James Gardner, "The Soft Touch of Robert Stern," *The New York Sun*, January 17, 2007, 15.

Paul Makovsky, "Movin' On Up," *Metropolis*, February 2007, 106-9.

Christopher Gray, "Taking the Long View," *The New York Times*, May 6, 2007, 11:2.

Michael Calderone, "The Master Architect," *Haute Living*, April / May 2007, cover, 90, 116-23.

Joy Y. Wang, "Selling High," *Avenue*, May 2007, 94-101.

Paul Goldberger, "Past Perfect: Retro Opulence on Central Park West," *The New Yorker*, August 27, 2007.

Max Abelson, "A Legend Comes Clean: Architect Robert A. M. Stern on 15 CPW, 99 Church, and George W. Bush," *The New York Observer*, October 29, 2007, 37, 42.

Kate Pickert, "Feeling the Stern Effect: Raising the Bar—and Prices—Around the Country," *The Real Deal*, October 2007, 36.

Justin Davidson, "The New Prewar Old-Style Luxury Returns (or Does It?) at Fifteen Central Park West and the Plaza," *New York*, November 5, 2007, 96-97.

James S. Russell, "Limestone Condo on Central Park Attracts Big Bucks, Needs Magic," *Bloomberg*, November 14, 2007.

Francis Morrone, "All About Context," *The New York Sun*, December 13, 2007, 18.

James Gardner, "The Skyline as Architectural History," *The New York Sun*, December 17, 2007, 18.

Justin Davidson, "Best New Prewar: 15 Central Park West," *New York*, December 17, 2007, 80-81.

Robert A. M. Stern: Buildings and Towns (New York: The Monacelli Press, 2007), 510-19.

Jill Priluck, "The Ralph Lauren of Architecture," *The New York Sun*, January 10, 2008, 14.

Francis Morrone, "At Home Among the Clouds," *The New York Sun*, February 14, 2008, 11, 13.

Clifford A. Pearson, "American Architecture Today: Six Critics Examine the State of American Architecture From Their Hometowns," *Architectural Record*, February 2008, 87-93.

Myron Magnet, "Architecture's Battle of the Modernisms... and What It Means for Gotham's Future," *City Journal*, Winter 2008, 105-10.

Philip Herrera, "Bob the Builder: Why Robert A. M. Stern, Formerly Dismissed as Old-Fashioned, Might Just Be the Architect of the Moment," *Town & Country*, May 2008, 107-8, 110, 112, 114.

Avihu Kadosh, "My God! I'm Going to Leave a Phallic Mark on the City," *Calcalist*, September 9, 2008, 28-29.

Paul Goldberger, "The King of Central Park West," *Vanity Fair*, September 2008, 348-53, 396-97.

"The Dean: Architect Robert A. M. Stern Is a Classicist Who Defies Classicism," *New York Spaces*, October 2008, 28.

D Fitzgerald, *Window on the Park: New York's Most Prestigious Properties on Central Park* (Mulgrave, Victoria, Australia: Images Publishing, 2008), 172-75.

"Rise Above: The Architecture of Robert A. M. Stern," *Robb Report Vacation Homes*, December 2008 / January 2009, 75.

David Kaufman, "The Old New," *Financial Times*, April 18–19, 2009, 4.

Candace Taylor, "The Closing: Robert A. M. Stern," *The Real Deal*, May 29, 2009.

Wasserstein Hall, Caspersen Student Center, and Clinical Wing
Harvard Law School, Cambridge, Massachusetts

Partners: Melissa DelVecchio, Alexander P. Lamis, Kevin M. Smith, Graham S. Wyatt. Project Senior Associates: Kurt Glauber, Jennifer Stone.. Project Associates: Sophia Cha, Don Johnson, Christopher LaSala, Kim Yap. Project Team: Taytana Albinder, Thomas Brady, George de Brigard, Andrew Donaldson, Lorenzo Galati, Dennis George, Natalie Goldberg, Milton Hernandez, William Holloway, Jennifer Lee, Victor Marcelino, Oliver Pelle, William Perez, Kaveri Singh, Brian Taylor. Interior Design Associate: Shannon Ratcliff. Interior Design Assistants: Tina Hu, Marissa Savarese, Aruni Weerasinghe. Landscape Architect: Halvorson Design Partnership.

"Strict Construction: New 'Northwest Corner' Development Takes Shape," *Harvard Law Today*, September 2006, 1, 2.

James M. O'Neill, "Lazard's Wasserstein Gives $25 Million to Harvard Law," *Bloomberg*, March 22, 2007.

"Wasserstein Gives $25 Million for Academic Center," *Harvard Law Today*, May 2007, 1.

Joan Wickersham, "Bricks and Politics," *Harvard*, September — October 2007, 50-58.

Robert Campbell, "Solving an Identity Crisis," *The Boston Globe*, February 10, 2008.

Robb London, "Northwest Passage," *Harvard Law Bulletin*, Fall 2008.

Farmer Hall
Richard T. Farmer School of Business, Miami University, Oxford, Ohio

Partners: Preston J. Gumberich, Graham S. Wyatt. Project Senior Associate: Jeffery Povero. Project Associate: George Punnoose. Project Manager: Sean Foley. Project Assistants: Daniel Arbelaez, Afzal Hossain, Jill Lagowski, Meredith Micale, Michael Ryan, Yok Saowasang, Jeremy Shannon, Michael Tabacinic, Rob Teeters. Interior Design Associate: Shannon Ratcliff. Interior Design Assistants: Michelle Everett, Taylor Stein. Landscape Architect: James Burkart Associates. Associate Architect: Moody Nolan.

"The Richard T. Farmer School of Business Breaks Ground for New Building," *Miami University News*, October 31, 2006.

Residence
Highland Park, Illinois

Partner: Grant F. Marani. Project Senior Associate: Charles Toothill. Project Associate: Rosa Maria Colina. Project Manager: Megan St. Denis. Project Assistants: Peter Lombardi-Krieps, Mark Pledger, Zong Ji Zhan. Interior Designer: Semel Snow Interior Design. Landscape Architect: Douglas Hoerr Landscape Architecture.

Sunstone
Quogue, New York

Partner: Randy M. Correll. Project Manager: Thomas Morbitzer. Interior Designer: Scott Salvator.

Robert A. M. Stern: Buildings and Projects 1987–1992 (New York: Rizzoli International Publications, 1992), 46-49.

Museum for African Art
Museum Mile, New York, New York

Partners: Daniel Lobitz, Paul L. Whalen. Project Associates: Gaylin Bowie, Mike Soriano. Project Architect: Chenhuan Liao. Project Assistants: Lina Ayala, Ravi D'Cruz, Jorge Fontan, Gemma Kim, Wing Yee Ng Fung, Aileen Park, Kurt Roessler, Ellen Willis. Interior Design Associate: John Boyland. Interior Design Assistant: Mitra Moshari. Associate Architects: SLCE Architects, G Tects.

Celia McGee, "Out of Africa, Architecture Founded on Art," *New York Daily News*, September 30, 2005, 59.

Sewell Chan, "Museum for African Art Finds Its Place on Fifth Avenue," *The New York Times*, February 9, 2007, E:34.

Kate Taylor, "Museum Mile Expands," *The New York Sun*, February 9–11, 2007, 1, 18.

James Gardner, "African Art Joins the Museum Mile," *The New York Sun*, February 13, 2007, 14.

"Museum for African Art Gets Permanent Home After 22 Years," *World Architecture News*, February 19, 2007.

Sarah F. Cox, "Museum for African Art's Harlem Home," *The Architect's Newspaper*, March 7, 2007, 1, 6.

C.J. Hughes, "Robert A. M. Stern Has Designed a New Building for the Museum for African Art," *Architectural Record*, April 2007, 46.

"Robert A. M. Stern Designs New Museum for African Art," *A+U (Architecture and Urbanism)*, April 2007, 7.

A.L. Gordon, "Building a Future for African Art," *The New York Sun*, May 25–27, 2007, 2.

"Celebrating African Art," *a+ (Architecture Plus)*, 2007, Issue 15, 22.

Richard Staub, "Shape Shifting: New York's Cultural Institutions Are Finding Ingenious Ways to Expand and Reenergize Their Facilities," *Oculus*, Winter 2008/2009, 30-32.

International Quilt Study Center and Museum
University of Nebraska, Lincoln, Nebraska

Partner: Grant F. Marani. Project Associates: Goil Amornvivat, Rosa Maria Colina. Project Assistants: Lourdes Bernard, Thomas Morbitzer, Matthew Schaeffer, Brian Stromquist, Kayin Tse. Landscape Architect: Hargreaves Associates. Associate Architect: Alley Poyner Macchietto Architecture.

Dan Feuerbach, "Companies Compete to Design Quilt Center," *Daily Nebraskan*, January 11, 2005.

Bill Hord, "UNL Pieces Together Plan to House Quilts," *Omaha World-Herald*, April 14, 2005, B:1, 2.

"Quilt Museum Architects Are Chosen," *The New York Times*, April 16, B:7, 8.

"Patchwork Design," *Contract*, May 2005, 28.

Sam Lubell, "Quilt Center in the Works," *Architectural Record*, June 2005, 43.

"Robert A. M. Stern Architects: International Quilt Study Center and Ithaca College School of Business Building," *e-Oculus*, July 11, 2005, 12-13.

Kate Taylor, "Uncovering the Quilt: New Yorkers Back a New Museum," *The New York Sun*, December 11, 2007, 1, 17.

Mark McMenamin, "Quilting Bee," *Interior Design*, February 2008, 42.

Lawrence Biemiller, "U. of Nebraska Prepares to Open Quilt Center by Stern," *The Chronicle of Higher Education*, March 6, 2008.

Megan Holloway Fort, "Quilt Study Center," *Antiques*, March 2008, 16.

Stacie Stukin, "Patch Patch Patch: The Art of Quilting Finally Gets Its Due," *The New York Times Style Magazine*, Spring 2008, 38.

Judy Horan, "Big Red Goes Green," *Omaha World-Herald*, March 30, 2008, in "Quilts: A New Story Unfolds," 4.

Judy Horan, "They Call It 'Quilt House'," *Omaha World-Herald*, March 30, 2008, in "Quilts: A New Story Unfolds," 5.

Laura Chapman, "A Common Thread: Quilt Center Draws Crowd of 1,500 from Several Countries for Its Grand Opening," *Lincoln Journal Star*, March 31, 2008, 1.

Bobbie Leigh, "Dispatches: Quilting Beehive," *Culture + Travel*, March / April 2008, 22.

Michael Allan Torre, "Defying Gravity," *Art & Antiques*, June 2008, 70-79.

"The Right Fabric," *Metal Architecture*, February 2009.

"Quilting in a Time of Change," *The Chronicle of Higher Education*, June 12, 2009, A:4.

The Century
Los Angeles, California

Partners: Daniel Lobitz, Paul L. Whalen. Project Senior Associates: Victoria Baran, Sargent C. Gardiner. Project Associates: Johnny Cruz, Enid De Gracia, Mike Soriano. Project Assistants: Merced Baumer, Ravi D'Cruz, Seher Erdogan, Dax Gardner, Peter Garofalo, Russell Grant, Bryan Hale, Jie Huang, Stuart Johnson, Miyun Kang, Gemma Kim, David Nguyen, Kurt Roessler, Sebastian Snyder. Interior Design Associates: John Boyland, Ken Stuckenschneider. Interior Design

Assistants: Jana Happel, Lisa Koch, Nathaniel Pearson, Alys Stephens Protzman. Landscape Architect: Pamela Burton and Company. Associate Architect: HKS.

Roger Vincent, "Condo Tower Will Replace St. Regis Hotel," *Los Angeles Times*, October 9, 2006.

Robin Pogrebin, "New Los Angeles Dream Factories Design Buildings," *The New York Times*, December 25, 2006, E:1, 11.

Kate Pickert, "Feeling the Stern Effect: Raising the Bar—and Prices—Around the Country," *The Real Deal*, October 2007, 36.

Richard Staub, "From Villain to Hero," *Oculus*, Winter 2007 / 2008, 32-33.

Roger Vincent, "Los Angeles Condo Sells for $2,848 (per Square Foot)," *Los Angeles Times*, July 22, 2008.

Mireya Navarro, "Downsizing in Los Angeles: From Mansion to $47 Million Condo," *The New York Times*, August 21, 2008, A:1, 16.

Jim Crockett, "Custom Column Forms Allow Condo Class," *Architectural Products*, September 2008, 14.

"Rise Above: The Architecture of Robert A. M. Stern," *Robb Report Vacation Homes*, December 2008 / January 2009, 75.

Writers' Penthouse
New York, New York

Partner: Grant F. Marani. Project Associate: Julie Nymann. Project Assistant: Matthew Schaeffer. Interior Design Associate: John Boyland. Landscape Design Senior Associate: Kendra Taylor. Landscape Design Associate: Michael Weber. Landscape Design Assistant: Susie Grossman.

Joseph Giovannini, "Miracle on 34th Street," *Architectural Digest*, July 2007, 12, 30, 32, 36, 40, 164.

The Mansion on Peachtree
Atlanta, Georgia

Partners: Daniel Lobitz, Paul L. Whalen. Project Associates: Diane Burkin, Mike Soriano, Rosalind Tsang. Project Assistants: Merced Baumer, Seher Erdogan, Thomas Fletcher, Dennis George, Russell Grant, Robert HuDock, Gemma Kim, Chenhuan Liao, Ulises Liceaga, Tin Yiu Lo, Matthew Meehan, Meredith Micale, Rizwana Neem, Daivd Nguyen, David Winterton, Paul Zembsch. Interior Designers: Harrison Design Associates, Wilson & Associates. Landscape Design Project Manager: Michael Weber. Landscape Architect: Park Landscape Services. Associate Architect: Milton Pate Architects.

Bryan Long, "Buckhead Lands 50-Story Tower," *Atlanta Business Chronicle*, February 3-9, 2006, A:1, 34.

Maria Saporta, "John Williams, Arthur Blank Team Up for Project," *The Atlanta Journal-Constitution*, March 16, 2006, F:2.

"The Mansion Takes Shape on Peachtree Street," *Atlanta Business Chronicle*, August 18–24, 2006.

Marcia Sherrill, "Real Estate Update: New Heights," *Atlanta Homes & Lifestyles*, September 2006, 122-24.

Meg Sparwath, "Sky High," *Atlanta Homes & Lifestyles*, September 2006, 125.

Nick Kaye, "The Mansion on Peachtree," *The New York Times*, September 15, 2006, F:5.

Eileen Freeman, "Moonlighting," *Southern Seasons*, Fall 2006, 46-51.

Rachel Tobin Ramos, "Bite of the Big Apple Coming to Atlanta," *Atlanta Business Chronicle*, April 13–19, 2007, A:1, 31.

Nancy Staab, "Atlanta: Good Manners and Glamour Too," *Elle Décor*, May 2008, 144, 146, 148, 150, 152, 154.

Alison Miller, "The Mansion on Peachtree," *Southern Accents*, October 2008, 142, 144.

Laura Landro, "Two Helpings of New Southern Splendor," *The Wall Street Journal*, June 13-14, 2009, W:5.

Park Center for Business and Sustainable Enterprise
Ithaca College School of Business, Ithaca, New York

Partners: Kevin M. Smith, Graham S. Wyatt. Project Senior Associates: Dennis Sagiev, Jennifer Stone. Project Associate: Sue Jin Sung. Project Assistants: Roland Sharpe Flores, Lorenzo Galati, Natalie Goldberg, Lara Kailian, Eric Silinsh, Saul Uranovsky. Interior Design Associate: John Boyland. Interior Design Assistant: Leah Taylor. Landscape Architect: Hargreaves Associates.

Chris White, "Business Designer Selected," *The Ithacan*, April 7, 2005.
"Robert A. M. Stern Architects: International Quilt Study Center and Ithaca College School of Business Building," *e-Oculus*, July 11, 2005, 13.
Lawrence Biemiller, "Sustainability Tops the Agenda as College Planners and Architects Meet," *The Chronicle of Higher Education*, August 5, 2005, A:25.
Sharon Shinn, "The B-School's New Home," *BizEd*, November / December 2005, 30-32, 35-36.
"Green Mansions," *BizEd*, November / December 2005, 33-34.
William Morgan, "Ithaca Goes Modern: A New School of Business by Robert A. M. Stern," *Competitions*, Winter 2005 / 2006, 32-39.
Nancy Solomon, "The Hidden Life of Green," *GreenSource*, April 2007, 44-49.
Aaron Seward, "In Detail: Ithaca School of Business," *The Architect's Newspaper*, May 9, 2007, 10, 11.
Scott Carlson, "Two New Buildings at Ithaca College Meet High Environmental Standards," *The Chronicle of Higher Education*, October 26, 2007, A:32.
Peter W. Bardaglio, "A Moment of Grace: Integrating Sustainability Into the Undergraduate Curriculum," *Planning for Higher Education*, October / December 2007, 16-22.
Melbourne Garber, "An Education in Going Green," *Structural Engineer*, September 2008, cover, 34-35.

Greenspun Hall
Greenspun College of Urban Affairs, University of Nevada, Las Vegas, Las Vegas, Nevada

Partners: Augusta Barone, Graham S. Wyatt. Project Senior Associate: Jeffery Povero. Project Assistants: Bradley Gay, Erin Murphy, Alicia Reed, Dongju Seo, Brian Stromquist, Michael Tabacinic. Interior Design Associate: Shannon Ratcliff. Interior Design Assistants: Michelle Everett, Marissa Savarese. Landscape Architect: SWA Group. Associate Architect: HKS.

"On the Boards: UNLV's Greenspun College of Urban Affairs Building," *Architecture Las Vegas*, 2006, 98.
Christina Littlefield, "College of Urban Affairs to Get New Home," *Las Vegas Sun*, January 25, 2007.
Charlotte Hsu, "At UNLV, Building a Monument to Forward Thinking," *Las Vegas Sun*, December 3, 2008.
Leslie V. Hemby, "LEEDing the Way to Gold: Structural Engineering Design Innovations Graduate With Honors at the University of Nevada, Las Vegas," *Structural Engineer*, June 2009, cover, 12-17.

Flinn Hall and Edelman Hall
The Hotchkiss School, Lakeville, Connecticut

Partners: Gary L. Brewer, Graham S. Wyatt. Project Manager: Gregory Shue. Project Assistants: Tae Kim, Brendan Lee. Interior Design Associates: Shannon Ratcliff, Ken Stuckenschneider. Interior Design Assistants: Alys Stephens Protzman, Aruni Weerasinghe. Landscape Architect: Towers Golde.

Nancy Solomon, "The Hidden Life of Green," *GreenSource*, April 2007, 44-49.
Witold Rybczynski, "Green But Not Ugly," *Slate*, July 17, 2007.
Charlotte Leib, "Georgian Gems: New Dorms Grace Hotchkiss Campus With Beauty and Functionality," *The Hotchkiss Record*, September 27, 2007, 1, 3.

Residences on South Flagler Drive
West Palm Beach, Florida

Partners: Paul L. Whalen. Project Senior Associate: Hernán Chebar. Project Assistant: Ching-Chyi Yang.

Front Street District
Hartford, Connecticut

Partners: Preston J. Gumberich, Meghan L. McDermott, Graham S. Wyatt. Project Senior Associate: Jeffery Povero. Project Associates: George Punnoose, Rosalind Tsang. Project Manager: Mark Van Brocklin. Project Assistants: Lorjan Agalliu, Tatyana Albinder, Danny Chiang, Enid De Gracia, Andrew Donaldson, Roland Sharpe Flores, Anthony Furino, Bram Janaitis, Ranjit Korah, Meghan Leininger, Trevor Laubenstein, Jennifer Smith, Mike Soriano, Marek Turzynski. Landscape Architect: BSC Group. Associate Architect: Ismael Leyva Architects.

Mike Swift, "New Front-Runner on Front Street," *Hartford Courant*, July 18, 2005.
Eleanor Charles, "Downtown Hartford's New Centerpiece," *The New York Times*, September 18, 2005, 11:10.
Jane Gordon, "A Suburb's Big Project Is Outpacing Hartford's," *The New York Times*, December 20, 2006, C:9.
Leonard Felson, "Riverside Cleanup: Major Hartford Redevelopment Hinges on Site Recovery," *New York Construction*, February 2007, 67 -69.
Leonard Felson, "Climbing Back: Development on the Rise in Hartford," *New York Construction*, April 2007, 111-15.
Jeffrey B. Cohen, "Designs Done: Developer Offers $60 Million Plan for Front Street," *Hartford Courant*, December 15, 2007.
Jeffrey B. Cohen, "A $7 Million Jump Start for Hartford's Front Street," *Hartford Courant*, May 9, 2008.

Del Sur Village
San Diego, California

Partner: Daniel Lobitz. Project Assistants: Saul Hayutin, Joel Mendelson, Kleber Salas, Raymond Sih.

Bavaro Hall
Curry School of Education, University of Virginia, Charlottesville, Virginia

Partners: Preston J. Gumberich, Graham S. Wyatt. Project Manager: Connie Osborn. Project Assistants: Kanu Agrawal, Noel Angeles, Matthew Blumenthal, Emilia Ferri, Sean Foley, Megan Fullagar, George Punnoose, Christopher Heim, Stephanie Mena, Michael Ryan, Yok Saowasang, Mike Soriano, Charles Toothill, Marek Turzynski. Interior Design Associate: Shannon Ratcliff. Interior Design Assistant: Michelle Everett. Landscape Architect: Ann P. Stokes Landscape Architects.

Adam Goodheart, "Expanding on Jefferson," *The New York Times Magazine*, May 21, 2006, 80-86.

Improvements at Abraham Goodman House
Kaufman Center, New York, New York

Partner: Alexander P. Lamis. Project Senior Associate: Michael D. Jones. Project Associates: Thomas Lewis, Salvador Peña. Project Assistants: Doreen Adengo, Gali Osterweil, Vanessa Sanchez.

Brian Wise, "Kaufman Center to Undergo $15.5M Renovation," *Musical America*, February 1, 2007.
Lawrence Van Gelder, "Merkin Concert Hall Makeover," *The New York Times*, February 21, 2007, E:2.
Jesse Oxfeld with Michael Idov, "Robert A. M. Stern Tweaks the Upper West Side," *New York*, February 21, 2007.
Stephen Martin, "Unveiled: Kaufman Center," *The Architect's Newspaper*, March 21, 2007, 11.
Elisa Niemack, "Robert Stern's Modern Touch," *The New York Sun*, June 19, 2007, 19.
James Gardner, "A Modernist Revival," *The New York Sun*, January 8, 2008, 18.
Anthony Tommasini, "The Kaufman Center: Something New for Both Ear and Eye," *The New York Times*, January 10, 2008, E:3.
Justin Davidson, "Reconstructionist Judaism: Two Jewish Cultural Centers Reinvent Themselves for the Demographics of a Changing City," *New York*, January 14, 2008, 62-63.
Brian Wise, "Merkin Concert Hall Reopens," *Musical America*, January 14, 2008.
Barrymore Laurence Scherer, "Cause to Celebrate at Merkin Hall," *The Wall Street Journal*, February 19, 2008, D:6.
"Frozen Music," *Interior Design*, February 2008, 240.
David Barbour, "Grace Notes for the Kaufman Center," *Lighting and Sound America*, May 2008, 76-81.

North Instructional Building and Library
Bronx Community College, Bronx, New York

Partners: Augusta Barone, Alexander P. Lamis, Graham S. Wyatt. Project Senior Associates: Jeffery Povero, Dennis Sagiev. Project Assistants: David Abecassis, Tatyana Albinder, Natalie Goldberg, Zachary Heaps, William Holloway, Bruce Lindsay, Katherine LoBalbo, Erin Murphy, Alicia Reed, Michael Ryan, Dongju Seo,

Michael Tabacinic. Interior Design Assistant: Phillip Chan. Landscape Design Senior Associates: Kendra Taylor, Michael Weber. Landscape Design Project Manager: Joelle Byrer. Landscape Assistant: Noy Lamb. Associate Architect: Ismael Leyva Architects.

Christopher Gray, "Bronx Community College: Not What Stanford White Envisioned, but Notable," *The New York Times,* November 26, 2006, 11:9.

The Brompton
New York, New York

Partners: Michael D. Jones, Paul L. Whalen. Project Associate: David Winterton. Project Assistants: Moheb Abdelmaseeh, Aaron Boucher, Bryan Hale, Carlos Hurtado, Catie Liken, Camellia Tian. Interior Design Associates: John Boyland, Hyung Kee Lee. Interior Design Assistants: Lisa Koch, Mitra Moshari. Landscape Architect: Mathews Nielsen. Associate Architect: Ismael Leyva Architects.

James Gardner, "Reinventing East 86th Street," *The New York Sun,* February 28, 2006, 15.
Katherine Dykstra, "The Upper East Side Smackdown," *New York Post,* June 21, 2007.
Joseph Dobrian, "Manhattan's Newest Luxury Condos," *New York Living,* June 2007, 40-43.
Rosalie Genevro, "The Next New York," *The Architect's Newspaper,* August 1, 2007, 38-41.
Kate Pickert, "Feeling the Stern Effect: Raising the Bar—and Prices—Around the Country," *The Real Deal,* October 2007.
Melissa Dehncke-McGill, "The Tale of Two Upper East Sides," *The Real Deal,* December 2007, 1, 110.
James Gardner, "Pre-War Pastiche," *The New York Sun,* July 1, 2008, 11, 14.
"Exclusive First Look at Robert Stern's The Brompton as It Nears Completion," *World Architecture News,* March 4, 2009.

Barnett Residential Life Center
Florida Southern College, Lakeland, Florida

Partner: Alexander P. Lamis. Project Senior Associate: Jeffery Povero. Project Associates: Thomas Lewis, James Pearson, Salvador Peña-Figueroa. Project Manager: Susan Ryder. Project Assistants: Doreen Adengo, Sara Rubenstein.

Julia Crouse, "Famed Firm to Design FSC Dorms," *The Ledger,* January 5, 2006.
Amy L. Edwards, "Just the Right Touch," *Orlando Sentinel,* June 11, 2006.
Lloyd Jackson, "Frank Lloyd Wright's College of Tomorrow," *Home Miami,* June 2006, 92-97.
Sandra Dimsdale, "Moving in the Wright Direction," *The Ledger,* July 16, 2006.
Noah Bierman, "School Does Right by Architect Wright," *Miami Herald,* August 12, 2006.
Jennifer LeClaire, "Florida Southern College Begins Large-Scale Restoration of Wright Campus," *Architectural Record,* October 2006, 32.
Cary McMullen, "At Home With Frank Lloyd Wright: Wide Influence After 50 Years," *The Ledger,* April 5, 2009, A:1, 10-11.
Cary McMullen, "In Later Years, Wright Designed FSC Structures; 12 Were Built," *The Ledger,* April 5, 2009, A:11.
Zeynep Pamuk, "Wright: A Legend," *Yale Daily News,* April 7, 2009.
Gary White, "Not Wright, But Perfect: New Luxury Dorm Keeps With Design Standards," *The Ledger,* August 12, 2009, B:1.
Chris Sherman, "If Frank Lloyd Wright Built Your Dorm Room . . .," *Florida Trend,* August 18, 2009.
Lawrence Biemiller, "Florida Southern Opens a New Dorm in the Spirit of Frank Lloyd Wright," *The Chronicle of Higher Education,* August 24, 2009.

Christoverson Humanities Building
Florida Southern College, Lakeland, Florida

Partner: Alexander P. Lamis. Project Senior Associate: Jeffery Povero. Project Associate: James Pearson. Project Manager: Susan Ryder. Project Assistants: Doreen Adengo, Roland Sharpe Flores, Anthony Polito, Sara Rubenstein, Vanessa Sanchez. Associate Architect: Wallis, Murphey, Boyington.

"FSC Holds Groundbreaking for Christoverson Humanities Building," *Florida Southern College News,* October 24, 2007.

Long Wharf
Saint John, New Brunswick, Canada

Partners: Preston J. Gumberich, Graham S. Wyatt. Project Associate: Breen Mahony. Project Manager: Douglas Neri. Project Assistants: Daniel Arbelaez, Rebecca Atkin, Seher Aziz, Alexander Boardman, Danny Chiang, Jonas Goldberg, Natalie Goldberg, Anya Grant, Milton Hernandez, Emily Jones, Leonid Khanin, Nasung Kim, Ranjit Korah, Katherine LoBalbo, Victor Marcelino, Tehniyet Masood, Sho Okajima, Katherine Richardson, Sara Rubenstein, Nasheet Rumy, Jennifer Smith, Marek Turzynski, Bruce Yao, Charles Yoo. Interior Design Associate: Shannon Ratcliff. Interior Design Assistants: Phillip Chan, Jamie Murphy. Landscape Design Senior Associates: Kendra Taylor, Michael Weber. Landscape Design Project Manager: Mark Rodriguez. Landscape Design Assistants: Joelle Byrer, Lily Dong, Susie Grossman, Kevin Hasselwander, Meredith Lawton. Associate Architect: TOSS Solutions.

Josh O'Kane, "On the Waterfront," *Telegraph-Journal,* June 21, 2008, B:1.
Bruce Bartlett, "City Should 'Make It Happen'," *Telegraph-Journal,* June 21, 2008, B:1.
Josh O'Kane, "Long Wharf Project Could Mean $1 Million for City," *Telegraph-Journal,* June 21, 2008, B:3.
Andrew McGilligan, "ILA Slams Long Wharf Deal," *Telegraph-Journal,* June 21, 2008, B:3.
Josh O'Kane, "Politicians Call for Public Consultation on Proposal," *Telegraph-Journal,* June 21, 2008, B:3.
John Mazerolle, "Business Leaders Agree Decision Should Not Be Rushed," *Telegraph-Journal,* June 23, 2008, C:1.
Reid Southwick, "Rejecting Land Deal Would Send Wrong Message – Rocca," *Telegraph-Journal,* June 23, 2008, C:2.
Bruce Bartlett, "City Merchants Thrilled at Thought of Bustling Uptown," *Telegraph-Journal,* June 23, 2008, C:3.
Daniel Leblanc, "Irving Oil Wharf Deal Ruffles Port Workers," *The Globe and Mail,* August 13, 2008, B:2.

Miller Hall
The Mason School of Business, The College of William and Mary, Williamsburg, Virginia

Partners: Kevin M. Smith, Graham S. Wyatt. Project Manager: Lara Kailian. Project Assistants: Kanu Agrawal, Hee-Young Cho, Christopher Heim, Antonio Salvador, Saul Uranovsky. Interior Design Associate: Shannon Ratcliff. Interior Design Assistants: Michelle Everett, Sandra Fayadel, Sam Mason, Mitra Moshari. Landscape Architect: Ann P. Stokes Landscape Architects. Associate Architect: Moseley Architects.

John T. Wallace, "Building Unlimited Possibilities," *William & Mary Alumni Magazine,* Spring / Summer 2007, 26-27.

Resorts
Hvar, Croatia

Partners: Sargent C. Gardiner, Daniel Lobitz, Paul L. Whalen. Project Associate: Johnny Cruz.

"Velike Gradevine Hvaru ne Trebaju," *Slobodna Dalmacija,* April 26, 2006.

Our Lady of Mercy Chapel
Salve Regina University, Newport, Rhode Island

Partner: Grant F. Marani. Project Senior Associate: Charles Toothill. Project Associate: Goil Amornvivat. Project Assistants: Mario Cruzate, Kenneth Frank, Elle Lee, Megan St. Denis, Kayin Tse. Associate Architect: Richard Quinn.

"Salve Regina Community Gathering Wednesday to Bless Our Lady of Mercy Chapel Site," *Salve Today,* November 4, 2008.
"An Act of Faith: Our Lady of Mercy Chapel Fulfills a Long-Awaited Dream," *Report from Newport,* Spring 2009, 26-31.
Eve M. Kahn, "Art-Glass Luminaries Reunited for Exhibition," *The New York Times,* August 28, 2009, C:25.

The Harrison
New York, New York

Partners: Michael D. Jones, Paul L. Whalen. Project Manager: Carlos Hurtado. Project Assistants: Noel Angeles, Mario Cruzate, Russell Grant, Adele Lim, Seema Malik, Tad Roemer. Interior Design Associates: John Boyland, Hyung Kee Lee. Interior Design Assistants: Lisa Koch, Mitra Moshari. Landscape Architect: Mathews Nielsen. Associate Architect: Ismael Leyva Architects.

Christopher Faherty, "Advocates Try to Rein in Stable Destruction," *The New York Sun*, October 18, 2006, 2.
Thomas J. Lueck, "2 Former Stables on the Upper West Side Get Opposite Verdicts on Landmark Status," *The New York Times*, November 15, 2006, B:5.
Tom Wolfe, "The (Naked) City and the Undead," *The New York Times*, November 26, 2006, 4:10-11.
Joseph Dobrian, "Manhattan's Newest Luxury Condos," *New York Living*, June 2007, 40-43.
Christopher Gray, "The Architect Who Turned a Railroad Bridge on Its Head," *The New York Times*, July 1, 2007, 11:2.
Rosalie Genevro, "The Next New York," *The Architect's Newspaper*, August 1, 2007, 38-41.
J. Alex Tarquinio, "New Buildings That Embrace the Old," *The New York Times*, October 3, 2007, C:7.
Kate Pickert, "Feeling the Stern Effect: Raising the Bar—and Prices—Around the Country," *The Real Deal*, October 2007, 36.
"Related Cos.' the Harrison to Feature 132 LEED-Certified Residences," *Northeast Real Estate Business*, November 2007, 19.
"Luxe Living: An Evening at the American Museum of Natural History to Preview the Harrison," *Avenue*, November 2007, 40.
Suzanne Stephens, "Abstract Incarnations of Place," *Architectural Record*, August 2008, 76-81.
Robin Pogrebin, "Preservationists See Bulldozers Charging Through a Loophole," *The New York Times*, November 29, 2008, C:1, 5.
Robin Pogrebin, "Preservation and Development in a Dynamic Give and Take," *The New York Times*, December 2, 2008, C:1, 5.
James Gardner, "Paying Homage to Fit In: Robert Stern Extends Ode to Contextualism With the Harrison," *The Real Deal*, May 2009, 62, 90.

100 Montgomery Street
San Francisco, California

Partners: Meghan L. McDermott, Graham S. Wyatt. Project Managers: Grace Chang, Robie Wood. Project Assistants: Emilia Ferri, Milton Hernandez, Afzal Hossain, Victor Marcelino, Helen Tout, Marek Turzynski, Bruce Yao, Charles Yoo. Interior Design Associate: John Boyland. Interior Design Assistants: Phillip Chan, Jamie Murphy. Associate Architect: Kendall/Heaton Associates.

John King, "Updated 1955 Tower Respects the Past, Present," *San Francisco Chronicle*, April 7, 2009.

Villanova Heights
Riverdale, The Bronx, New York

Partner: Gary L. Brewer. Project Associate: Kevin Fitzgerald. Project Assistants: Kathleen Casanta, Clay Hayles, Robert Holub, Eunice Kim, Tae Kim, Maryann Kril, Tin Yiu Lo, David Rinehart, Greg Shue, Winnie Yen. Landscape Design Senior Associates: Kendra Taylor, Michael Weber. Landscape Design Project Managers: Joelle Byrer, Susie Grossman. Associate Architect: Li Architect Associates.

Joshua Payne, "Board Grill's Chapel Farm's Developer," *The Riverdale Press*, February 8, 2007.
Max Gross, "A Bronx 'Dale," *New York Post*, July 1, 2008.
N. Clark Judd, "Developer Seeks Buyers for High-End Homes," *The Riverdale Press*, December 25, 2008.
Amy Rowland, "Smile When You Call Them McMansions," *The New York Times*, June 7, 2009, Real Estate:11.
Kevin Deutsch, "Builder Has Big Hopes for Big Houses: Villanova Heights Goes on Sale at Last," *The Riverdale Press*, June 18, 2009.

Superior Ink
New York, New York

Partners: Michael D. Jones, Paul L. Whalen. Project Manager: Robert HuDock. Project Assistants: Aaron Boucher, Adrian Coleman, Clarisa Diaz, Stuart Johnson, Michael Leocata, Ulises Liceaga, Chenhuan Liao, David Nguyen, Kurt Roessler, Russell Grant. Interior Designer: Yabu Pushelberg. Associate Architect: Ismael Levya Architects.

S. Jhoanna Robledo and Rebecca Milzoff, "The Next . . . Celebrity-Magnet Condo," *New York*, September 3–10, 2007, 160.
Steve Cutler, "Downtown Buildings," *New York Living*, September 2007, 46-49.
Kate Pickert, "Feeling the Stern Effect: Raising the Bar—and Prices—Around the Country," *The Real Deal*, October 2007, 36.
Jason Sheftell, "Village People: Do Modern Buildings Threaten the West Village's Historic Charm or Enhance Its Design Heritage?" *New York Daily News*, December 7, 2007, "Your Home":4-5.
Kate Pickert, "Mixing Townhouses With Towers: A Popular Combo Provides Residents With More Amenities and Services," *The Real Deal*, December 2007, 78.
Richard Staub, "From Villain to Hero," *Oculus*, Winter 2007 / 2008, 32-33.
"Superior Ink Condominiums and Townhouses," *New York Living*, April 2008, 20-21.
"Sophia Salaman Chooses the Best Merchandise and Events Worldwide," *The World of Interiors*, July 2008, 54.
"The Dean: Architect Robert A. M. Stern Is a Classicist Who Defies Classicism," *New York Spaces*, October 2008, 28.
"Superior Living," *Avenue*, November 2008, 138.
Robin Pogrebin, "Preservation and Development in a Dynamic Give and Take," *The New York Times*, December 2, 2008, C:1, 5.
David Kaufman, "The Old New: The Latest Residential Projects in Manhattan Are Clad in Prewar-Style Limestone, Granite, and Brick," *Financial Times*, April 18–19, 2009, 4.
Alison Gregor, "A New Personality for West 12th Street," *The New York Times*, May 17, 2009, Real Estate:8.
Candace Taylor, "The Closing: Robert A. M. Stern," *The Real Deal*, May 29, 2009.

Berwyn Residences
Berwyn, Pennsylvania

Partner: Graham S. Wyatt. Project Associates: Breen Mahony, Jack Robbins. Project Assistants: Dennis George, Natalie Goldberg, Katherine LoBalbo, Marek Turzynski, Bruce Yao.

Natalie Kostelni, "Berwyn Plan Would Replace Housing," *Philadelphia Business Journal*, June 30, 2006.

Ritz-Carlton Hotel and Residences
Almaty, Kazakhstan

Partners: Grant F. Marani, Meghan McDermott. Project Senior Associate: Charles Toothill. Project Associate: Goil Amornvivat. Project Assistants: Doreen Adengo, Lorjan Agalliu, Seher Aziz, Katarina Carlin, Thomas DiNatale , Alena Kereshun, Dylan Kuo, Anthony Polito, Jack Robbins, Nasheet Rumy, Matthew Schaefer, Yoko Suzuki. Interior Design Associates: John Boyland, Shannon Ratcliff. Interior Design Assistant: Lisa Koch. Landscape Design Senior Associate: Kendra Taylor. Landscape Design Assistants: Joelle Byrer, Daniel Evans. Associate Architect: Kazgor Design Academy, MAER and Partners.

Yekaterina Panchenko, "American Architect Held Master Class in Almaty," *Kazinform*, November 23, 2006.
Alec Appelbaum, "Kazakhstan: New Architecture Reflects Rising Prosperity," *Eurasia Insight*, July 20, 2007.
Candace Jackson, "The Search for the Next Hot Spot," *The Wall Street Journal*, August 18-19, 2007, P:1, 6-7.
Alec Appelbaum, "New Kids on the Bloc," *The Architect's Newspaper*, October 3, 2007, 21-23.

Ritz-Carlton Hotel and Residences
Astana, Kazakhstan

Partners: Grant F. Marani, Meghan L. McDermott. Project Associate: Rosa Maria Colina. Project Assistants: Lorjan Agalliu, Maya Akeho, Vivian Au, Mario Cruzate,

Anthony Goldsby, Susan Law, Mako Maeno, Sho Okajima, Sung Park, Nasheet Rumy, Matthew Schaefer, Veronica Varella, Albert Yadao, Bruce Yao. Interior Designer: Peter Silling Limited. Associate Architect: Design Group.

Candace Jackson, "The Search for the Next Hot Spot," *The Wall Street Journal,* August 18–19, 2007, P:1, 6-7.

Residence
Saint John, New Brunswick, Canada

Partner: Roger H. Seifter. Project Associate: David Solomon. Project Assistants: Laura Lisa DeLashmet, Todd Sullivan. Interior Design Associate: Ken Stuckenschneider. Interior Design Assistant: Michelle Everett.

Venus Rock
Paphos, Cyprus

Partners: Daniel Lobitz, Paul L. Whalen. Project Manager: Miyun Kang. Project Assistants: Joshua Barkan, Gerard Beekman, Alexander Boardman, Edward Hsu, Dylan Kuo, Franklin Nunez, Jin Park, Benjamin Salling, Daniel Siegel, Raymond Sih. Associate Architect: UDS.

Gwenda Brophy, "Swing-time in Cyprus," *Financial Times,* June 7, 2008.

Greenberg Conference Center
Yale University, New Haven, Connecticut

Partner: Graham S. Wyatt. Project Senior Associates: Jeffery Povero, Dennis Sagiev, Jennifer Stone. Project Assistants: Jennifer Bailey, Maria Gonzalez, Bram Janaitis, Lara Kailian, Brendan Lee, Tehniyet Masood, Wendy Yeung, Charles Yoo. Interior Design Associate: Shannon Ratcliff. Interior Design Assistant: Tina Hu. Landscape Design Senior Associates: Kendra Taylor, Michael Weber. Landscape Design Assistants: Daniel Evans, Demetrios Staurinos.

Ilana Seager, "May Opening for Stern Project," *Yale Daily News,* January 28, 2009, 3. Paul Needham, "Short on Details, but Big on Value," *Yale Daily News,* September 29, 2009, 1, 4.

Mas Fleuri
Saint-Jean-Cap-Ferrat, France

Partner: Grant F. Marani. Project Associate: Rosa Maria Colina. Project Assistants: Lauren Bollettino, Brian Fell, Peter Lombardi-Krieps, Esther Park. Interior Design Associate: John Boyland. Interior Design Assistants: Alexandra Rolland, Aruni Weerasinghe. Landscape Design Senior Associate: Kendra Taylor. Landscape Design Assistant: Meredith Lawton. Associate Architect: Lino Barone / Studio Laura Tibald.

Shir Hadash Center for Jewish Life
German Colony, Jerusalem, Israel

Partner: Alexander P. Lamis. Project Associate: Salvador Peña-Figueroa. Project Manager: Sara Rubenstein. Project Assistant: Vanessa Sanchez.

Residences at Albany Marina
New Providence, The Bahamas

Partner: Paul L. Whalen. Project Senior Associate: Michael D. Jones. Project Manager: Miyun Kang. Project Assistants: Kohilam Chandrahasan, David Nguyen, Jonathan Pettibone, Benjamin Salling. Landscape Senior Associate: Michael Weber. Landscape Design Assistants: Terrie Gamble, Kevin Hasselwander, Noy Lamb, Mark Rodriguez. Associate Architect: HKS.

Nick Kaye, "Breaking Ground: Albany," *The New York Times,* February 27, 2009, D:6.

Silo Ridge
Amenia, New York

Partners: Daniel Lobitz, Paul L. Whalen. Project Senior Associate: Joel Mendelson. Project Associate: Johnny Cruz. Project Managers: Gaylin Bowie, Bryan Hale. Project Assistants: Saul Hayutin, Robert HuDock, Kleber Salas, Benjamin Salling. Landscape Design Senior Associate: Kendra Taylor. Landscape Design

Project Manager: Joelle Byrer. Landscape Design Assistants: Susie Grossman, Kevin Hasselwander, Noy Lamb, Demetrios Staurinos. Land Planner: Chazen Engineering and Land Surveying.

Darryl Gangloff, "Silo Ridge Design Concepts Presented," *Harlem Valley Times,* July 6, 2007.

Pequot Library
Southport, Connecticut

Partner: Alexander P. Lamis. Project Senior Associate: Julie Nymann. Project Associate: James Pearson. Project Assistants: Caroline Graf Statile, Vanessa Sanchez, Addie Suchorab. Landscape Design Senior Associate: Michael Weber.

Robert A. M. Stern: Buildings and Projects 1999–2003 (New York: The Monacelli Press, 2003), 568.

50 Connaught Road
Hong Kong, China

Partners: Daniel Lobitz, Paul L. Whalen. Project Senior Associate: Hernán Chebar. Project Associate: David Winterton. Project Assistants: Armando Amaral, Joshua Barkan, Franklin Nunez, Jin Park, Camellia Tian. Associate Architect: Aedas.

Crown Heights High School
Brooklyn, New York

Partners: Augusta Barone, Melissa DelVecchio, Graham S. Wyatt. Project Senior Associate: Dennis Sagiev. Project Assistants: Jennifer Bailey, Timothy Carroll, Kathryn Everett, Natalie Goldberg, Isabel Gonzalez, Jennifer Lee, Tehniyet Masood, Anthony McConnell, Michael Ryan, William West. Associate Architect: Gensler.

Sophie Brickman, "Brand New Uncommon High School Building to Open in 2010," *Uncommon Schools E-Newsletter,* January 2008.

Four Seasons Downtown Hotel and Private Residences at 30 Park Place
New York, New York

Partners: Sargent C. Gardiner, Daniel Lobitz, Paul L. Whalen. Project Associates: Johnny Cruz, Mike Soriano. Project Assistants: David Abecassis, Adrian Coleman, Saul Hayutin, Scott Hines, Rebecca Morgan, David Nguyen, Jonathan Palmer-Hoffman, Tad Roemer, Kurt Roessler, Roberto Rossi, Kleber Salas, Benjamin Salling, Heather Spigner, Hilary Tate. Interior Design Associate: John Boyland. Interior Design Assistant: Marissa Savarese. Landscape Architect: Lee Weintraub Landscape Architecture. Associate Architect: SLCE Architects.

David M. Levitt, "Silverstein Picks Stern to Design Manhattan Tower," *Bloomberg,* October 15, 2007.
Bradley Hope, "Silverstein Is Going Upscale Downtown," *The New York Sun,* October 15, 2007, 1, 3.
Max Abelson, "A Legend Comes Clean: Architect Robert A. M. Stern on 15 CPW, 99 Church, and George W. Bush," *The New York Observer,* October 29, 2007, 37, 42.
"Silverstein Gets Stern Look," *The Architect's Newspaper,* October 31, 2007, 20.
Robin Pogrebin, "Building Respect at Yale," *The New York Times,* December 16, 2007, Arts & Leisure:1, 38.
Jill Priluck, "The Ralph Lauren of Architecture," *The New York Sun,* January 10, 2008, 14.
Tom Acitelli, "Silverstein to Unveil Stern's 99 Church Design," *The New York Observer,* January 25, 2008.
Eliot Brown, "Larry Loves 'Em Large," *The New York Observer,* January 29, 2008.
Peter Slatin, "The Four Seasons of Silverstein," *The Slatin Report,* January 29, 2008.
Tom Topousis, "Four Seasons Plans 80-Story Tower," *New York Post,* January 30, 2008, 12.
Peter Kiefer, "City's Tallest Residential Tower Planned for Church Street," *The New York Sun,* January 30, 2008, 4.
Douglas Feiden, "Livin' High Life: The City's Tallest Apt. Tower Planned," *New York Daily News,* January 30, 2008.

"A Wall Street Classic: Silverstein Properties Unveil Stern-Designed Tower at Ground Zero," *World Architecture News,* January 31, 2008.

Bradley Hope, "Living the Highest Life," *The New York Sun,* February 14, 2008, 11, 13.

Francis Morrone, "At Home Among the Clouds," *The New York Sun,* February 14, 2008, 11, 13.

Aaron Seward, "A Tall Order," *The Architect's Newspaper,* February 20, 2008, 6.

James Murdock, "Stern's 99 Church Street to Soar Near WTC Site," *Architectural Record,* March 2008, 29.

Terry Pristin, "The Optimistic (and Long) View of Larry A. Silverstein," *The New York Times,* May 14, 2008, C:8.

Philip Herrera, "Bob the Builder: Why Robert A. M. Stern, Formerly Dismissed as Old-Fashioned, Might Just Be the Architect of the Moment," *Town & Country,* May 2008, 107-8, 110, 112, 114.

Avihu Kadosh, "My God! I'm Going to Leave a Phallic Mark on the City," *Calcalist,* September 9, 2008, 28-29.

"Stern para Silverstein, el más alto de Manhattan," *Arquitectura Viva,* 120 (2008): 13.

Steve Cuozzo, "Silver Lining for 99 Church Street," *New York Post,* March 31, 2009, 28.

Tour Carpe Diem
La Défense, Courbevoie, France

Partners: Meghan L. McDermott, Kevin M. Smith, Graham S. Wyatt. Project Associate: Fred Berthelot. Project Manager: Renaud Magnaval. Project Assistants: Rebecca Atkin, Anya Grant, Milton Hernandez, Trevor Laubenstein, Douglas Neri, Kaveri Singh, Charles Yoo, Young Jin Yoon. Associate Architect: SRA Architects.

Paul Petrunia, "Stern Selected for Tour Carpe Diem, an Environmentally Responsible Office Tower at La Défense," *Archinect,* January 11, 2008.

"Stern Seizes the Day: Tour Carpe Diem by Robert A. M. Stern Architects," *ArchNewsNow,* January 18, 2008.

"Paris Win for Stern," *World Architecture News,* January 26, 2008.

Aaron Seward, "Vive La Stern: American Architect's Tower Chosen to Rise in Paris," *The Architect's Newspaper,* February 6, 2008, 1, 10.

"Stern Architects sélectionnés pour la Tour Carpe Diem à La Défense," *Le Moniteur,* February 13, 2008.

Kim A. O'Connell, "The French Connection: Designers of a Parisian Skyscraper Hope to Exceed French Green-Building Standards," *eco-structure,* June 2008, 43-46.

Michèle Trimont, "La Défense Pushes Sustainability: Robert A. M. Stern Wins Paris Highrise Competition," *Competitions,* Spring 2008, 28-35.

Hélène Bédon-Rouanet, "3 questions à Joëlle Chauvin, Directeur Immobilier du Groupe Aviva France," *Le Figaro,* July 7, 2008, 30.

Alexander Gorlin, "And the Band Played On: Forget the Film Festival—the Gaudiest Display of Power and Money in Cannes Involves Real Estate," *Metropolis,* September 2008, 102, 104, 106.

Christophe Leray, "La Tour Carpe Diem s'inscrit de manière singulière à La Défense," *Cyber Archi,* March 23, 2009.

Hancock Technology Center
Marist College, Poughkeepsie, New York

Partners: Kevin M. Smith, Graham S. Wyatt. Project Associate: Fred Berthelot. Project Manager: Bram Janaitis. Project Assistants: Noel Angeles, Rebecca Atkin, Matthew Blumenthal, Isabel Gonzalez, Celeste Hall, Christopher Heim, Silas Jeffrey, Seema Malik, Ian Mills, Michael Ryan, Dongju Seo. Interior Design Project Manager: Phillip Chan. Interior Design Assistant: Tina Hu. Landscape Design Senior Associate: Kendra Taylor. Landscape Design Project Manager: Mark Rodriguez. Landscape Design Assistants: Joelle Byrer, Meredith Lawton, Demetrios Staurinos.

"Ahead of the Curve: The Hancock Technology Center," *Marist,* Fall 2008, 7-13.

"Ground Is Broken on Hancock Center," *Marist,* Summer 2009, 8.

McCann Center
Marist College, Poughkeepsie, New York

Partners: Kevin M. Smith, Graham S. Wyatt. Project Associate: Fred Berthelot. Project Assistant: Rebecca Morgan, Michael Ryan, Antonio Salvador. Interior Design Project Manager: Phillip Chan. Interior Design Assistant: Tina Hu. Associate Architect: Hastings + Chivetta.

Tenth Square
New Haven, Connecticut

Partners: Michael D. Jones, Paul L. Whalen. Project Associate: Bina Bhattacharyya. Project Assistants: Brian Fell, Bryan Hale, Carlos Hurtado, Adele Lim, Amneris Rasuk.

Andrew Mangino, "Will Downtown Grow to Ten Squares?" *New Haven Independent,* June 17, 2008.

Leonard Honeyman, "Newman's Out; Stern, Pelli Remain," *New Haven Independent,* August 12, 2008.

Eric Gershon, "Developers Northland, Archstone Have Plans for New Haven Site," *Hartford Courant,* August 19, 2008.

Victor Zapana, "Future for Coliseum Site: Stern or Pelli?" *Yale Daily News,* September 5, 2008.

"Northland Chosen to Develop Coliseum Site," *The New Haven Register,* September 12, 2008.

Martine Powers and Victor Zapana, "A 10th Square?" *Yale Daily News,* September 12, 2008, 1, 5.

Paul Zeng, "At Old Coliseum Site, Locals Buzz," *Yale Daily News,* September 17, 2008, 3.

Nicolas Niarchos, "Developers Aim for '10th Square' to Fit Right In," *Yale Daily News,* September 23, 2008, 9.

Sarah Nutman, "Building Blocks: New Haven Models New Development on an Old Urban Ideal," *The New Journal: The Magazine About Yale and New Haven,* October 2008, 12-16.

New College House
Franklin & Marshall College, Lancaster, Pennsylvania

Partners: Preston J. Gumberich, Graham S. Wyatt. Project Associate: George Punnoose. Project Manager: Sean Foley. Project Assistants: George de Brigard, Kevin Fitzgerald, Melanie Fox, Milton Hernandez, Jennifer Lee, Thomas Lewis, Sung Chan Park, David Rinehart, Mike Soriano, Rosalind Tsang, Young Jin Yoon. Interior Design Associate: Shannon Ratcliff. Interior Design Assistants: Phillip Chan, Sandra Fadayel, Ann Johnson.

Jennifer Todd, "Planners OK Dorms at F&M," *(Lancaster) Intelligencer Journal,* February 19, 2009, B:1.

Caruthers Biotechnology Building
University of Colorado at Boulder, Boulder, Colorado

Partners: Sargent C. Gardiner, Paul L. Whalen. Project Associates: Bina Bhattacharyya, Johnny Cruz, Paul Zembsch. Project Manager: Bryan Hale. Project Assistants: Armando Amaral, Joshua Barkan, Adrian Coleman, Nikki Hartle, Jonathan Palmer-Hoffman, Amneris Rasuk, Tad Roemer, Kleber Salas, Raymond Sih. Associate Architect: HDR.

"CU to Celebrate Groundbreaking of World-Class Biotechnology Facility," *Colorado (University of Colorado at Boulder News Center),* September 3, 2009.

Ryan Dionne, "CU Bioscience Building Breaks Ground," *Boulder County Business Report,* September 18, 2009.

Classical Opera and Ballet Theater
Astana, Kazakhstan

Partners: Gary L. Brewer, Michael D. Jones, Grant F. Marani. Project Assistants: Lorjan Agalliu, Kathleen Casanta, Mario Cruzate, Nicholas DeRosa, Thomas DiNatale, Hussam Jallad, Bruce Lindsay, Yoko Suzuki.

George W. Bush Presidential Center
Southern Methodist University, Dallas, Texas

Partners: Augusta Barone, Alexander P. Lamis, Graham S. Wyatt. Project Architect: James Pearson. Project Senior Associates: Jennifer Stone, Charles Toothill. Project Associate: Thomas Lewis, Salvador Peña-Figueroa. Project Assistants: David Abecassis, Seher Aziz, Jennifer Bailey, Elizabeth Bondaryk,

Seth Burney, Deirdre Cerminaro, Mario Cruzate, Megan Fullagar, Anya Grant, Ruth Irving, Hussam Jallad, Bradley Jones, Emily Jones, Kathryn Lenehan, Bruce Lindsay, Peter Lombardi-Krieps, Victor Marcelino, Mary Martinich, Anthony McConnell, Wing Yee Ng Fung, Jung-Yoon Park, William Perez, Susan Ryder, Karen Rizvi, Vanessa Sanchez, Jessica Saniewski, Daniel Siegel, Heather Spigner, Addie Suchorab, Albert Yadao. Interior Design Assistant: Phillip Chan. Landscape Design Assistants: Susie Grossman, David Weissman. Landscape Architect: Michael Van Valkenburgh Associates.

David Dillon, "Bush Library Architect Selection Begins," *Architectural Record,* August 2007, 42.

"Architect Chosen for Bush Library," *The New York Times,* August 29, 2007, A:16.

"Stern's Firm Will Design Bush Library at Southern Methodist U." *The Chronicle of Higher Education,* August 28, 2007.

Brendan McKenna, "Bush Library Design Firm Chosen," *The Dallas Morning News,* August 29, 2007.

Dave Montgomery, "Famed N.Y. Architect Picked to Design Bush Library," *(Fort Worth) Star-Telegram,* August 29, 2007.

Mark Norris, "Architect Selected for Bush Library Project," *SMU Daily Campus,* August 29, 2007.

David Dillon, "Stern to Design Bush Presidential Library," *Architectural Record,* August 29, 2007.

Rachel Boyd, "Architecture Dean to Design Bush Library," *Yale Daily News,* August 31, 2007, 5.

Cathleen McGuigan, "Picking the President's Architect," *Newsweek,* September 6, 2007.

Sarah Williams Goldhagen, "Bush's Architect Is a Perfect Match for His Presidency," *The New Republic,* September 7, 2007.

Alan G. Brake, "Stern in the Bush League," *The Architect's Newspaper,* September 19, 2007, 1, 5.

Max Abelson, "A Legend Comes Clean: Architect Robert A. M. Stern on 15 CPW, 99 Church, and George W. Bush," *The New York Observer,* October 29, 2007, 37, 42.

John Gendall, " 'No Bombast or Boredom' for Bush Library, Stern Says," *Architect,* October 2007, 16.

David Dillon, "News Briefs," *Architectural Record,* October 2007, 57.

"NYC's Stern to Design Bush Library," *Texas Architect,* November / December 2007, 14.

Scott Carlson, "The Back-of-the-Envelope Design Contest," *The Chronicle of Higher Education,* March 7, 2008, B: cover, 14-15.

Brendan McKenna, "PRD Group to Shape Legacy at George W. Bush Presidential Library," *The Dallas Morning News,* March 14, 2008.

Philip Herrera, "Bob the Builder: Why Robert A. M. Stern, Formerly Dismissed as Old-Fashioned, Might Just Be the Architect of the Moment," *Town & Country,* May 2008, 107-8, 110, 112, 114.

Leonard Kniffel, "First Lady Laura Bush Reveals Post-White House Agenda," *American Libraries,* May 2008, 18-19.

Ned Cramer, "People Who Design Glass Houses ....," *Architect,* May 2008, 16.

Robin Pogrebin, "I'm the Designer. My Client's the Autocrat," *The New York Times,* June 22, 2008, Arts & Leisure:1, 25.

William Hanley, "Newsmaker: Robert A. M. Stern," *Architectural Record,* August 2008.

Dan Stewart, "Robert Stern: Designing Dubya's Library," *Building,* November 7, 2008.

"Ubiquitous," *The Chronicle of Higher Education,* November 14, 2008, A:3.

Lori Stahl, "Bush Library, Freedom Institute to Share Building at SMU," *The Dallas Morning News,* January 10, 2009.

New Residential Colleges
Yale University, New Haven, Connecticut

Partners: Melissa DelVecchio, Graham S. Wyatt. Project Senior Associates: Kurt Glauber, Jennifer Stone. Project Assistants: Rebecca Atkin, Jennifer Bailey, Alexander Boardman, Gary L. Brewer, Kathleen Casanta, Yolanda Cheung, George de Brigard, Preston J. Gumberich, Clay Hayles, Milton Hernandez, Lara Kailian, Jonathan Kelly, Mia Gorretti Layco, Kathryn Lenehan, Tin Yiu Lo, Christopher McIntire, George Punnoose, William West, Young Jin Yoon. Landscape Architect: Olin.

Thomas Kaplan, "Stern to Design New Colleges," *Yale Daily News,* September 4, 2008.

C.J. Hughes, "Yale Taps Stern for Major Project," *Architectural Record,* September 4, 2008.

Lawrence Biemiller, "Stern Will Design 2 New Residential Colleges, Yale U. Says," *The Chronicle of Higher Education,* September 4, 2008.

Robin Pogrebin, "New Buildings for Yale," *The New York Times,* September 5, 2008, E:5.

Nora Wessel, "Stern Pick Incites Debate," *Yale Daily News,* September 5, 2008.

"News' View: Eli Aesthetic Renders Stern Best for Job," *Yale Daily News,* September 5, 2008.

Nathan Harden, "Stern Offers Elegance Over Absurdity," *Yale Daily News,* September 8, 2008.

"Architecture Dean to Design New Colleges," *Yale Bulletin & Calendar,* September 12, 2008, 1-2.

Thomas Kaplan, "Fourteen Colleges: Design Allows for 850 Elis," *Yale Daily News,* September 12, 2008, 1, 6.

Ryan Caro, "Stern Should Trade Luxury for Novelty," *Yale Daily News,* September 15, 2008.

Paul Needham, "For New Colleges, Stern Prepped at the Taft School," *Yale Daily News,* September 24, 2008.

Isaac Arnsdorf, "Stern Shares Vision on Nos. 13, 14," *Yale Daily News,* October 30, 2008, 1, 4.

C.J. Hughes, "Yale University Has Turned Within Its Own Ranks," *Architectural Record,* October 2008, 47.

Sarah Nutman, "Building Blocks: New Haven Models New Development on an Old Urban Ideal," *The New Journal: The Magazine About Yale and New Haven,* October 2008, 12-16.

"In Stern We Trust," *Yale Daily News,* November 13, 2008.

"Ubiquitous," *The Chronicle of Higher Education,* November 14, 2008, A:3.

Witold Rybczynski, "When Buildings Try Too Hard," *The Wall Street Journal,* November 22–23, 2008, W:1, 3.

Isaac Arnsdorf and Paul Needham, "New Colleges Delayed: A Decade's Work Derailed," *Yale Daily News,* February 25, 2009, 1, 4.

Paul Needham, "The Architecture of Richard Levin: Levin Works to Restore a Crumbling Campus and Add New Gems," *Yale Daily News,* April 16, 2009, 1, 8-9.

Isaac Arnsdorf, "College Planning Continues," *Yale Daily News,* April 16, 2009, 3.

Paul Needham, "Drawings Give First Look at New Colleges," *Yale Daily News,* May 13, 2009.

R.J. O'Hara, "Sketches of Yale's New Residential Colleges," *Collegiate Way,* May 13, 2009.

Carole Bass, "New Colleges Will Be Gothic, Sketches Reveal," *Yale Alumni Magazine,* May 15, 2009.

Esther Zuckerman, "Construction Continues at Yale," *Yale Daily News,* May 25, 2009, 9.

Candace Taylor, "The Closing: Robert A. M. Stern," *The Real Deal,* May 29, 2009.

Jay Dockendorf, "Stern Unveils Models of New Colleges," *Yale Daily News,* May 29, 2009.

Dorie Baker, "New Colleges Designed to Be 'Bridge' Between Campuses," *Yale Bulletin & Calendar,* June 12, 2009, 1, 3.

Duo Dickinson, "New Colleges' Homage to Gothic Style Adds to Yale 'Brand,' " *The New Haven Register,* June 29, 2009.

Carole Bass, "Preservationists Object to Plan for New Colleges," *Yale Alumni Magazine,* July 7, 2009.

Mark Alden Branch, "New Colleges Aim to Match the Old," *Yale Alumni Magazine,* July / August 2009, 12.

Philip Langdon, "New College Plans Razing a Fuss at Yale," *Hartford Courant,* September 6, 2009.

ADDITIONAL PROJECTS

Santa Monica UCLA Medical Center / Orthopaedic Hospital Replacement Project
Santa Monica, California

Partner: Paul L. Whalen. Project Associates: Johnny Cruz, Diane Burkin. Project Assistants: Bina Bhattacharyya, Carmen Gonzalez, Sara Ridenour. Interior

Design Associate: Kathleen Mancini-Ferrigno. Landscape Architect: Pamela Burton & Company. Associate Architect: CO Architects (formerly Anshen + Allen Los Angeles).

Robert A. M. Stern: Buildings and Projects 1999–2003 (New York: The Monacelli Press, 2003), 560.

55 Railroad Avenue
Greenwich, Connecticut

Partner: Graham S. Wyatt. Project Senior Associate: Adam Anuszkiewicz. Project Managers: Gregory Christopher, Thomas Salazar. Project Assistants: Jennifer Berlly, Fred Berthelot, Marcus Carter, Enid De Gracia, John Ellis, Qu Kim, Jack Robbins, Corina Rugeroni, Ahmad-ali Sarder-Afkhami. Landscape Design Associate: Marsh Kriplen. Landscape Design Project Manager: Michael Weber. Landscape Design Assistant: Christina Belton.

Peter Healy, "Railroad Ave. Building Gets Makeover," Greenwich Time, January 8, 2002, B:7, 8.
"NOP's 55 Railroad Avenue Gets Remade, Remarketed," Hinesight, January / March 2002, 4.
Sana Siwolop, "Greenwich Offices, and Rents, Are Sprucing Up," The New York Times June 5, 2002, C:5.
"Hines, CalPERS Upgrade Asset," Real Estate Forum, May 2002, 28.
Robert A. M. Stern: Buildings and Projects 1999–2003 (New York: The Monacelli Press, 2003), 568.
"Arts Council Selects Buildings for Architecture Awards," Greenwich Time, May 26, 2006, C:8.

Residence
Atherton, California

Partner: Roger H. Seifter. Project Manager: Glenn Albrecht.

Office Building
Centre du Val d'Europe, Marne-la-Vallée, France

Partner: Paul L. Whalen. Project Senior Assistant: Kevin O'Connor. Project Assistant: Evanthia Dova. Associate Architect: Inter Faces.

Robert A. M. Stern: Buildings and Projects 1999–2003 (New York: The Monacelli Press, 2003), 569.
David Rothnie, "Liberté, Liquidité, Diversité," Urban Land Europe, Winter 2003, 38.

Residence
Bristol, Virginia

Partner: Roger H. Seifter. Project Associate: Victoria Baran.

Middle School and Gymnasium, Madison Country Day School
Waunakee, Wisconsin

Partner: Gary L. Brewer. Project Assistant: Anthony Goldsby. Landscape Architect: Ken Sail Design.

Cube-Is-Mmm

Project Manager: Nancy Thiel.

Chee Pearlman, "Creations in the Cake Pan," The New York Times, June 12, 2003, F:7.
"Cakes for a Cause," Architectural Record, June 2003, 42.
Emilie W. Sommerhoff, "It Took So Long to Bake It . . ." Architecture, July 2003, 16.

Lyons View Gardens
Knoxville, Tennessee

Partner: Gary L. Brewer. Project Senior Associate: Julie Nymann. Project Assistant: Kayin Tse. Landscape Architect: Ryan Gainey & Company.

Amy McRary, "Growing the Gardens," Knoxville News Sentinel, June 15, 2003.

Grumble Knot
Meredith, New Hampshire

Partner: Graham S. Wyatt. Project Assistant: Mark Haladyna. Associate Architect: Pinnacle Hill Architects.

Kensington Manor
Bronxville, New York

Partners: Daniel Lobitz, Paul L. Whalen. Project Senior Associate: Hernán Chebar.

Lakefields
Michigan

Partner: Roger H. Seifter. Project Associates: Jacob Morrison, Josh Bull. Project Assistants: Joshua Coleman, Troy Curry, Henry Gunawan, Thomas Hickey, David Solomon, Daniel Wolfskehl. Landscape Architect: Ann P. Stokes Landscape Architects.

Residence in Tulsa
Tulsa, Oklahoma

Partner: Randy M. Correll. Project Associate: Pamela McGirr. Project Assistant: Holly Zeiler. Landscape Design Project Manager: Michael Weber. Landscape Design Senior Assistant: Ashley Christopher.

Working Dog's Weekend House

Partner: Daniel Lobitz. Project Assistants: Matt Casey, Carlos Hurtado, Colin Martin. Interior Design Associate: Ken Stuckenschneider.

Birdhouse, Litchfield Historical Society

Partner: Daniel Lobitz.

Street Furniture for JCDecaux

Partner: Daniel Lobitz. Project Assistant: Gemma Kim.

"Outdoor-Ad Company to Bid on Contract in New York City," The Wall Street Journal, March 20, 2004, A:12.

The Houses at Greenwich Armory
Greenwich, Connecticut

Partners: Graham S. Wyatt. Project Senior Associates: Jonas Goldberg, Jeffery Povero. Project Associate: Fred Berthelot. Project Assistants: Tatyana Albinder, Noel Angeles, Matthew Blumenthal, Melanie Domino, Kathryn Lenehan, Anthony McConnell, Jennifer Smith. Landscape Design Senior Associate: Michael Weber. Landscape Design Senior Assistant: Mark Rodriguez. Landscape Design Assistant: Susie Grossman.

Hoa Nguyen, "Old-Style Armory Slated for High-Style Makeover," Greenwich Time, May 17, 2006.
Hoa Nguyen, "Geothermal System Slated for Armory Complex," Greenwich Time, July 19, 2007, A:1, 4.
"Deeds and Don'ts: Connecticut Report," Hamptons Cottages and Gardens, July 1–15, 2008, 98, 102, 104.

School of Business and Technology
Webster University, Webster Groves, Missouri

Partner: Kevin M. Smith. Project Associate: Sue Jin Sung. Project Assistants: Daniel Arbelaez, Leo Khanin, Eric Silinsh, Michael Tabacinic, Saul Uranovsky. Interior Design Associates: Hyung Kee Lee, Ken Stuckenschneider. Associate Architect: Mackey Mitchell Associates.

World Expo 2010
Shanghai, China

Partners: Grant F. Marani. Project Associates: Goil Amornvivat, Paul Zembsch. Project Assistants: Marcus Carter, Oliver Pelle. Landscape Architect: Hargreaves Associates. Associate Architect: Frederic Schwartz Architects.

"Winners All," *e-Oculus*, December 3, 2004, 7.
G. Stanley Collyer, "Frederick Schwartz," *Competitions*, Spring 2006, cover, 42-51.

Residential Development at Reston Town Center
Reston, Virginia

Partner: Daniel Lobitz. Project Associates: Gaylin Bowie, Mike Soriano. Project Assistants: Kanu Agrawal, Roberto Burneo, Russell Grant, Kurt Roessler. Interior Design Associate: Hyung Kee Lee. Landscape Architect: Urban Engineering & Associates. Associate Architect: WDG.

Alan Ward, ed., *Reston Town Center: A Downtown for the 21ˢᵗ Century* (Washington, DC: Academy Press, 2006), vi-vii, 1-3, 170-77, 203.
Philip Langdon, "Reston Town Center: A Downtown for the 21ˢᵗ Century?" *New Urban News*, October / November 2006, 2-3.

Science and Engineering Quad 2, Stanford University
Palo Alto, California

Partners: Preston J. Gumberich, Kevin M. Smith, Graham S. Wyatt. Project Associate: Fred Berthelot. Project Assistant: Sue Jin Sung.

East River Park Showboat, NYC 2012 Cultural Olympics

Partner: Grant F. Marani. Project Manager: Goil Amornvivat. Project Assistants: Thomas Morbitzer, Jack Robbins.

Hindsight 20/20

Project Designers: Goil Amornvivat, Thomas Morbitzer.

Gwenda Blair, "Designers Redefine the Political Machine," *The New York Times*, Thursday October 7, 2004, F:1, 7.
Celia McGee, "Every Voting Machine Counts as Art," *New York Daily News*, October 8, 2004, 73.
"Around Town: The Voting Booth Project," *Metro*, October 12, 2004, 14.
"Reimagining the Vote," *The New York Sun*, October 13, 2004, 16.
David Segal, "Voters' Revenge: A Smashing Show," *The Washington Post*, October 16, 2004, C:1, 2.
Peter Plagens, "Tools of Democracy," *Newsweek*, October 18, 2004, 12.
Richard Johnson, "Charity Chads," *New York Post*, October 28, 2004.
James Murdock, "A Vote for Better Design," *Architectural Record*, November 2004, 46.

Metropolitan Spice

Partner: Grant F. Marani. Project Senior Associate: Joel Mendelson.

Sura Wood, "Artists Give the Spice Box a Modernist Slant," *San Francisco Arts Monthly*, August 2005, 1, 3.

Westport Weston Family Y
Westport, Connecticut

Partner: Kevin M. Smith. Project Senior Associate: Dennis Sagiev. Project Assistants: Kanu Agrawal, Dennis George, Lara Kailian, Michael Tabacinic.

Will Rowlands, "Mahackeno Architect Chosen," *Westport News*, January 28, 2005, A:1, 21.
James Lomuscio, "Plans for New YMCA in Westport Progressing," *Stamford Advocate*, June 11, 2006.
Matthew J. Malone, "Plan to Move Family Y Is Drawing Opposition," *The New York Times*, March 25, 2007.

Apartment at Lost Tree Village
Palm Beach, Florida

Partner: Roger H. Seifter. Project Associate: Josh Bull. Interior Designer: John Gilmer Architecture and Interior Design.

Fudu Mansion
Shanghai, China

Partner: Grant F. Marani. Project Associate Partner: Meghan L. McDermott. Project Associate: Goil Amornvivat. Project Assistant: Kayin Tse. Associate Architect: Frederic Schwartz Architects.

Takanassee Beach
Long Branch, New Jersey

Partners: Sargent C. Gardiner, Daniel Lobitz. Project Associates: Bina Bhattacharyya, Johnny Cruz, Enid De Gracia. Project Manager: Nikki Hartle. Project Assistants: Gerard Beekman, Seher Erdogan, Peter Garofalo, Stuart Johnson, Rizwana Neem, Hilary Tate. Landscape Design Senior Associate: Michael Weber. Landscape Design Assistants: Susie Grossman, Aileen Park. Associate Architect: Smith Maran.

Residential Towers on the New River
Fort Lauderdale, Florida

Partner: Paul L. Whalen. Project Senior Associate: Hernán Chebar. Project Associate: Johnny Cruz. Project Assistants: Armando Amaral, Amneris Rasuk.

Center for the Arts
University of Virginia, Charlottesville, Virginia

Partners: Alexander P. Lamis, Graham S. Wyatt. Associate Partner: Kevin M. Smith. Project Associates: James Pearson, Salvador Peña-Figueroa. Project Assistants: Roland Sharpe Flores, Natalie Goldberg, Katherine LoBalbo, Meredith Micale.

Melanie Mayhew, "UVa Selects Design Finalists," *Daily Progress*, September 9, 2005.

Dunwalke Farms
Far Hills, New Jersey

Partner: Grant F. Marani. Project Associate: Rosa Maria Colina. Project Assistants: Doreen Adengo, Peter Lombardi-Krieps.

Athletics and Events Center, Ithaca College
Ithaca, New York

Partners: Kevin M. Smith, Graham S. Wyatt. Project Manager: Eric Silinsh.

200 North Riverside
Chicago, Illinois

Partners: Meghan L. McDermott, Graham S. Wyatt

Capital Park
Trenton, New Jersey

Partner: Grant F. Marani. Project Associate: Goil Amornvivat. Landscape Designer: Balmori Associates.

Pool Pavilion, Lily Pond Lane
East Hampton, New York

Partner: Randy M. Correll. Project Senior Associate: Lenore Passavanti. Project Assistant: Anthony Furino.

Carissa Katz, "Neighbor Says 'Terrace' may be a Stretch," *The East Hampton Star*, August 24, 2006, A:3.
Carissa Katz, "No Objections at Lily Pond," *The East Hampton Star*, September 28, 2006, A:3.

Residence in Watch Hill
Watch Hill, Rhode Island

Partner: Randy M. Correll. Project Manager: Damon Van Horne. Project Assistant: Ben Herzog. Landscape Design Senior Associate: Kendra Taylor. Landscape Design Assistants: Joelle Byrer, Meredith Lawton.

Balfour Cosmopolitan Club
Denver, Colorado

Partner: Paul L. Whalen. Project Senior Associate: Hernán Chebar. Project Manager: Roberto Burneo. Project Assistants: Moheb Abdelmaseeh, Armando Amaral, Noel Angeles, Seema Malik, Amneris Rasuk, Benjamin Salling, Sonia Siaw, Camillia Tian. Interior Designer: Dorothy Draper & Company. Landscape Architect: studioINSITE. Associate Architect: Klipp Architects.

Mary Voelz Chandler, "Preservation Projects Make Progress," *Rocky Mountain News*, August 5, 2006.
John Rebchook, "Seniors to Get Riverfront Digs," *Rocky Mountain News*, November 24, 2006.
Thaddeus Herrick, "Urban Developers Target Seniors," *The Wall Street Journal*, December 13, 2006, B:1, 6.

Tuxedo Reserve Welcome Center
Tuxedo, New York

Partner: Gary L. Brewer. Project Associate: Kevin Fitzgerald. Project Assistants: Tae Kim, Maryann Kril, Anthony McConnell, Tyler Vigil. Interior Design Associate: John Boyland. Interior Design Senior Assistant: Phillip Chan. Landscape Architect: EDAW

East Hampton Town Hall
East Hampton, New York

Partner: Randy M. Correll. Project Manager: Christian Dickson. Project Assistants: Aiyla Balakumar, Hannah Cho, Caroline Graf Statile, Wing Poon, Todd Sullivan. Interior Design Associate: Shannon Ratcliff. Interior Design Assistant: Marissa Savarese.

Joanne Pilgrim, "History Will Be the New Face of Town Hall," *The East Hampton Star*, October 5, 2006, A:1, 13.
Pilar Viladas, "Past / Present," *New York Times Magazine*, October 22, 2006, 104-9.
Joanne Pilgrim, "A Historic East Hampton Gift That Keeps on Giving," *The East Hampton Star*, November 30, 2006, A:18.
Joanne Pilgrim, "Free House Hangover: Jubilation Tembered by Criticism, Cost Estimates," *The East Hampton Star*, January 11, 2007, A:1, 13.
Joann Pilgrim, "Historic Gift Made Official," *The East Hampton Star*, January 25, 2007.
Susan J. Greenberg, "Saved Twice, Historic Structures to Be Part of E. Hampton Town Hall," *Suffolk Life*, January 10, 2007, A:2.
Nicole Cotroneo, "Historic East Hampton Buildings Gain New Life," *The New York Times*, February 18, 2007, Long Island: 7.
Joann Pilgrim, "A Herd of Houses Hits the Highway," *The East Hampton Star*, April 5, 2007, A:3.
James Fanelli and Angela Montefinise, "East End Town Haul," *New York Post*, April 15, 2007.
Alex McNear, "Moving-Day Parade Will Remake Municipal Complex," *The East Hampton Press*, April 18, 2007, A: 1, 6.
Michael Braverman, "Compliments of the House," *Hamptons*, June 1 – 7, 2007, 46.
Ellen Keohane, "Futuristic Vision for Colonial Houses," *The East Hampton Star*, August 2, 2007, A: 1, 13.
T. J. Clemente, "Building Begins at East Hampton Town Hall," *Dan's Papers*, August 10, 2007.
Joanne Pilgrim, "Cuts for Town Hall: Bids Push Estimate $1 Million Over Budget," *The East Hampton Star*, July 17, 2008, 1.
Carissa Katz, "Town Hall Project: Board Goes With Hand Out to de Menil," *The East Hampton Star*, November 13, 2008, A: 12.

Echo Bay
New Rochelle, New York

Partner: Paul L. Whalen. Project Senior Associate: Joel Mendelson. Project Assistant: Saul Hayutin.

Kathy Gilwit, "Echo Bay Developers Show Their Stuff," *The New Rochelle Sound Report*, June 30, 2006, 1, 8.
"Four Plans for New Rochelle's Echo Bay," *The LoHud Journal News*, July 24, 2006.

Nelson Fitness Center and Smith Swim Center, Brown University
Providence, Rhode Island

Partner: Gary L. Brewer. Project Managers: Roland Sharpe Flores, Nalina Moses. Project Assistants: Eunice Kim, Dominic Lidl, Tin Yiu Lo, David Rinehart, Tyler Vigil. Interior Design Associate: Hyung Kee Lee. Interior Design Assistant: Tina Hu. Landscape Design Project Manager: Joelle Byrer. Landscape Architect: Quennell Rothschild.

Scott Lowenstein, "U. Names Robert A.M. Stern as Fitness Center Architect," *Brown Daily Herald*, March 19, 2007.
"The Nelson Fitness Center," *Boldly Brown*, May / June 2007, 8-11.
Michael Skocpol, "How 'Building Brown' Will Change the Face of College Hill," *Brown Daily Herald*, December 6, 2007.
Ben Bernstein, "Building a Mystery: Examining the Nelson Fitness Center," *Brown Daily Herald*, February 15, 2008.
Robert Emlen, "The Great Wall of Providence," *The Providence Journal*, March 30, 2008, D:7.
Peter Mackie, "Save the Wall!" *The Providence Journal*, April 9, 2008.
David Brussat, "Don't Tear Down That Wall!" *The Providence Journal*, May 1, 2008.

Penthouse at One St. Thomas Street
Toronto, Ontario

Partner: Randy M. Correll. Project Senior Associate: Lenore Passavanti. Project Manager: Christiane Gallois. Project Assistants: Anthony Furino, Timothy Kirkby. Interior Design Associate: John Boyland. Interior Design Assistants: Ann Baumgartner, Sam Mason, Mitra Moshari, Aruni Weerasinghe.

Baisetova Square
Almaty, Kazakhstan

Partner: Grant F. Marani. Project Senior Associate: Charles Toothill. Project Associate: Salvador Peña-Figueroa. Project Assistants: Mario Cruzate, Alena Kereshun, Renaud Magnaval, Jeff Morrical, Yoko Suzuki, Jessica Swan. Landscape Design Senior Associate: Kendra Taylor. Landscape Design Project Manager: Joelle Byrer. Landscape Design Assistant: Kevin Hasselwander. Associate Architect: Boyut Architecture.

Kaplankaya
Bozbuk, Turkey

Partner: Grant F. Marani. Project Manager: Rebecca Atkin. Project Assistants: Juan Ayala, Brian Fell, Kenneth Frank, Natalie Golnazarians, Nasung Kim, Mako Maeno, Brian Murphy, Wing Yee Ng Fung, Gali Osterweil, Aileen Park. Landscape Design Senior Associate: Kendra Taylor. Landscape Design Assistants: Joelle Byrer, Terrie Gamble, Kevin Hasselwander, Demetrios Staurinos, David Weissman. Associate Architect: Design Group.

"Capital Partners to Develop US$1.5bn Mixed-Use Project in Turkey," *Turkey Real Estate*, August 7, 2007.

Tole Bi
Almaty, Kazakhstan

Partner: Grant F. Marani. Project Senior Associate: Charles Toothill. Project Manager: Anthony Goldsby. Project Assistants: Lorjan Agalliu, Katarina Carlin, Elle Lee, Gali Osterweil. Landscape Design Senior Associate: Kendra Taylor.

Hun-In Village
Seoul, Korea

Partner: Kevin M. Smith. Project Associate: Sue Jin Sung. Project Assistants: Anya Grant, Christopher Heim, Wing Poon, Michael Ryan, Michael Tabacinic, Charles Yoo. Associate Architect: Mooyoung Architects & Engineering.

Chapel Hill Public Library
Chapel Hill, North Carolina

Partners: Alexander P. Lamis, Kevin M. Smith. Project Associate: James Pearson. Project Assistants: Tehniyet Masood, Susan Ryder, Vanessa Sanchez, Toby Shirard,

Addie Suchorab. Landscape Architect: OBS Landscape Architects. Associate Architect: Corley Redfoot Zack.

Rob Shapard, "Library Design Plan Back on Table," *The Chapel Hill Herald*, June 17, 2007, 1, 3.
Jesse DeConto, "Is Library Design Futuristic Enough?" *The Chapel Hill Herald*, June 20, 2007.

Las Olas
Coral Isles, Florida

Partner: Roger H. Seifter. Project Associate: Josh Bull. Project Assistants: Tiffany Barber, Josh Bartlett, Natalia Galvis, Megan St. Denis. Interior Designer: Perlmutter-Freiwald. Landscape Architect: Rhett Roy.

Apartment on Park Avenue
New York, New York

Partner: Randy M. Correll. Project Senior Associate: Lenore Passavanti. Project Assistants: Anthony Furino, Allen Robinson. Interior Designer: Pamela Pantzer Interiors.

Apartment on Park Avenue
New York, New York

Partner: Randy M. Correll. Project Senior Associate: Lenore Passavanti. Project Associate: Damon Van Horne. Project Assistants: Anthony Furino, Franklin Nunez, Allen Robinson.

Shymbulak Mountain Resort
Medeu Valley, Kazakhstan

Partner: Grant F. Marani. Project Associate: Breen Mahony. Project Assistants: Katherine LoBalbo, Jen Simmons, Elizabeth Sweeney, Marek Turzynski. Landscape Design Senior Associate: Kendra Taylor. Landscape Design Assistant: Daniel Evans. Associate Architect: Kinetik Grubu.

Candace Jackson, "The Search for the Next Hot Spot," *The Wall Street Journal*, August 18–19, 2007, P:1, 6-7.

Leninville
Almaty, Kazakhstan

Partner: Grant F. Marani. Project Manager: Bruce Yao. Project Assistants: Maya Akeho, Vivian Au, Jack Robbins, Veronica Varela. Landscape Design Senior Associate: Kendra Taylor. Landscape Design Assistant: Kevin Hasselwander.

House in Southampton
Southampton, New York

Partner: Randy M. Correll. Project Managers: Timothy Deal, Marc Rehman. Project Assistants: Hannah Cho, Nicholas DeRosa, Alexis Ryder.

House on Edgartown Harbor
Martha's Vineyard, Massachusetts

Partner: Randy M. Correll. Project Managers: Christian Dickson, Damon Van Horne. Project Assistants: Hannah Cho, Nicholas DeRosa, Wing Poon.

Moon Dance
Park City, Utah

Partner: Paul L. Whalen. Project Associates: Diane Burkin, Rosalind Tsang. Project Assistants: Laura Boutwell, Jin Park, Benjamin Salling, Sonia Siaw. Landscape Design Senior Associate: Michael Weber. Landscape Design Assistants: Kevin Hasselwander, Mark Rodriguez. Interior Designer: Denton House Interiors. Associate Landscape Architect and Associate Architect: IBI Group.

Harrison MetroCentre
Harrison, New Jersey

Partner: Meghan L. McDermott, Graham S. Wyatt. Project Manager: Trevor Laubenstein. Project Assistants: Emilia Ferri, Meghan Leininger, Victor Marcelino, Sung Chan Park.

Patricia L. Kirk, "Mixed-Use Musings," *Urban Land*, August 2007, 84-90.

Residence
Almaty, Kazakhstan

Partner: Grant F. Marani. Project Associate: Rosa Maria Colina. Project Assistant: Brian Murphy. Landscape Design Senior Associate: Kendra Taylor. Landscape Design Assistant: Susie Grossman.

Block "O", Southeast Federal Center
Washington, D.C.

Partners: Sargent C. Gardiner, Paul L. Whalen. Project Associate: Johnny Cruz. Project Manager: David Winterton. Project Assistants: Peter Garofalo, Russell Grant, Stan Gray, Bryan Hale, Franklin Nunez.

Residence
Toronto, Ontario

Partner: Roger H. Seifter. Project Associate: Josh Bull. Project Assistants: Brian Murphy, Ying Li.

Hudson Point
Esopus, New York

Partner: Gary L. Brewer. Project Associate: Kevin Fitzgerald. Project Assistants: Kathleen Casanta, Clancy McGilligan, David Rinehart, Greg Shue, Winnie Yen. Landscape Architect: Chazen Engineering and Land Surveying. Associate Architect: Duany Plater-Zyberk & Company.

18 Gramercy Park South
New York, New York

Partner: Paul L. Whalen. Project Senior Associates: Victoria Baran, Hernán Chebar. Project Manager: Roberto Burneo. Project Assistants: Armando Amaral, Laura Boutwell, Russell Grant, Franklin Nunez, Jin Park. Interior Design Associate: John Boyland. Interior Design Assistants: Tina Hu, Aruni Weerasinghe. Associate Architect: John Schimenti.

Manny Fernandez and Kate Hammer, "Twist in Eviction Fight: Charity as Landlord," *The New York Times*, September 16, 2007.
Eric Konigsberg, "The Guardian of Gramercy Park's Leafy Seclusion," *The New York Times*, June 19, 2008, B: 1, 2.

Opera House Residences
Almaty, Kazakhstan

Partner: Grant F. Marani. Project Senior Associate: Charles Toothill. Project Manager: Anthony Goldsby. Project Assistants: Roberto Burneo, Katarina Carlin, Thomas DiNatale, Dylan Kuo, Nasheet Rumy, Yoko Suzuki, Chung Yang. Landscape Design Senior Associate: Kendra Taylor. Landscape Design Assistant: Kevin Hasselwander.

University of Kentucky College of Law
Lexington, Kentucky

Partners: Kevin M. Smith, Graham S. Wyatt. Project Senior Associate: Melissa DelVecchio. Project Associate: Kim Yap. Project Manager: Michael Ryan. Project Assistants: Timothy Carroll, Megan Fullagar, Erin Murphy, Michael Tabacinic.

Art Jester, "University of Kentucky Proposes Three New Buildings," *Lexington Herald-Leader*, January 2, 2008.
Dick Levine, "What Image Will Planned Buildings Help UK Present?" *Lexington Herald-Leader*, January 23, 2008.

Waterview Cottage
Martha's Vineyard, Massachusetts

Partner: Randy M. Correll. Project Manager: Christian Dickson. Project Assistant: Hannah Cho. Interior Design Project Manager: Marissa Savarese. Interior Design Assistants: Cristina Berusch, Nicholas DeRosa, Tina Hu, Alexis Ryder.

Hanwha Jiri Resort
Jirisan National Park, Korea

Partner: Kevin M. Smith. Project Associate: Sue Jin Sung. Project Assistants: Christopher Heim, Peter Lombardi-Krieps, Asdren Matoshi, Dongju Seo. Associate Architect: Gansam Partners.

Miramar Resort
Santa Barbara, California

Partner: Kevin M. Smith. Project Associate: Sue Jin Sung. Project Assistants: Christopher Heim, Peter Lombardi-Krieps, Asdren Matoshi, Dongju Seo. Associate Architect: Gansam Partners

Alexandra Laviada, "Beachfront Tear-Down," Key: *The New York Times Magazine,* September 9, 2007, 86-89.

215 Brazilian Avenue
Palm Beach, Florida

Partners: Daniel Lobitz, Roger H. Seifter. Project Senior Associate: Victoria Baran. Project Associates: Gaylin Bowie, Mike Soriano. Project Assistants: Jorge Fontan, Scott Hirshson, Tehniyet Masood. Interior Designer: William T. Georgis. Landscape Architect: DS Boca Landscape Architects & Planners. Associate Architect: Oliver, Glidden, Spina & Partners.

House
Cape May, New Jersey

Partner: Randy M. Correll. Project Associate: Timothy Deal. Project Manager: Damon Van Horne. Project Assistants: Hannah Cho, Alexis Ryder. Landscape Design Senior Associate: Kendra Taylor. Landscape Design Assistant: Meredith Lawton.

Gurgaon City Center
Gurgaon, Haryana, India

Partners: Meghan L. McDermott, Graham S. Wyatt. Project Senior Associate: Don Lee. Project Associate: Breen Mahony. Project Assistants: Kanu Agrawal, Megan Fullagar, Lara Kailian, Magdalena Mroz. Landscape Architects: Hargreaves Associates. Associate Architect: Architect Hafeez Contractor.

"New & Notable," *Hinesight,* July / September 2007, 16-17.
Nayantara Rai, "DLF Plans Another 'Connaught Place'," *(New Delhi) Business Standard,* August 23, 2007.
Nalina Moses, "Sun, Stone, Glass, and New Wealth: A Critical Overview of New Architecture in India," *Harvard Design Magazine,* Spring / Summer 2009.

At Last
Long Branch, New Jersey

Partner: Roger H. Seifter. Project Senior Associate: Victoria Baran. Project Associate: David Winterton. Project Assistants: Josh Bartlett, Natalia Galvis, Matt Gerlins, Scott Hirshson. Interior Designer: Jamie Drake. Landscape Designer: Abe Jerome.

Hotel in Westwood
Los Angeles, California

Partners: Daniel Lobitz, Paul L. Whalen. Project Associates: Johnny Cruz, Enid De Gracia. Project Assistants: Moheb Abdelmaseeh, Gerard Beekman, Peter Garofalo, Hussam Jallad, Amneris Rasuk

"Robert A.M. Stern Tower Proposed for Wilshire Corridor," *Curbed Los Angeles,* June 10, 2009.

Barn
Jamestown, Rhode Island

Partner: Gary L. Brewer. Project Associate: Kevin Fitzgerald. Project Assistants: Kathleen Casanta, Omar Clennon, Roland Sharpe Flores, Robert Holub, Nalina Moses. Interior Design Project Manager: Michelle Everett. Landscape Design Senior Associate: Kendra Taylor. Landscape Design Project Manager: Susie Grossman.

House at Wickapogue
Southampton, New York

Partner: Randy M. Correll. Project Associates: Timothy Deal, Marc Rehman. Project Assistants: Hannah Cho, Alexis Ryder. Landscape Design Senior Associate: Kendra Taylor. Landscape Design Assistant: Meredith Lawton.

Strawberry Hill
Victoria Peak, Hong Kong

Partner: Grant F. Marani. Project Manager: Rebecca Atkin. Project Assistant: Kenneth Frank. Landscape Design Senior Associate: Kendra Taylor.

Hanwha Resort
Seorak, Korea

Partner: Kevin M. Smith. Project Senior Associate: Jonas Goldberg. Project Associate: Sue Jin Sung. Project Assistants: Juan Ayala, Timothy Carroll, Christina Fazio, Melanie Fox, Jennifer Smith.

House in East Hampton
East Hampton, New York

Partner: Randy M. Correll. Project Associate: Timothy Deal. Project Assistant: Alexis Ryder.

Houses on Lake Geneva
Lake Geneva, Wisconsin

Partner: Randy M. Correll. Project Associate: Timothy Deal. Project Assistants: Lauren Bollettino, Hannah Cho. Landscape Design Senior Associate: Kendra Taylor. Landscape Design Assistant: Meredith Lawton.

350 Boylston Street
Boston, Massachusetts

Partner: Graham S. Wyatt. Project Associate: Breen Mahony. Project Manager: Bruce Yao. Project Assistants: Doreen Adengo, Natalie Goldberg, Kathryn Lenehan, Bruce Lindsay, Oliver Pelle.

Executive Office
Saint John, New Brunswick

Partner: Alexander P. Lamis. Project Assistant: Gali Osterweil. Interior Design Associate: Shannon Ratcliff. Interior Design Assistant: Jamie Murphy.

Campus Gates, Marist College
Poughkeepsie, New York

Partner: Kevin M. Smith. Project Manager: Benjamin Salling. Project Assistants: Alexander Boardman, Christopher Heim.

Pedestrian Crossing, Marist College
Poughkeepsie, New York

Partner: Kevin M. Smith. Project Manager: Benjamin Salling. Project Assistants: Alexander Boardman, Christopher Heim. Associate Architect: New York State Department of Transportation.

Illustration Credits

Photographers

Peter Aaron / Esto: cover, 2, 34-41, 44-131, 139-43, 148-75, 178 (bottom), 179-80, 181 (bottom), 182-97, 200-27, 234-45, 252-71, 274-79, 289-99, 302-7, 312-17, 320-27, 330-33, 356-61, 367-84, 386-92, 399-409, 414-21, 427-33, 438-41, 442 (bottom), 443-59, 464, 475, 477 (top, middle), 480-85, 487-91, 504-6, 512-15, 530-33, 537-39, 582 (2), 586 (5), 588 (5), 591 (4, 5).

Joe Aker: 228-31, 354-55.

Aveq Fotografie: 133-34, 135 (bottom), 136-37.

John Bartelstone: 477 (bottom).

California Coastal Commission: 42-43.

C. Taylor Crothers: 177.

John Davis: 246-51.

Nick D'Emilio: 338-39.

Marcelo Grillo: 232-33.

Chris Kendall: 460-63, 465.

R. Bradley Maule: 178 (top).

Peter Mauss / Esto: 181 (top).

Norman McGrath: 474 (top).

Michael Moran: 586 (2 right).

Jock Pottle: 472, 529 (right), 584 (3), 586 (2 left, 3), 592 (5 right).

Mike Rixon: 362-63.

Walt Roycraft: 144-46.

David Soliday: 318-19.

Hans Spuijt: 135 (top).

Eric Taylor: 442 (top).

Jeffrey Totaro: 176.

Albert Večerka/Esto: 280-81, 284-87, 348-53, 474 (bottom).

David Wakely: 509.

Renderers

Luis Blanc: 340-41, 589 (5).

Ernest Burden III: 342, 585 (4).

Frank Costantino: 335 (bottom), 568-69.

dbox: 516-19, 525-27, 555-56, 594 (1).

The Drawing Studio: 583 (5).

Gil Gorski: 501, 589 (2), 592 (5 left), 596 (2).

David Huang: 424.

Andre Junget: 592 (4).

Kingsland Linassi: 535.

John Mason: 582 (3), 583 (3).

Michael McCann: 199, 272, 396-97, 411 (top, middle), 413, 466-70, 473, 495, 546-47, 551, 575-77, 590 (1), 591 (1), 595 (2), 597 (5).

Neoscape: 335 (top left), 337, 422-23, 498, 545, 590 (3).

Rad Marketing: 434-37.

Rendering House: 510, 511 (bottom).

Thomas Schaller: 309-11, 328-29, 347, 364-65, 385, 479, 492-93, 499, 522-23, 541 (top), 543, 549, 583 (1), 585 (1, 2, 5), 586 (4), 587 (4), 590 (4), 592 (1, 2), 593 (2), 594 (3), 597 (2).

Clark Smith: 345, 503, 584 (2), 588 (1), 589 (1), 590 (5), 594 (2), 595 (3), 596 (4), 597 (4).

Dick Sneary: 393, 511 (top), 593 (5).

Jeff Stikeman: 411 (bottom), 565-67, 571, 578-79, 588 (2), 589 (4), 594 (5), 598 (2, 3).

studio amd: 558-63.

Vlad Yeliseyev: 300-1.